UNDERSTANDING SEEKING FAITH
Essays on the Case of Judaism

Volume Two
Literature, Religion and the Social Study of Judaism

Program in Judaic Studies
Brown University
BROWN JUDAIC STUDIES
Edited by
Jacob Neusner,
Wendell S. Dietrich, Ernest S. Frerichs,
Calvin Goldscheider, Alan Zuckerman

Project Editors (Project)

David Blumenthal, Emory University (Approaches to Medieval Judaism)
William Brinner (Studies in Judaism and Islam)
Ernest S. Frerichs, Brown University (Dissertations and Monographs)
Lenn Evan Goodman, University of Hawaii (Studies in Medieval Judaism) (Studies in
Judaism and Islam)
William Scott Green, University of Rochester (Approaches to Ancient Judaism)
Ivan Marcus, Jewish Theological Seminary of America
(Texts and Studies in Medieval Judaism)
Marc L. Raphael, Ohio State University (Approaches to Judaism in Modern Times)
Norbert Samuelson, Temple University (Jewish Philosophy)
Jonathan Z. Smith, University of Chicago (Studia Philonica)

Number 73
UNDERSTANDING SEEKING FAITH
Essays on the Case of Judaism

Volume Two
Literature, Religion and the Social Study of Judaism
by
Jacob Neusner

UNDERSTANDING SEEKING FAITH
Essays on the Case of Judaism

Volume Two
Literature, Religion and the Social Study of Judaism
by
Jacob Neusner

Scholars Press
Atlanta, Georgia

UNDERSTANDING SEEKING FAITH
Essays on the Case of Judaism

Volume Two
Literature, Religion and the Social Study of Judaism

Library of Congress Cataloging in Publication Data

Neusner, Jacob, 1932-
   Understanding seeking faith.

   (Brown Judaic studies ; no. 116,   )
   Includes indexes.
   Contents: v. 1. Debates on method, reports of results --
v. 2. Literature, religion, and the social study of Judaism.
   1. Judaism--Essence, genius, nature. 2. Rabbinical
literature--History and criticism. 3. Judaism--History--Talmudic
period, 10-425. 4. Judaism--Historiography. I. Title.
II. Series: Brown Judaic studies ; no. 116, etc.

BM565.N485   1986   296   86-20316
ISBN 1-55540-053-1 (v. 1. : alk. paper)

Printed in the United States of America
on acid-free paper

For

Our neighbors on Vassar Avenue
in Providence, Rhode Island

THE KENYONS
THE FLESCHERS
THE EUSTISES
THE BERGELS

and, up the street a bit,

THE FRERICHSES

Better than family, they're fun!

A token of thanks for nearly two
decades of friendship and fellowship

CONTENTS

Preface

This book presents studies within the academic discipline of religion. Specifically, I undertake the religious study of Judaism. In my judgment the exercise of trying to describe, anayze, and interpret Judaism as a species of the genus, religion, presents important opportunities for humanistic learning. Specifically, the religious study of Judaism within the comparative framework of other religions provides perspective upon data that, viewed by themselves, yield nothing beyond themselves. Seeing Judaism as an example allows us to explain why this, not that, which is to say, permits us to propose theses of interpretation and understanding. But for me, the study of religion, in the case of Judaism, bears profoundly human meaning, and that accounts for the goal of the enterprise: understanding seeking faith. For as a religious and observant Jew, I affirm that that same study bears rich implications for the inner life of faith. In this book I carry forward the former of the two enterprises – the academic – in full awareness of the goal, which builds upon and transcends the merely academic. I choose my subject out of love, respect, affirmation, even in proper time and place celebration. Mine is a quest for understanding of religion, in my case, Judaism, with full appreciation for the human testimony that religion – Judaism – offers to the life of faith. That accounts for my program, the pursuit of understanding, but with a goal beyond, understanding in search, at the end, of faith's full and whole meaning and object: the one in whose image, after whose likeness, we are created.

By the religious study of Judaism, therefore, I mean a very specific thing. It is the study of the Jews' systems of organizing themselves as a social group characterized by a distinctive world view and way of life. Those systems before our own day conformed in their basic structure to the genus, religion, of which they, in the aggregate, formed a species, itself articulated in a variety of subspecies. In the religious study of Judaism, therefore, I propose to describe, analyze, and interpret Judaic systems – structures of belief and behavior formed by a distinct Jewish group (an "Israel"), specifically aiming at an explanation of the relationship of the contents of a given structure to the context in which it endured. That study draws my attention to matters of literature, specifically the description of documents and their traits, as well as to problems in the history of religions. In Parts One and Two of this book, I address both sorts of matters.

That same study, furthermore, requires a measure of self-aware definition of method: what we are doing while we are doing it. Debates on the social description and analysis of Judaism, discussion of the data to be addressed, criticism of the methods used in the interpretation of the sources – these methodological concerns, taken up in Part Three of this book, form the third pillar that holds up the composition.

In the introduction, I place into context the essays collected in this book as well as in the series of which it is a part. Specifically, I explain why these essays address the questions that they do, and spell out alternative approaches to the study of the Jews and Judaism to the one that guides my work.

Many of these essays began in telephone conversations with dear friends at other universities, beginning with Professor William Scott Green, University of Rochester, Professor Marvin Fox, Brandeis University, Dr. Michael Berenbaum, Georgetown University, Professor David Altshuler, George Washington University, Dr. Robert Berchman, University of Virginia, Professor Manfred Vogel, Northwestern University, Professor Ivan Marcus, Jewish Theological Seminary of America, and many others.

It was Professor Green who drew my attention to the work on Midrash addressed in Chapter One, that is, the publications of James Kugel and others of that school, and he also framed for me the issue of the civil war in Jewish learning spelled out in the introduction. My discussion of problems of Midrash and Literature are in these books: *What Is Midrash?* (Philadelphia, 1987: Fortress); *Invitation to Midrash. The Working of Rabbinic Bible Interpretation. A Teaching Book* (San Francisco, 1987: Harper & Row); *Literature and Midrash: The Primacy of Documentary Discourse* (1987).

Matters of mnemonics, which have retained my interest for fifteen years, were discussed at length at a conference at Brown University on the occasion of the visit of Professor Mauro Pesce, University of Bologna, in response to a major paper by Professor Brian Stock, University of Toronto. I owe them much for renewing my appreciation of the importance of that subject, and I found unusually stimulating and suggestive the remarks of the several dozen colleagues who were kind enough to join us for two days of conversation on Professor Stock's paper. Since the National Endowment for the Humanities provided a grant for the conference, my colleagues join me in expressing thanks to that pillar of humanistic learning and education.

I owe to Professor Marc Lee Raphael the suggestion that I reread Nathan Glazer's *American Judaism* and reevaluate it thirty years later.

My essay on art will appear, in revised form, in a volume edited by Diane Apostolos-Cappadona, and I appreciate her permission to print a somewhat different version in the present volume.

On matters of intertextuality and the issues involved in that interesting approach to the reading of the received texts, I have enjoyed guidance from a number of colleagues at Brown University; Professor Robert Scholes introduced me to the important work of Professor Thais Morgan, Arizona State University, who was kind enough to send me a draft of her paper on the subject. The chapter on intertextuality goes over matters covered at greater length in my *Religious Study of Judaism*, Volume III (Lanham, 1987: University Press of America *Studies in Judaism* series). This briefer version seems to me to make its own statement. A much more sustained and detailed study on the same matter is my *Canon and Connection: Intertextuality in Judaism* (Lanham, 1987: University Press of America Studies in Judaism series).

Chapters One and Ten overlap in dealing with James Kugel's characterization of Midrash, though each makes its own point in its own context. The one concerns a thesis tested against the evidence of a specific document, the other offers a more general theoretical statement. I beg the reader's indulgence for the recurrence of a few paragraphs.

I express my thanks to Joshua Bell of Verbatim, Providence, Rhode Island, for his, and his staff's, conscientious work in preparing camera-ready copy of my essays. I am grateful also to Dr. Dennis Ford of Scholars Press and to Dr. Conrad Cherry, press director. Working with these two loyal and effective friends has given only pleasure, and I state publicly my high esteem not only for their professionalism but also for their critical judgment. Brown Judaic Studies, working its way toward its one hundred fiftieth title, could not have achieved the standing and acceptance that it now enjoys without the guidance of Dr. Cherry and the effective everyday management of Dr. Ford. My colleagues and I are proud to associate ourselves with them.

None of these papers has received a printing to this time, though some of them in revised form in the future will serve diverse purposes, and, as I said, Chapters Six and Seven in quite different form serve in other contexts.

JACOB NEUSNER

9 Heshvan 5747
November 11, 1986

Program in Judaic Studies
Brown University
Providence, Rhode Island 02912-1826

Introduction

What Is at Stake in the Religious Study of Judaism

I

The Ethnic and the Academic

In order to understand the approach followed in the essays in this book, the reader will wish to ask about the alternative. Mine is an academic approach, formed in the secular university of America, familiar in the academy throughout the West. Part of the comparative study of religion, the religious study of Judaism proposes to describe, analyze, and interpret Judaic systems of religion in the larger context of religion. It treats the Jews and their Judaisms as subject to the same laws of humanistic and social scientific inquiry as apply to all other groups and their social systems. That accounts for my interest in problems of method, on the one side, and my concern for the close analysis of documents read as a whole not for their lessons but for their testimony on large issues of culture and social reality. The alternative position, characteristic of Jewish institutions of Jewish learning (though not by any means of everyone who pursues scholarship within those institutions) treats as special and self-validating the data produced by the Jews. That same approach, which is ethnic under some circumstances, theological under others, tends to read all of the documents out of context and as framing their own circumstance of meaning. Much scholarship under ethnic, and all scholarship under theological, auspices furthermore reads in an uncritical spirit the allegations of the received holy books. In these and other ways the present essays testify to an approach to Judaic Studies essentially different from the more familiar one characteristic of the field conducted (even in universities) as an exercise in ethnic celebration or, in seminaries and yeshivot, as an expression of religious conviction.

During the past two decades the ethnic and theological subject, Jewish studies, formerly conducted mostly under Jewish auspices and for Jewish purposes, found entry into Universities under secular auspices and for academic purposes of analysis and criticism. The Jews, in their history, literature, and religion, as well as in their modern and contemporary society, gained access to common discourse and so could contribute examples of interest in the exploration of propositions of general intelligibility. But what has happened is not that a new academy has replaced an old. Rather, a second academy has entered competition with an existing (and I think, intellectually decaying) one. The result has been an increase not of peace but of vitality and debate, a net gain for the intellectual life of Judaism, if not for the peace of mind of the formerly dominant ethnic scholars. The debates represented in the books of this series of mine, The Religious Study of Judaism, represent only one chapter in the larger story of the new academy.

I have tried to make myself a voice for the new academy, or, really, for the first *academy* of Judaic studies in the history of Judaism. For the world of the Yeshivas and rabbinic schools, Israeli universities and ethnic colleges, never formed an academy in the Western sense. It has other tasks and performed them admirably. But when the academy of the universities of the West opened the doors to Judaic studies, I have aspired to raise one voice for the debates and discussions of the new issues. I tried to understood and attempted to meet the challenge of the new setting for Judaic learning. In this volume as in others, I have tried to allow issues to come to the fore which the existing establishment did not wish to see debated. Consequently, in a time of enormous conflict, when one party wished to destroy the other not through reasoned argument but through the death of silence, I have tried to bring light where others wished to preserve only darkness.

II
The Debate between the Ethnic and the Academic
Schools of Judaic Studies

The alternative to this persistence in public debate should not be missed. There has been among the ethnic and theological circles alike a policy of *Todschweigen*, a German word meaning to kill by ignoring (leave it to the Germans to have a word for academic assassination), carried on in Jerusalem and among the ethnic and theological Jewish scholars of Judaism in Europe and the USA. In accord with that policy "we" shall not argue, "we" shall ignore. We – our crowd – shall not acknowledge and debate and seek civil exchange of reasoned viewpoints. Rather, "we" shall condemn, vilify, degrade, trivialize, and otherwise in silence assassinate the other side – because "we" have nothing better to say – or to do. A few examples of *Todschweigen* show the character of the last quarter-century. Judah Goldin's bibliography of the twenty-five years of scholarship in Judaic studies since 1960, in the Charles Adams' *Religion*, presenting bibliographies on world religions published by Macmillan, for example, cited no work done after 1960 thus misrepresenting the fact that over twenty-five years things had happened – whether or not approved by the bibliographer. Salo W. Baron's footnotes in his *Relevance of History,* just now published by Columbia University Press, treats as null everything done in the history of religion, including Judaism, for nearly two decades. When James Kugel offers two introductions to Midrash, in the Hartman and Buddick volume

Midrash and Literature (Yale University Press, 1986), he utterly ignores Gary G. Porton's and Addison Wright's introductions to Midrash, from which he learned nothing; these do not appear even in his footnotes. Nor do the standard bibliographies of Midrash gain even a reference; they were done under the wrong auspices. "We do not have to cite you, you are not on the scholarly canon" – that is the prevailing ethos of the ethnics. The famous "ignoring of Jacob Neusner" carried on in Jerusalem is now remarked upon regularly by reviewers of such books as the Jerusalemites produce in the field of Talmudic history and religion, in German, Holland, Britain, and even the USA.

The list of those subjected to *Todschweigen* is easy to compile. Just make a list of everyone who does not teach at the Hebrew University, Harvard, Yale, the Jewish Theological Seminary, Hebrew Union College, or in a Yeshiva. These unfortunates employed in secular universities are condemned to outer darkness. So much for the record, for twenty-five years, of the Jewish scholarly establishment of 1960. There is now, however, a second scholarly establishment, a competing academy of Judaic studies, and one that has done reasonably well in defining for itself (if not for its enemies) a useful and productive scholarly program – and carrying out that program.

How have matters worked out during this period? As a principal advocate of one position on the definition of Judaic studies, I look back on the past two decades with some satisfaction, but look toward the future with no certainty. We have indeed established and made normative the academic definition of Judaic studies. That is certainly so for most serious universities, if not for Harvard and Yale, the one a preserve of Orthodoxy, the other of ethnic celebration of the Holocaust in particular. In most Universities in which Jewish money has not purchased for the Jewish community a privileged place in faculty appointments and curriculum, the academic definition of the field thrives. In all Universities in which the ethnics control matters, the academic definition of the field is excluded and the ethnic-celebratory-apologetic definition prevails, as it does, of course, in the mishmash that calls itself the Association for Jewish Studies (whatever that is, and is not).

In the academic side of Judaic Studies, like in all other academic subjects, teachers teach about a subject to whom it may concern. In the ethnic side, Jews teach Jews Jewish things, the value of knowing those things is self-evident, and ethnic celebration takes place instead of academic learning. As with Black Studies and Women's studies conducted for essentially apologetic purposes, so Jewish Studies are declining. As with Black Studies and Women's Studies conducted for essentially academic purposes, so Judaic Studies thrive. In my view that is how it should be. For Judaism now endures in a free society. The intellectual life of Judaism therefore finds itself in an unprecedented situation. Entry of Judaic Studies into the academy marks only one measure of the new circumstance, but makes acute, not merely chronic, the crisis of freedom confronting the received tradition of learning in Judaism.

III
The Canons of Critical Learning in the Academy

The Jewish-ethnic scholars have not yet taken up the challenges of freedom to the intellect, in the academy in particular: the public, shared, reasoned, even civil discourse about what was formerly private and parochial to the Jews. They commit one simple error. They ignore the canons of criticism that govern academic scholarship. They celebrate facts – Jewish facts – rather than investigating their meaning. They approach the Jewish sources with inappropriate gullibility. The sources are self-evidently valid, and rehearsing the holy words by itself suffices. The ethnics take for granted that pretty much everything they read is true – except what they decide is not true. They cannot and do not raise the question of whether an authorship knows what it is talking about, and they do not address the issue of the purpose of a text: historical or imaginative, for example. For them the issue always is history, namely, what really happened, and that issue was settled, so to speak, at Sinai: it is all true (except, on an episodic basis, what is not true, which the scholars somehow know instinctively). As a result the generality of Jewish ethnic scholars of Jewish studies end up telling fairy tales instead of conducting serious research, play an unending game of showing and telling, collecting and arranging, to keep themselves busy.

In fact, they all remain well within the walls of the old intellectual ghetto. They exercise their monopoly, celebrating themselves among themselves and by themselves and excluding outsiders to their viewpoint. Their most trivial achievements they magnify and sanctify, as they get their named chairs on the strength of their published dissertations – that alone. In their scholarly work in the study of the classical sources, they exhibit the credulity characteristic of the traditional settings of Judaic studies, Yeshivot and Jewish universities and seminaries in the diaspora and in the State of Israel, and they take not only as fact but at face value everything in the holy books.

To them "Judaism" is special and need not undergo description, analysis, and interpretation in accord with a shared and public canon of rules of criticism. "We all know" how to do the work, and "we" do not have to explain to "outsiders" either what the work is or why it is important. It is a self-evidently important enterprise in the rehearsal of information. Knowing these things the way "we" know them explains the value of knowing these things. That is the mentality of a ghetto, a closed circle, and the generality of Jewish scholars of Judaism have not left the ghetto, nor do they even admit to themselves that they presently reside therein. The old order endures, not everywhere to be sure, but in places in which it otherwise does not belong, specifically, in the academy in the West.

Let me dwell on the matter of the pure credulity brought to the Jewish sources by the Jewish scholars of Jewish studies. In biblical studies in Jerusalem (with many noteworthy exceptions) and in historical studies in

Talmud and Midrash done nearly everywhere except within my school, a pious gullibility reigns supreme. People who are gullible generically believe everything they hear, and gullibility as generic generates belief in whatever the holy books say. If, therefore, a canonical ("holy") book says a holy man said something, he really said it, and if the book says he did something, he really did it. That is gullibility. Scholarship in the service of gullibility frames questions that implicitly affirm the accuracy of the holy books, asking questions, for example, that can only be answered in the assumption that the inerrant Scriptures contain the answers – therefore, as a matter of process, do not err. By extension holy books that tell stories produce history through the paraphrase of stories into historical language: this is what happened, this is how it happened, and here are the reasons why it happened. Scholarship of a credulous character need not serve God, it may serve Satan. Lives of Jesus may portray him as son of God or as magician. Both statements are equally fundamentalist in scholarly premise, the one white, the other black gullibility, the one positive, the other negative. There is no methodological or epistemological difference.

Total gullibility about what sources tell us, incapacity critically to analyze those sources, an attitude that it suffices to paraphrase the sources and that it is not necessary to analyze them, presently characterize the Jewish studies in general, and the study of the history of Judaism, in particular. Believing Jews of Orthodox or Conservative or Reform, or secular origin, whether young or old, use these sources in ways in which no reputable scholar of the Old or New Testaments would condone in the scholarly reading the biblical writings. Eminent scholars take for granted that we may ignore the entire critical program of biblical learning. So the study of ancient Judaism in its formative centuries produces results in no way based on the principles of scholarship universally honored. The character of critical attitudes in other areas is difficult to assess, though in studies of medieval times the level of work seems somewhat more mature, and I can point to much excellent work in that area.

Can we draw an analogy to how things would be done in biblical studies if the same epistemological premise governed? Indeed we can. Working along the same lines, in like manner Old Testament scholars would analyze tales of conversations between Moses and Aaron or Pharaoh as if they really took place, and not as the imaginary compositions of great writers of religious fiction. The scholars, young and old, from whom we shall hear at some length, invoke arguments from the *plausibility* of the contents of a statement for the veracity of that statement. New Testament scholars following that program would tell us that Jesus really made such-and-such a statement, because it sounds like something he would say. So the *"if-I-were-a-horse,-I'd-like-to-eat-oats-too"* school of anthropology finds company in the great stables of Jewish scholarship. The scholars under discussion furthermore invoke the claim that they can identify the point of origin of a statement, without also telling us how we would know if we were wrong. The works of scholarship under discussion recapitulate the mode of historical thought of the Talmud – "since this statement uses this language, it must have been said before such and such a point, after which such language cannot have been used." So they blunder into minefields of pure guesswork.

An analogy in biblical studies may be drawn. In like manner, biblical scholars would tell us that such and such a proposition has the ring of truth; or "if such and such a proposition is true, then we can solve a further problem," or, "since text X knows nothing of the rule in text Y, therefore text X must come before text Y." That may be so – but not on the basis of argument alone. At some point, evidence must make its contribution, not to mention tests of falsification and verification. Otherwise we shall never know whether we are right. Deductive logic untested by evidence and unchallenged by skeptical analysis rules supreme. To state matters simply as the work is done in my field of specialization: if biblical history were written the way the history of the Jews and Judaism in late antiquity (which used to be called "Talmudic history") is written today, the histories of ancient Israel would begin with the creation of the world – in six days, of course. If complete indifference to the history of the writings in hand were to characterize New Testament scholarship, as that indifference governs Talmudic-historical scholarship, we should be reading more and more harmonies of the Gospels. For the recognition that the four Evangelists preserve viewpoints distinctive to themselves should never have shaped the interpretation of the Gospels, and we should be left with ever more complicated restatements of the Diatesseron. New Testament scholars know full well that when they come to the rabbinic sources, they tend to use it in ways in which they do not utilize the New Testament. But they may take comfort in the simple fact that since the specialists in the Talmudic writings read the documents in a fundamentalist way, the New Testament scholars do no worse. Nonetheless, both Old and New Testament scholarship, with its keen interest in questions of formulation and transmission of sayings, composition of sayings into documents, preservation of documents, and other critical issues must find primitive and alien the traits of mind to which I shall now point. *In contemporary Judaic studies, we routinely deal with premises last found plausible in biblical and historical studies more than one hundred and fifty years ago.*

IV

The Jews as Exemplary

At the same time, I should maintain, in the past twenty years we have in various areas developed new methods. Social science has drawn us out of the ethnic ghetto, through imposing tests of comparison and rejecting special appeals to theological or ethnic, that is, racist celebration. The history of various specific fields has rightly drawn attention to the Jews' experience as worth knowing and investigating. So what we have witnessed is not twenty years of retrogression, nor has the academy found reason to reject, out of hand, all of Judaic studies. What we see is quite different. It is the development out of the single world of Jewish studies under ethnic auspices and for ethnic purposes a second and quite separate world of Judaic studies. The new academy of Judaic studies has erstablished itself firmly. It has its journals, its monograph series, its regular occasions for meeting. Of course it has no Judaic studies association, since its members join the professional societies of their disciplines, whether religion, history, literature, or social science, and find nothing of interest among the ethnics with their Talmud side-by-side with American Jewish history next to Rashi, with their articles on X's view of Y and the conception of C in W. The old academy celebrates itself and bores the world. The new academy addresses the world and learns from everyone all the time. Who is wise? We try at least to learn from everybody. That may not mean we are wise. But it should mean we are not hopelessly paralyzed by insularity and ethnocentrism, self-referential and self-reverential.

V

The Civil War in Jewish Studies

These remarks make clear that there are really two academies in Judaic or Jewish Studies, the academic and the ethnic. What no one anticipated thirty years ago, as Judaic Studies first made their way into universities, or twenty years ago, when Leon Jick, Marvin Fox, Nahum Sarna, Arnold Band, and I, with others, organized the Association for Jewish Studies, was a development we should have predicted. It is the complete split that has now taken place between Jewish and gentile scholars of Judaic studies in universities and Jewish scholars of Judaic studies (there are no gentiles to speak of) in institutions under Jewish auspices in the USA and Europe as well as most Israeli scholars of Judaic studies in the humanistic mode (as distinct from the social scientific). A civil war – fought on uncivil terms, of course – has broken out. There is no more a single field of Jewish learning, whether called Jewish or Judaic Studies. Two separate academies have taken shape, the ethnic and the genuinely academic, and discourse between them is becoming increasingly strained. The one side addresses issues of humanistic learning, engages in no special pleading, and treats the Jewish or the Judaic data as exemplary of broader issues. The other side takes for granted the interest and importance of the Jewish and the Judaic data and regards incremental erudition, whether or not formed for a purpose, as self-evidently interesting.

Professor William Scott Green, University of Rochester, writing in *Midstream*, October, 1986, p. 39, states matters as follows:

From the perspective of ethnic Jewish studies, materials are deemed interesting because they are Jewish. This school of thought is marked by a fundamentally romantic view of all things it defines as Jewish. Ethnic scholarship tends to be avenging and celebratory. Ethnic education at whatever level makes learning into a ritual attachment to the heroic people. Ethnic intellectual discourse tends to be restricted...and directed primarily to those within the ethnic group or those who share its romantic suppositions. In short, ethnic Jewish Studies is a self-validating enterprise, designed to preserve Jewish distinctiveness. Ethnic Jewish scholarship serves a powerful communal purpose and therefore is highly charged. It aims to teach the Jews about themselves and thereby to create a usable Jewish past, a workable Jewish present, and a viable Jewish future. Wirthin this framework, reasoned intellectual dissent is all too often ignored or censored, or discounted and dismissed, as a form of disloyalty and disrespect.

I am inclined to think that, in the coming decade, Judaic Studies will break apart into two essentially irreconcilable camps, with little interchange between them. The size of the two camps is roughly the same in numbers, but the distribution is different. The Jewish ethnic scholars of Judaic Studies are concentrated in a few places, the Jewish seminaries, for example, along with the Hebrew teachers colleges, Yeshivas, and the like (so far as yeshivas participate in the scholarly world at all), and in the State of Israel and its universities. The academic scholars of Judaic studies, both Jewish and otherwise, are widely distributed among universities, with from one to ten at any one place, but no sizable number anywhere.

They are scattered in a second sense. In their universities, they are not assembled in a single department, but they serve in a variety of disciplines and therefore also disciplinary departments, e.g., as at Brown, history, religion, literature, language, sociology, political science, and the like. In some places there may be a program or center or even interdisciplinary department. But it is not the same thing as a yeshiva or a seminary or the Hebrew University of Jerusalem and its confreres, in which dozens of scholars, not differentiated as to discipline, form a unified and large cadre in a single school.

But while widely distributed, the academic and discipline-oriented scholars of Judaic studies are numerous. By definition they want no journals of "their own," since they propose to address the scholarly universe formed by their particular disciplines. They also do not form organizations of Jewish studies, nor do many of them join such organizations. But that is not because the academic scholars of Judaic studies do not concur or constitute a community. They form a vital consensus on the basic issues of learning. They view the Jews as exemplary, and they address a broad audience of interested but neutral scholars, in a variety of fields, on a common and shared agenda of inquiry. They do not treat the Jews as self-evidently interesting, and the data do not validate themselves without analysis. The academic sector of Judaic studies proves as productive as other parts of the humanities and social sciences; debates go forward; theses are presented and tested; much, for learning, is at stake. Green explains matters in this way:

> Disciplinary Jewish Studies...apply to Jewish sources and materials the standardized inquiries, analytical criteria, and...skepticisim of university studies in the humanities and social sciences. These disciplines attempt to address common questions to various texts, cultures and societies, and thus deny special privilege to any ofthem. They reject in principle private, self-validating worlds of experience whose meaning is pertinent and can be transmitted only to initiates. Within a disciplinary freamework, the study of discrete Jewish materials is shaped by general questions about human imagination and behavior, questions extrinsic to particular Jewish needs, concerns, and preoccupations.

The ethnic or theological or Israeli sector, by contrast, which emphasizes other matters altogether, tends to a certain aridity in both method and result. While – if not very witty – wonderfully erudite, little is at stake in debates conducted under the ethnic and theological auspices, and in a broad range of subjects, publication is limited. What is more consequential than the absence of publication is the poverty of a scholarly program characteristic of the ethnics, since most of the articles in *Tarbiz* and *Zion* – to take two prominent journals of the ethnics – can – and should – have been written a century ago, so far as program and problem are concerned. The range of publication limited, the volume spare, the ethnic sector of Jewish or Judaic studies finds little to contribute to common discourse, when work on X's view of Y or on the Jews in Z in the year 1904 has been placed on display.

Proof of the complete break between the two academies may be adduced from the conduct of the ethnics toward the academics. The former condemn without reading, receive with sedulous silence major statements, and violate the accepted norms of academic debate. As Professor William Scott Green comments:

> Strong criticism of others' work is an academic commonplace. It is the principal form of public intellectual engagement – the way scholars transact their business – and is supposed to promote the understanding of ideas, the assessment of theories, and the advancement of knowledge. When criticism degenerates into mere condemnation and overt insult, the dispute is political or personal, not academic and professional. When criticism aims simply to discredit rather than to discern, the conflicting positions are irreconcilable, perhap incommensurable.

The mode of criticism of the ethnics is to point to "mistakes," which may or may not be mistakes at all, of which much is made. That is a form of discrediting. To prove plausible, however, lists of mistakes should be joined with lists of non-mistakes. Otherwise the mistakes may prove – if in fact errors at all, and the great authorities pass their opinion on the basis of remarkable disinterest in facts – adventitious. Reviews that list errors but do not list correct statements are invidious and present mere innuendo; they do not persuade anyone who is not already persuaded.

When, again, the ethnics invite the other side to conferences and then rescind the invitation on meretricious grounds – or no grounds at all! – as was the case with the Israel Historical Society and the Jewish Theological Seminary of America in 1984 and 1985, respectively, then we stand in the presence of not debate but something else entirely. And the something else, as Green says, has no scholarly or academic interest. That is why the future will witness the fruition of what has already taken place, the complete and final break between two completely unrelated scholarly camps, both working on the same sources and data, the one ethnic, the other academic, or, as Green says, disciplinary.

What we have now to accept, in my view, is that the world of Jewish learning has broken in half, with a few strong and segregated centers of the ethnic, and many, diffused and integrated presences of the disciplinary and academic. The two sides can no longer meet and transact business, because there is no business to be done any more, and, if truth be told, there probably never was. As Green says,

> There is a surrealism to the entire dispute. Ethnic and disciplinary Jewish Studies operate in incongruous worlds, have incompatible motivations, and address disparate constituencies. The dispute between them is bitter because it is pointless. Not enough is shared between them to allow the possibility of communication, much less persuasion.

I find the development of the two worlds of Judaic Studies a perfectly natural outcome of that free academy which welcomes Judaic learning on its terms, alongside that Jewish world which nurtures Judaic learning for its purposes. Both are valid terms and purposes. But the absolute and final division between the one and the other has now to be recognized, so that we can get on with the work and see for what it really is the rather overstated and overwrought statement with which the ethnic scholars have dismissed their enemy and competition.

What we see is simply the end of a monopoly and the beginning of competition. Our side has broken the monopoly, which cannot be regained. What can be wrong with that? I see nothing so healthy as the free market place in which ideas compete, as they must compete, and in which people make up their own minds. The disciplinary scholars will learn what the ethnics have to teach, when (and that is often) they come up with new facts. They will not be much affected by the imprecations of the ethnics; they will go on with their work, and they already do. As Green says,

> Ethnic Jewish Studies, which serve communal political needs and have communal support, will continue. But disciplinary Jewish Studies have taken firm root in American universities, and they will endure there. No amount of ethnic resentment, hosility, or anger can change that.

Green is surely right. I am not inclined to regret what has happened. On the contrary, I believe it is healthy for the Jewish people to preserve both kinds of learning, since there is a vital role for each, the one for the inner world, the other for the sheltering academy beyond. My purpose in publishing these books of essays is to bring to that academy in a convenient form some of the results of a large and on-going scholarly enterprise. I learn from the efforts of others to teach me about the worlds on which they work, and I mean in this way to address to them the lessons of the world of Judaism as I have been able to describe, analyze, and interpret that world.

Part One

LITERATURE

Chapter One

The Primacy of Documentary Discourse

The Case of Sifra, its Plan and Program

I
The Issue

The basic unit of the Bible, for the midrashist, is the verse:
this is what he seeks to expound, and it might be said that
there simply is no boundary encountered beyond that of the
verse until one comes to the borders of the canon itself.

James Kugel

James Kugel maintains that the principal mode of generating, formulating and transmitting midrash-exegeses was not documentary but discrete. So he states, *And so midrashic explications of individual verses no doubt circulated on their own, independent of any larger exegetical context* . He does not tell us for how long these "explications of individual verses" circulated on their own, independent of any larger exegetical context, or how, or why, they then formed into aggregates. He does not indicate whether or not he thinks that the (later) conglomeration of exegeses of verses into larger composites, then into still larger ones, and finally into complete documents, persisted even after (some) documents took shape. Indeed, the position he wishes to maintain does not intersect with analysis of any document as a whole or even as to its larger parts, so we cannot be certain we have understood precisely what, if anything, Kugel has in mind. Let me turn, therefore, to the contrary proposition, to be stated with precision and then demonstrated thoroughly and in detail.

While the data of rhetoric prove suggestive, the principle that documents define the initial limits of discourse stands or falls upon a single claim. It is that a given document establishes through a *cogent* program of rhetoric, topic, and logic the point that, through all detailed discourse within the document, the authorship of the document wishes to make. The proportions of the whole, the cogency of the parts, the integrity of detail and proposition, of rhetoric, topic, and logic – all form a whole and distinctive entity, speaking metaphorically, a book with beginning, middle, and end. If that principle does not hold in the description of midrash-literature, then a hermeneutic that ignores documentary limits and treats as primary not the document but components – the atoms, not the molecules, so to speak – proves congruent to the character of the literature's program, if not to its rhetorical plan. If I cannot demonstrate documents' fundamental cogency, in rhetoric, logical principle of intelligible discourse, and program and proposition, then Kugel is right that *midrashic explications of individual verses no doubt circulated on their own, independent of any larger exegetical context*. But a principle of interpretation that imposes on the literature premises contradictory of the character of the literature cannot stand and must be set aside. In the present exercise, I shall test Kugel's hypothesis against the facts of a single case, that of Sifra. I shall show that that document follows a uniform rhetorical plan to effect a powerful and cogent syllogistic program, on which takes the form of exegesis. The exegesis as to its rhetoric and logic, begins not with the atom, the verse itself, but with the generative proposition important to the authorship of the document as a whole.

II

The Cogency of a Document

Kugel treats the midrash-compilations as scrapbooks, not collages. In my view the midrash-compilations of the canon of Judaism in late antiquity form cogent documents of integrity, and that that fact can be demonstrated. Specifically, when we uncover what holds a document together, we may state what we conceive to be the logic of intelligible discourse of that document. And others may devise tests of verification and falsification as well. That is, we may explain what turns discrete sentences into paragraphs, paragraphs into chapters, chapters into a book: a whole and complete statement, one cogent within itself and exhibiting integrity, one also congruent to those patterns of judgment and argument that govern discourse beyond the pages of the book and so allow us to read that book among other books: the deep syntax and structure of intellect of one kind rather than some other. Under discussion therefore is the mode of shared intelligibility leading to the possibility of making sense of, and accepting, the propositions at hand. The matter of logic proves central, for it is through the logic of intelligible and cogent discourse that an authorship proposes to communicate – and succeeds in doing so. When we grasp the distinctive principles of intelligibility, we also uncover what is common between the authorship of the document and its readership beyond. Then the context becomes clear, the original setting known, and the power of the literature to transcend the limits of context and setting affects even us, so long afterward.

The criteria for analyzing midrash as literature – rhetoric, topic, and logic – therefore draw us onward to the issue of logic, as is now clear, the logic of shared intelligibility that lends proportion and position to the parts and a proposition of cogency and integrity to the whole The questions we therefore bring to our documents are these:

1. structure: how, overall, does the document organize its materials? do the framers follow a clearly discernible principle or organization, through which they wish to establish a proposition? or are matters haphazard?

2. plan: does the document at hand follow a fixed and limited plan, a repertoire of rhetorical forms? or do the framers simply use whatever comes to hand, without attention to the rhetorical traits of their materials?

3. program: do these forms yield cogent and intelligible proposition(s), one(s) that, in some recurrent interest(s) or point(s) of emphasis, may make of the whole if not more than, then at least, the sum of the parts? or does the authorship simply assemble this and that on whatever subject comes to mind?

Affirmative answers to these questions yield the hermeneutic that the document defines the lines of structure, therefore dictates the opening questions of analysis and interpretation. Negative answers justify ignoring documentary lines and attending solely to the smallest whole units of discourse, the completed units of thought, inclusive of proposition, that we may discern one by one.

How shall we identify what I claim to be evidences of a well-composed plan for the rhetoric, logic, and topic of a document? It is by uncovering, on the basis of systematic inquiry, the fundamental literary structures inherent in a document. A literary structure is a set of rules that dictate recurrent conventions of expression, organization, proportion, as well as modes of cogent and intelligible discourse even encompassing an implicit syllogism, that are *extrinsic* to the message of the author. The conventions at hand bear none of the particular burden of the author's message, which is delivered only or mainly in the details, so they are not idiosyncratic. They convey in their context the larger world-view expressed within the writing in which they are used, so prove systemic and public. That is because a literary structure conforms to rules that impose upon the individual writer a limited set of choices about how he will convey whatever message he has in mind. Or the formal convention will limit an editor or redactor to an equally circumscribed set of alternatives about how to arrange received materials. These conventions then form a substrate of the literary culture that preserves and expresses the world-view and way of life of the system at hand.

On the basis of what merely appears to us to be patterned or extrinsic to particular meaning and so entirely formal, we cannot allege that we have in hand a fixed, literary structure. Such a judgment would prove subjective. Nor shall we benefit from bringing to the text at hand recurrent syntactic or grammatical patterns shown in other texts even of the same canon of literature to define conventions for communicating ideas in those other texts. Quite to the contrary, we find guidance in a simple principle: *A text has to define its own structures for us*. This its authors do by repeatedly resorting to a given set of linguistic patterns and literary conventions and no others.. On the basis of inductive evidence alone we testify the thesis that the authors at hand adhere to a fixed canon of literary forms. If demonstrably present, we may conclude that these forms will present an author or editor with a few choices on how ideas are to be organized and expressed in intelligible – again, therefore, public – compositions.

So internal evidence and that alone testifies to the literary structures of a given text. When, as in the present exercise, we draw together and compare five distinct documents, each one to begin with has to supply us with evidence on its own literary structures. It follows that the adjective "recurrent" constitutes a redundancy when joined to the noun "structure." For we cannot know that we have a structure if the text under analysis does not repeatedly resort to the presentation of its message through that disciplined structure external to its message on any given point. And, it follows self-evidently, we do know that we have a structure when the text in hand repeatedly follows recurrent conventions of expression, organization, or proportion *extrinsic* to the message of the author. How shall we proceed to identify the structures of the documents before us? It seems to me that, as we did in Chapter Three, we had best move first to the analysis of a single whole and large unit of a document, e.g., a *pisqa* or *parashah*. We seek, within that *parashah*, to identify what holds the whole together. The second step then is to see whether we have identified something exemplary, or what is not an example of a fixed and formal pattern, but a phenomenon that occurs in fact only once or at random.

III
The Case of Sifra
And A Sample

Before proceeding to the analysis of a sample of Sifra, covering the *parashiyyot* of Negaim and Mesora, or 13% of the whole, I provide for the reader a brief extract of the document. In this way the reader may have a clear notion of the traits of Sifra, for, as I shall show in the next section, the document follows a statistically demonstrable rhetorical pattern, on the one side, and, in working out the relationship of the Mishnah (tractate Negaim) to Scripture (Leviticus 13-14, for our sample) makes a systematic and sustained argument for a single proposition. The case adduced in opposition to Kugel's proposed description, analysis, and interpretation of midrash as literature then will call into question his most fundamental premise as to the character of the literature.

In my abstract I give the biblical verses in italics, citations of the Mishnah or the Tosefta in bold face type. My translation in square brackets introduces under GRA the comments of Elijah of Vilna.

PARASHAT NEGAIM PEREQ 1

A. *And the Lord spoke to Moses and to Aaron saying, A man (Adam) when there will be on the skin of his body* (Lev. 13:1-2) –

B. Why does Scripture say so [speaking of Adam + *will be*]?

C. Because it is said, *And a man or a woman, when there will be on the skin of his flesh bright spots [the priest shall make an examination, and if the spots on the skin of his body are of a dull white, it is tetter that has broken out in the skin; he is clean]* (Lev. 13:38-9) –

D. [This refers to] clean bright spots.

E. It is hardly necessary to speak [in Lev. 13:2] of [GRA: I know only about] bright spots which do not exhibit the colors of plagues and which have not come into the category [of uncleanness, for Lev. 13:38-9 includes them].

F. But [there are, in accord with Lev. 13:2, clean] bright spots which do [nonetheless] exhibit the colors of plagues [namely]:

G. **Which were on him and he converted –
on the infant and he was born –
on the crease [of the flesh] and it was unfolded –
on the head and on the beard –
on the festering boil and burning and blister –**

H. **Their [those items in G] colors changed, whether to produce a lenient or a stringent ruling –
R. Eleazar b. Azarah declares clean.
R. Eleazar b. Hisma says, To produce a lenient ruling – it is clean, and to produce a stringent ruling – let it be examined afresh.
R. Aqiva says, Whether to produce a lenient or a stringent ruling, it is examined afresh [M. Neg. 7:1].**

I. Therefore it is said, *A man (Adam) – when there will be* (Lev. 13:1).

N1:1

A. *When there will be* (Lev. 12:2) –

B. From the [time at which this law is] proclaimed [namely, Sinai] onward.

C. And is it not logical?

D. It [Scripture] has declared unclean with reference to Zabim and has declared unclean with reference to plagues.

E. Just as in the case of Zabim, it declared clear [such appearances of uncleanness as occurred] before the pronouncement [of the Torah], so in reference to plagues, it declared clear [such appearances of uncleanness as occurred] on them before the pronouncement.

N1:2

F. It [moreover] is an argument *a fortiori*:

If in the case of Zabim, whose uncleanness and uncleanness may be determined by anyone, it [Scripture] has declared free before the declaration, plagues, the uncleanness or cleanness of which may be declared only by a priest, is it not logical that it should declare them clear before the declaration?

G. No. If you have so stated concerning Zabim, whom it [Scripture] did not declare unclean when [the flux is] accidental, will you say so concerning plague, which is declared unclean [even when the uncleanness is] accidental?

H. Since is declared unclean [even when the uncleanness is] accidental, will it declare them clear before the pronouncement [of the Scriptural law]?

I. Therefore Scripture says, When it well be, meaning, from the pronouncement [at Sinai] and onward.

N1:3

A. *On the skin of his flesh* (Lev. 13:2).

B. What does Scripture mean to say?

C. Because it is said, *And hair in the diseased spot has turned white* (Lev. 13:3), might one say I have reference only to a place which is suitable to grow white hair? But a place which is not suitable to grow white hair – how do we know [that it is susceptible]?

D. Scripture says, *On the skin of his flesh* – as an inclusionary clause.

[E. *A swelling or an eruption or a spot* (Lev. 13:2).]

F. *A swelling* – this is a swelling.

G. *A spot* – this is a spot.

H. *An eruption (SPHT)* – this is secondary [in color] to the bright spot.

I. *And its shade is deep [Lev. 13:3: And the shade of the plague is deep]* – [the color of the SPHT is] secondary to that of the swelling.

J. What is the meaning of the word eruption (ST)? Prominent (MWBHQT) (GRA: MWGBHT).

K. **Like the shades of the shadow, which are higher than the appearance of the sun.**

L. What is the meaning of the word deep (MWQ)?

M. **Deep as the shades of the sun, which are deeper than the shadow.**

N. What is the meaning of the work eruption (SPHT)? Secondary (TPYLH).

O. As it is said, *Put me (SPHYNY), I pray you, in one of the priest's places...* (I Sam. 2:36).

P. *And it will be* (Lev. 13:2) – teaches that **they [the colors] join together with one another to declare clear and to certify and to shut up.**

Q. *On the skin of his flesh* (Lev. 13:2) – on the skin of that flesh which can be seen [or: in accord with its appearance].

R. On this basis have they said:
    A bright spot appears dim on a German and the dim one on the Ethiopian appears bright.

S. R. Ishmael says, The house of Israel – lo, I am atonement for them – lo, they are like box-wood, not black and not white but intermediate.

T. R. Aqiba says, The artists have pigments with which they color skin black, white, and intermediate.   One brings the intermediate pigment and surrounds it [the bright spot] on the outer perimeter, and it will appear like the intermediate.

U. R. Yose says, One Scripture says, *On the skin of the flesh* (Lev. 13:2), and another Scripture says, *On the skin of the flesh* (Lev. 13:2).

V. We therefore find that the specification of colors of plagues are meant to produce a lenient ruling, but not to produce a strict ruling.   One therefore examines the German in accord with his skin-tone to produce a lenient ruling.

W. It comes out that [thereby] one carries out, *On the skin of his flesh.*

X. And the Ethiopian is adjudged in accord with the intermediate pigment to produce a lenient ruling.

Y. It comes out that [thereby] one carries out, *On the skin of the flesh.*

Z. And sages say, This [and this are adjudged in accord with] the intermediate [M. Neg. 2:1].

A. *And it will be on the skin of his flesh [for a plague]* (Lev. 13:2).

B. This teaches that he is pained by it.

C. And how do we know that also others are pained by it?

D. They see him, that he is pained by it.

E. Scripture says, *For a plague* (Lev. 13:2).

F. *A leprosy [sign]* (Lev. 13:2) – the size of a split bean.

G. And is it not logical?

H. It has declared unclean here [where there is white hair], and it has declared unclean in reference to quick flesh.

I. Just as quick flesh is the size of a split bean, so also here [we require] a sign the size of a split bean.

J. No. If you have said so concerning quick flesh, which must be the size of a lentil, will you say so concerning [a leprosy sign, marked as unclean by] white hair, for the space of white hair requires nothing [no specific area].

K. Scripture says, *Leprosy* (Lev. 13:2) – a sign the size of a split bean.

A. *And he will be brought to Aaron [the priest or to one of his sons the priests]* (Lev. 13:2).

B. I know only about Aaron himself.

C. How do we know to include another priest?

D. Scripture says, *The priest* (Lev. 13:2).

E. How do we know to include [as suitable examining priests] those [priests who are] injured?

F. Scripture says, *Among his sons* (Lev. 13:2).

G. Then perhaps should I also include profaned [disqualified priests, HLLYM]?

H. Scripture says, *The priests* (Lev. 13:2) – the disqualified priests are excluded.

I. And how do we know to include any Israelite [qualified to examine the plague]?

J. Scripture says, *Or to one.*

N1:8

K. If our end is to include every Israelite, why does Scripture say, Or to one of his sons the priests?

L. But to teach that the actual declaration of uncleanness or cleanness is only by a priest.

M. How so?

N. A sage who is an Israelite examines the plagues **and says to the priest, even though he is an idiot, Say, Unclean, and he says, Unclean.   Say, Clean, and he says, Clean [M. Neg. 3:1].**

O. Another matter:

P. Why does Scripture say, *Or to one of his sons the priests* (Lev. 13:2)

Q. Since it is said, *In accord with their instructions will be every dispute and every plague* (Deut. 21:5), controversies are linked to plagues. Just as plagues must be decided by day, so controversies must be judged by day.

N1:9

R. **Just as controversies may not be settled by relatives, so plagues may not be examined relatives [M. Neg. 2:5].**

S. If [we should now attempt to continue]: Just as controversies must be with three [judges] so plagues must be examined by three [priests] – it is an argument a fortiori.

T. If his property [dispute] is settled by a decision of three judges, should his body not be examined by three?

U. Scripture says, *Or to one of his sons the priests* (Lev. 13:2).

V. This teaches that a single priest examines the plagues.

N1:10

A few observations on our abstract prepare the way for the analysis of the plan and program of the document. The structure of Sifra is readily described. The document is organized as a sequence of exegeses of verses of the book of

Leviticus. A further important trait stands out. The document further introduces into the amplification of the chosen verses of Scripture citations of the Mishnah or the Tosefta. A substantive trait is a strong interest in showing that the rules of the Mishnah or the Tosefta in fact derive from Scripture, not from the working of processes of reason. Let me now survey the facts of rhetoric in my sample of Sifra, which covers *parashiyyot* Negaim and Mesora, or, as I have emphasized, 13% of the whole in volume.

IV

Rhetorical Plan

1. Use of Attributions

In the main Sifra tends not to attribute its materials to specific authorities, and most of the pericopae containing attributions are shared with Mishnah and Tosefta.

Of 354 items in my surveyed population, a total of 76 contain attributions, 21% of the whole. But of these, all but 20 are shared with Mishnah and Tosefta, 5% of the whole. We may say that it is highly uncommon for Sifra to attribute to named authorities materials peculiar to itself.

2. Non-Exegetical Pericopae

Sifra contains a fair sample of pericopae which do not make use of the forms common in the exegesis of specific Scriptural verses and, mostly do not pretend to explain the meaning of verses, but rather resort to forms typical of Mishnah and Tosefta. When Sifra uses forms other than those in which its exegeses are routinely phrased, it commonly, though not always, draws upon materials also found in Mishnah and Tosefta.

Of 87 pericopae which are non-exegetical but follow forms typical of Mishnah and Tosefta, all but 16, 18%, are in fact common to Sifra and Mishnah and Tosefta. Of these 16, moreover, Nos. 40, 48, 54, and 62 are exegetical in substance, that is, dispute-forms are applied to exegetical materials. That leaves not more than 12 items, 14% of the whole sample of non-exegetical pericopae, unique to Sifra and not concerning exegetical problems in a substantive manner. Accordingly, we may conclude that it is uncommon for Sifra to make use of non-exegetical forms for materials peculiar to its compilation.

3. Exegetical Pericopae. Simple Exegetical Form.

We now turn to those pericopae, predominant in Sifra, in which the center of interest is the exegesis of Scripture. These may be categorized as follows. First is the simple, in which a verse, or an element of a verse, is cited, and then a very few words explain the meaning of that verse. Second is the complex, in which a simple exegesis is augmented in some important way, commonly by questions and answers, so that we have more than simply a verse and a brief exposition of its elements or of its meaning as a whole.

Let us consider the possibility that the "original" or primary stratum of Sifra consisted of a set of continuous, simple exegeses of words or phrases of Leviticus 13-14, in the uncomplicated form: Citation of Scripture or element or clause + brief comment or explanation of the meaning of the verse or some element in it. We review all the important examples of the simplest possible exegetical form. But we now omit the many items which stand at the head of a dialectical exegesis, in which we ask either how we may prove a stated proposition, or how we may test a thesis, or how we may show that only through exegesis of Scriptures and not through reason a given rule is the case, and similar complex constructions. If we omit, therefore, all simple and uncomplex exegeses which form the foundations for dialectical structures, what we have left is as follows (* = associated with named authorities):

1. N1:2A-B(NIII:2A)
   When there will be – from the proclamation onward.

2. N1:4E-I
   Lev. 13:2 + swelling, spot, secondary color to each.

3. N1:6F(N3:1A, 7:9D, N14:2A)
   Leprosy is the size of split bean.

4. N2:1A(NIV:5A, N7:6A)
   Lev. 13:3 + his eyes should be upon it when he sees it.

5. N2:2A-B (NV:5C, N8:5A, 9:14D, MI:11A, M2:8A)
   Hair (Lev. 13:3) = two hairs

6. N2:4A-B (NV:5D, 9:14E)
   White (Lev. 13:3) = not red, green, black

*7. NII:7A-B, 8G-H(NIII:5A, 6A)
   Hair must be turned white by bright spot (Simeon).

8. N2*:4E-F, G-H (N15:6J-K)

9. N2:9
   Lev. 13:6 + even though colors did not change (Judah).

10. N2*:10 (N9:8)
    Lev. 13:6 + degrees of uncleanness.

11. NIII:11P
    Lev. 13:10 + *not* boil, tetter, etc.

12. N4:2A-B
    Lev. 13:13 + skin suitable to receive a diseased spot.

13. N4:3A-B, 4B-C

Lev. 13:12 + excluding private parts.

Lev. 13:12 + excluding priest with poor eyesight.

14. N5:1A-B (N6:1A-B, 6:2A)

Lev. 13:14 + if tips of limbs reappear, they are unclean.

*15. N5:4A-B, 5M

Lev. 13:14 + Living flesh which recurs is a token of uncleanness, white hair is not, tetter is not (Joshua).

*16. NIV:1

Lev. 13:19 + Boil appears after rising (Eliezer b. Jacob).

*17. NIV:8A-B (NIV:9D-E)

Lev. 13:20 + what is certainly unclean is declared unclean ('Aqiva).

18. NIV:9A-B

Lev. 13:23: It spreads to the place under it, not to surrounding skin.

19. N9:4A, %A, 6A

Lev. 13:33: Shaved by anyone, any object, even Nazir.

20. N12:5A

Lev. 13:45 + even a high priest.

21. N12:7A

Lev. 13:45 + cover head like a mourner.

*22. N12:10A-B

Lev. 13:46 + not the days + it was cut off (Eliezer).

23. N14:3A

Lev. 13:49 + and not the fringes.

24. N15:4A

Lev. 13:53 + this is what stands unchanged.

*25. N15:4C-D, MI:9A-B, M1:1A-C, MV:12A, etc.

Lev. 13:54 + commandment by a priest, Action by anyone (Rabbi, R. Judah b. R. Yose).

26. N15:8A

Lev. 13:55 + explanation of PHTT.

(26.* N15:13

Lev. 13:59 + Just as it is a *misvah* etc.)

27. MI:1-2

Lev. 14:2 + for the eternal house, not for a high place, in this time.

28. MI:6

Lev. 14:3 + his plague has left him, etc.

29. MI:12A-C

Lev. 14:4 + and not slaughtered, etc.

30. M1:3
    Lev. 14:5H + and not two, etc.

31. M1:7I
    Lev. 14:6 + and not killed by pinching.

32. MII:4A-B
    Lev. 14:8 + even in water of immersion pool.

*34. MII:11A-C
    Lev. 14:8 + he is to be like one who is excommunicated. (Rabbi, Yose b. R. Judah)

35. M2:9D-H
    Lev. 14:10 + various interpretations.

36. MIII:6
    Lev. 14:11 + he sets it up at Nicanor's gate.

37. M3:13A-B
    Lev. 14:19 + all deeds for the sake of the sin-offering.

38. M3:14A-B
    Lev. 14:20 + even though, etc.

*39. MIV:2G
    Lev. 14:21 + and not ... (Rabbi).

40. MV:7A
    Lev. 14:35 + he should send by a messenger.

41. MV:11E
    Lev. 14:35 + and not to ...

42. MV1:5
    Lev. 14:37 + colors.

43. M4:4A
    Lev. 14:40 + them ... but not ...

44. M4:9
    Lev. 14:42 + even bricks, etc.

45. M4:10A-B
    Lev. 14:42 + his fellow does not ...

46. M5:3A-C, E, F-H, K-M
    Lev. 14:45: citations of each word and exegeses.

If we now theorize that, in those long centuries of exegesis prior to the formulation of law in Mishnaic style without an exegetical support, simple exegetical form was followed, we find – at most – forty-six items. Of these we must omit those items which clearly are attributed to later authorities, e.g., after 70 or 132, Yavneh or Usha, Nos. 7, 9, 15, 16, 17, 22, 25, 34, 39, leaving thirty-seven. What emerges is nothing like a continuous exegetical treatise. The formally simple explanations remaining treat the following: Lev. 13:2, 3, 5, 6, 10, 12, 13, 14, 23, 33, 45, 49, 53, 55, 59; 14:2, 3, 4, 5, 6, 7, 8, 10, 11, 19, 20, 35, 37, 38, 40, 42, 45, that is, of the total of 116 verses, no more than 42, or 36%.

On the other hand, of the verses before us, the following are subjected to continuous commentary and do form a contiguous group: Lev. 13:2-6, Nos. 1-10 (omitting Nos. 7, 9), Lev. 13:10-14, Nos. 11-15 (omitting No. 15), Lev. 14:2-11, Nos. 27-36 (omitting No. 34), Lev. 14:25-42, Nos. 40-45. Of the 42 pericopae selected s likely to present the irreducible minimum of exegesis, therefore, and now including items omitted because they seem to derive from circles after 70, we see that as many as 31 are part of what appear to be continuous and contiguous sequences. That is a sizable proportion, 73% of the whole.

It therefore seems possible that the specified groups do form a primary stratum of Sifra's treatment of Leviticus 13-14. But, as is self-evident, even the most tightly organized sets are greatly enriched by the more complex forms and logical patterns intruded, in various ways and for various purposes, thereafter. The specified items will provide important means of testing our theories on conceptions which form the earliest theoretical stratum in the history of the law now in Mishnah. More than that cannot be suggested at this stage in the inquiry.

4.   Complex Form: Dialectical Exegesis

Every example of a complex form, that is, a pericopae in which we have more than a cited verse and a brief exposition of its meaning, may be called "dialectical," that is, moving or developing an idea through questions and answers, sometimes implicit, but commonly explicit. What "moves" is the argument, the flow of thought, from problem to problem. The movement is generated by the raising of contrary questions and theses. There are several subdivisions of the dialectical exegesis, so distinctive as to be treated by themselves. Let us begin with the largest catalogue. All of the items which follow are marked by the presence of more than a single unit of thought or the exposition of a range of questions, and all exhibit a flow of logical argument, unfolding in questions and answers, characteristic, in the later literature, of *gemara*.

5.   Dialectical Exegesis.   The Fallibility of Logic

One important subdivision of the stated form consists of those items, somewhat few in number but all rather large in size and articulation, intended to prove that logic alone is insufficient, and that only through revealed law will a reliable view of what is required be attained. The polemic in these items is pointed and obvious; logic (DYN) never wins the argument, though at a few points flaws in the text seem to suggest disjunctures in the flow of logic.

6. Dialectical Exegesis. The Perfection of Scripture

A further, unimportant subdivision of the stated form consists of those items whose primary purpose is to show that Scripture has good reasons for whatever it tells us. Each of the following begins, "Why does Scripture say so?"

7. Sifra's Joining Language

When Sifra makes use of materials common to Sifra and Mishnah and Tosefta, it commonly relies upon a fairly limited, and normally quite clear-cut, set of phrases which join an antecedent exegesis to a pericopae found also in Mishnah and Tosefta. The repertoire of joining language is as follows.

1. N1:1E-F: It is hardly necessary ... but there are ...
2. N1:4P: Lev. 13:2 + teaches that +material common to Sifra and M.
3. N1:4Q-R + 1:5: Verse plus explanatory matter + M.2:1.
4. N1:9M + N: How so? + M.3:1C.
5. N2:2H: On this basis + M.4:11.
6. N2:3: On this basis + M.4:4A-G, T.2:2.
7. N2:6D: We learned that + M.3:1F.
8. N2:9E: On this basis + M.6:7.
9. N.2:8D: That (S) + T.2:12E-G.
10. NII:4/O: On this basis + M.1:1, 2, 3, T.1:1.
11. NII:7: How so + M.4:6.
12. NII:8: How so + M.4:6.
13. N2*:3G: On this basis + M.2:2.
14. NIII:3C-D + III:4: Exegesis + M.5:3.
15. NIII:5: Exegesis + M.4:10Q-U.
16. NIII:6: Exegesis + M.4:10 L-P, M.4:10G-K.
17. NIII:11N-O: It comes out + M.6:1.
18. N4:3: On this basis have they said + M.2:4.
19. N4:4: On this basis have they said + M.2:3A.
20. N4:5J: On what basis do you rule + M.8:5H-K.
21. N5:1: No joining language to N5:1F-H = T.3:7-8.
22. N5:2: And how much + M.3:2.
23. N5:3: On what basis ... + M.8:5.
24. N5:4: That + T.3:9.
25. N6:1: How do we know + M.8:4E-F.

26. N6:6: How do we know + M.9:1C-D, M.7:1A.
27. N6:7: No joining language to M.9:3.
29. NIV:1-2: How + dispute.
29. NIV:6-7 = N7:9A-B: No joining language to M.5:2. Then: Therefore it is said.
30. NIV:8: How so + M.5:4E-K.
31. NIV:9: How so + M.5:5C-H.
32. NV:6: No joining language to M.10:1.
33. N8:7-8: On this basis + M.10:6-7.
34. N9:7: How so + M.10:5B-C.
35. N9:10: No joining language + M.10:5 + on this account it is said.
36. N10:2A: How do you know + M.10:9.
37. N10:6V: How do you know + M.10:10D.
38. N10:7: No joining language + T.4:9C.
39. N10:8: This teaches that + M.10:10.
40. N12:14: On this basis + M.13:7.
41. N13:7: When is + M.11:8.
42. N14:10: It comes out + M.11:7H.
43. N15:9: On this basis + M.11:11F-G.
44. N16:5: No link to M.11:5K-L-11:6.
45. N16:9: No link to M.11:7.
46. M1:5: What does he do + M.14:1E-F.
47. M1:6: How do we know that + M.14:5J-K.
48. M2:6 = M.14:4: No link to cited passage.
49. M3:4: You turn out to say + M.14:8.
50. M3:11-12 = M.14:9E-G, M.14:10H-K: No joining language whatsoever.
51. M3:13A-B, H-I.
52. M3:14.
53. MV:4: Excludes + M.12:1.
54. MV:11A-B: On this basis + M.2:3.
55. MVI:2-3: On this basis + M.12:1.
56. MVI:10: It comes out that one says +M.12:7.
57. M4:2: On this basis + M.12:6H-I.
58. M4:7: On this basis + M.12:6G.
59. MVII:2: You turn out to rule + M.12:7C-E.
60. MVII:12: How do I know + on this basis + M.12:1A-Q.
61. M5:1-2: This teaches that + M.12:2F, 12:3A-H.

62. M5:3I-J: On this basis + M.13:3A-E.
63. M5:3N-O: No clear joining language to T.6:10.
64. M5:8: No joining language to M.13:9E.
65. M5:10-13: On this basis + M.13:10, T.7:9J-K.
66. M5:16A-D: How do you know + T.1:2.

Of 66 items on this list, joining language of some precise formulaic quality links a pericope common to Sifra and Mishnah and Tosefta to antecedent materials in all but the following cases: Nos. 21, 27, 29, 32, 35, 38, 44, 45, 48, 50, 63, 64, 18% of the cited items, We may conclude that it is fairly common for Sifra, when introducing materials shared with Mishnah and Tosefta, to signify that two distinct units of tradition are in hand by the provision of some clear-cut joining language. But that fact, by itself, cannot prove that the materials common to Sifra and Mishnah and Tosefta invariably are secondary to, and intruded into, Sifra.

8.   Summary

First, Sifra does not commonly attribute its traditions to named authorities, and when it does, it is in the context of materials common to Sifra and Mishnah and Tosefta. Second, Sifra contains a predominance of exegetical pericopae, of 356 counted for the purposes of Part i, only 85 (23%) are non-exegetical in formal character and intent. Of these 85, fully 69 are shared by Sifra and Mishnah and Tosefta, and of the remainder, four are exegetical in substance, not in form (they are disputes). Accordingly, a negligible proportion of the whole – evidently approximately 12 items or 3% of the estimated total number of pericopae – in fact are both non-exegetical and also distinctive to Sifra. Where Sifra does not draw upon materials common to Mishnah and Tosefta, it is nearly wholly exegetical in character.

Third, in a fair number of items – 73 (20% of 356) – Sifra makes use of a very simple exegetical form, consisting of the citation of a verse followed by the provision of a few words explaining the meaning of the verse or of a word or phrase in the verse.

Fourth, all of the remaining exegetical items – 186 (52% + of the whole, but, taking account the fat that many entries in these lists cover more than a single pericope counted in the list in Part i, probably as much as 60-65% of the whole) – are characterized as dialectical. They present an argument which moves from point to point through a series of questions and answers.

Since Sifra is a composite document, with what I think is an early stratum of simple exegeses and a later, and much larger, stratum of dialectical ones, the purposes of the ultimate formulators of the dialectical materials and of the final redactors is revealed in particular in these dialectical constructions. It is to apply rigorous logic to the exegesis of Scripture and to demonstrate that revelation, not logic alone, is necessary for the discovery of the law. In doing so, the formulators and redactors of the late second and early third century probably made use of the inherited, simple form, spinning out their theses by presenting ideas in that uncomplicated form and then challenging those ideas in various ways but in equally simple, disciplined forms and formulaic usages. The final redaction also drew abundant materials from completed, free floating pericopae also utilized in the redaction of Mishnah and Tosefta. So far as we now can discern, these shared materials are prior to ultimate redaction to the work of compiling both Sifra and Mishnah and Tosefta. But they are, normally though not always, primary to the editorial and redactional purposes of Mishnah and Tosefta and secondary to those of Sifra.

The literary analysis strikingly distinguishes the literary traits of those shared pericopae from those of pericopae distinctive to Sifra. Pericopae found in both Sifra and Mishnah and Tosefta accord with the literary preferences and forms common to Mishnah and Tosefta and conflict with those peculiar to Sifra.

The materials common to Sifra and Mishnah and Tosefta nearly always take the forms and formulaic patterns characteristic of Mishnah and Tosefta and found in Sifra, with remarkably few exceptions, primarily in those shared materials. Sifra commonly makes not the slightest effort to link each element of the shared materials to the exegesis of Scriptures, which is its primary interest. Or if there is a connection between exegesis and the law stated in the materials common to both compilations, then that exegesis touches only one aspect, not always an important one, of the stated law.

Let me now generalize on the basis of the foregoing catalogues. The rhetorical plan of the Sifra, as the sample indicates, involves two fundamental rhetorical patterns,

> first, a citation of a verse followed by a few words that state the sense or meaning of that verse;

> second, the verbatim citation of a passage of the Mishnah in association with a verse of Scripture.

We may call the former plan exegetical, the latter polemical,[1] in that the latter rhetoric always serves to demonstrate the proposition stated just now, the priority of Scripture within the dual Torah of written and oral media. We may distinguish the two rhetorical forms by reference to the use of attributions. The former tends not to attribute its materials, the latter does. That is to say, in the main Sifra tends not to attribute its materials to specific authorities, and most of the pericopae containing attributions are shared with Mishnah and Tosefta. Of 354 items in my surveyed population, a total of 76 contain attributions, 21% of the whole. But of these, all but 20 are shared with Mishnah and Tosefta, 5% of

---

[1] In other contexts it may be preferable to call the counterpart form syllogistic or propositional, but in Sifra that form serves only a polemical purpose.

the whole. We may say that it is highly uncommon for Sifra to attribute to named authorities materials peculiar to itself.[2]

The polemical-syllogistic form requires differentiation in yet another way. Sifra contains a fair sample of pericopae which do not make use of the forms common in the exegesis of specific Scriptural verses and, mostly do not pretend to explain the meaning of verses, but rather resort to forms typical of Mishnah and Tosefta. When Sifra uses forms other than those in which its exegeses are routinely phrased, it commonly, though not always, draws upon materials also found in Mishnah and Tosefta. Of 87 pericopae of my sample of 13% of Sifra which are non-exegetical but follow forms typical of Mishnah and Tosefta, all but 16, 18%, are in fact common to Sifra and Mishnah and Tosefta. Of these 16, moreover, four are exegetical in substance, that is, dispute-forms are applied to exegetical materials. That leaves not more than 12 items, 14% of the whole sample of non-exegetical pericopae, unique to Sifra and not concerning exegetical problems in a substantive manner. Accordingly, we may conclude that it is uncommon for Sifra to make use of non-exegetical forms for materials peculiar to its compilation.

We may further differentiate within the exegetical pericope between the simplest exegetical form and somewhat more elaborate renditions of it. We now turn to those pericopae, predominant in Sifra, in which the center of interest is the exegesis of Scripture. These may be categorized as follows.

First is the simple, in which a verse, or an element of a verse, is cited, and then a very few words explain the meaning of that verse.

Second is the complex, in which a simple exegesis is augmented in some important way, commonly by questions and answers, so that we have more than simply a verse and a brief exposition of its elements or of its meaning as a whole. The complex form commonly involves a dialectical exegesis. Every example of a complex form, that is, a pericope in which we have more than a cited verse and a brief exposition of its meaning, may be called "dialectical," that is, moving or developing an idea through questions and answers, sometimes implicit, but commonly explicit. What "moves" is the argument, the flow of thought, from problem to problem. The movement is generated by the raising of contrary questions and theses.

One important subdivision of the complex form – as I showed in my classification of the forms – consists of those items, somewhat few in number but all large in size and articulation, intended to prove that logic alone is insufficient, and that only through revealed law will a reliable view of what is required be attained. The polemic in these items is pointed and obvious; logic (DYN) never wins the argument, though at a few points flaws in the text seem to suggest disjunctures in the flow of logic. A further, unimportant subdivision

---

[2]All factual statements in this chapter derive from my*History of the Mishnaic Law of Purities*. VII. *Negaim. Sifra* (Leiden, 1976: E. J. Brill). The sample is 13% of the whole of Sifra.

of the stated form consists of those items whose primary purpose is to show that Scripture has good reasons for whatever it tells us. Each of the following begins, "Why does Scripture say so?" When Sifra makes use of materials common to Sifra and Mishnah and Tosefta, it commonly relies upon a fairly limited, and normally quite clear-cut, set of phrases which join an antecedent exegesis to a pericopae found also in Mishnah and Tosefta.

The rhetorical plan of our sample of Sifra may be stated very simply.

First, the authorship of the Sifra responsible for items that occur only in Sifra and not in Mishnah or Tosefta does not commonly attribute its traditions to named authorities, and when it does, it is in the context of materials common to Sifra and Mishnah and Tosefta.

Second, Sifra contains a predominance of exegetical pericopae, of 356 counted in my sample,[3] only 85 (23%) are non-exegetical in formal character and intent. Of these 85, fully 69 are shared by Sifra and Mishnah and Tosefta, and of the remainder, four are exegetical in substance, not in form (they are disputes). Accordingly, a negligible proportion of the whole – evidently approximately 12 items or 3% of the estimated total number of pericopae – in fact are both non-exegetical and also distinctive to Sifra. Where Sifra does not draw upon materials common to Mishnah and Tosefta, it is nearly wholly exegetical in character. In a fair number of items – 73 (20% of 356) – Sifra makes use of a very simple exegetical form, consisting of the citation of a verse followed by the provision of a few words explaining the meaning of the verse or of a word or phrase in the verse. All of the remaining exegetical items – 186 (as much as 60-65% of the whole) – are characterized as dialectical. They present an argument which moves from point to point through a series of questions and answers.

The literary analysis strikingly distinguishes the literary traits of those shared pericopae from those of pericopae distinctive to Sifra. Pericopae found in both Sifra and Mishnah and Tosefta accord with the literary preferences and forms common to Mishnah and Tosefta and conflict with those peculiar to Sifra. The materials common to Sifra and Mishnah and Tosefta nearly always take the forms and formulaic patterns characteristic of Mishnah and Tosefta and found in Sifra, with remarkably few exceptions, primarily in those shared materials. Sifra commonly makes not the slightest effort to link each element of the shared materials to the exegesis of Scriptures, which is its primary interest. Or if there is a connection between exegesis and the law stated in the materials common to both compilations, then that exegesis touches only one aspect, not always an important one, of the stated law. How all of these facts may sustain Kugel's

---

[3] For complete texts, discussions, and catalogues see my *History of the Mishnaic Law of Purities*. VI. *Negaim. Sifra* (Leiden, 1976: E. J. Brill).

thesis about the priority and individuality of the discrete, free-floating exegesis of the individual verse I cannot say.[4]

V

Program

Sifra's authorship clearly has undertaken a well-considered program, arguing a set of quite cogent syllogisms, which guide them in their reading of the discrete verses of Scripture they have selected for exegesis. We may define that program solely in its relationship to the Mishnah and Tosefta, because, as the Sifra's formal plan has already indicated, a principal and recurrent point of interest is the relationship of Scripture's law to that in the Mishnah. One paramount polemic of the authorship of the Sifra maintains that Scripture, not logic, alone yields reliable conclusions. Logic by itself cannot be trusted. The exercises beginning *vehalo din hu* make that point and only that point.[5]

1.   Introduction

The first problem is, at what points do Sifra and Mishnah and Tosefta share a common agenda of interests, and at what points does one compilation introduce problems, themes, or questions unknown to the other? The answer to these questions will show that Sifra and Mishnah and Tosefta form two large concentric circles, sharing a considerable area in common. Sifra, however, exhibits interests peculiar to itself.

2.   Sifra and Mishnah and Tosefta

While as much as one third of the corpus of Sifra covers rules not known to Mishnah and Tosefta, when we eliminate refinements of laws known, explicitly or implicitly, to Mishnah and Tosefta., as well as narrowly exegetical

---

[4]It is simple to demonstrate the same rhetorical rules for all other midrash-compilations I have analyzed.   But the apply equally well to the Mishnah, Tosefta, and other halakhic compilations, so the formalization of rhetoric is a trait of the canonical literature of the Judaism of the dual Torah in general. When Kugel treats as distinct and uniquely indicative of "midrash" in particular the literary traits of midrash-exegeses collected in midrash-compilations, he errs.

[5]The same rhetorical-logical proposition characterizes Sifré to Numbers. Lest readers suppose that it is a commonplace, I hasten to add that it is a polemic utterly absent in Leviticus Rabbah, Genesis Rabbah, Pesiqta deRab Kahana, and The Fathers According to Rabbi Nathan, to name four documents at random. Those who read the rabbinic documents as interchangeable scrapbooks, which have made no impact upon their contents, have taken for granted a proposition against which every document I have analyzed beginning to end testifies. One wonders whether those who take the contrary view have analyzed any document beginning to end. Careful study of the impact of a document upon its exegetical contents is in Steven D. Fraade, "Sifre Deuteronomy 26 (ad Deut. 3:23): How Conscious the Composition?"*Hebrew Union College Annual* 1983, 54:245-302. See also my *Midrash in Context. Exegesis in Formative Judaism* (Philadelphia, 1983: Fortress). Neither of these two items occurs in Kugel's notes in his 1986 publication.

statements, we reduce the number to 56. 75% of all items peculiar to Sifra cover matters in which Mishnah and Tosefta cannot be said to be much interested. Sifra and Mishnah and Tosefta, where they do have common interests to begin with, are nearly wholly concentric. That is to say, with Sifra as the base and Mishnah and Tosefta as the variable, the two corpora seem to have in common 94% of all important items; a minimum of 81% of all pertinent items, important and unimportant, are shared in substance and even in exact language. The former figure will become still more important when we use Mishnah as the base and Sifra as the variable, for, as we shall see in a moment, the same procedure will yield nearly the same percentage of shared themes, interests, and pericopae using the same language. It would seem that, on the criterion of common themes and interests, with the sole omission of purification-rites, in which Sifra clearly has a unique and predominant concern, Mishnah and Tosefta and Sifra exhibit a remarkable unity. This underlines the conclusion reached in the examination of forms and the obvious implication of shared pericopae, which is that Mishnah and Tosefta and Sifra draw upon pretty much the same common stratum of materials and reflect a single set of conceptions and issues.

3. Mishnah and Sifra

Remarkably few pericopae in Mishnah will have surprised the pericopae unique to Mishnah go over ground. We may with some confidence say that, with Mishnah as the base and Sifra as the variable, Sifra covers nearly the whole 96% of Mishnah's themes and problems. On the surface, this would argue that Mishnah follows Sifra. But this is hardly a decisive consideration. Our earlier results make it far more likely that both compilations derive in their main conceptual traits from the last quarter of the second century and the first quarter of the third. Both documents make use of discrete pericopae completed in Ushan times and in the period of Rabbi – and cite them in pretty much identical language. As we now see, both documents also cover the same ground, sharing something like 90-95% of the same themes and ideas, not to mention laws.

The upshot of these studies may be stated very briefly. In describing the history of the laws of Negaim, we must now take full account of the materials of Sifra, which are to be regarded as chronologically and thematically correlative to those of Mishnah and Tosefta. Both major compilations share a common agenda of legal interests. Both evidently draw upon materials which reached their state before the redaction of either – as a whole or in large constitutive elements – commenced. Neither can be treated in isolation from the other.

VI

Document

In a few words we may revert to our opening issue and settle the questions raised there.

1. Structure: how, overall, does the document organize its materials? The framers of Sifra follow a clearly discernible principle or organization, citing verses one by one to amplify their sense or to join the verse to a passage of Scripture. The document is exegetical in a strict sense: it systematically explains the meaning of verses of Scripture and it organizes its materials in line with the order of those verses.

2. Plan: does the document at hand follow a fixed and limited plan, a repertoire of rhetorical forms? There are two – and only two – rhetorical patterns, and these govern throughout.

3. Program: do these forms yield cogent and intelligible proposition(s), one(s) that, in some recurrent interest(s) or point(s) of emphasis, may make of the whole if not more than, then at least, the sum of, the parts? We can discern at least one important polemic, and, beyond that, we see a systematic picture of the sense and meaning of the cited passage. There is nothing random or casual about the propositional program of the document.

It follows that the overall plan and program of the authorship of our document do impart to the parts a cogency of rhetoric, syllogistic logic of cogent discourse, and even proposition or topic, making of the parts something that joins and therefore transcends them all. Ignoring the plan and program of the authorship of Sifra renders incomprehensible what is in fact an intelligible and cogent statement. I look in vain for evidence in support of Kugel's allegation that *Our midrashic compilations are in this sense potentially deceiving, since they seem to treat the whole text bit by bit; but with the exception of certain patterns, these "bits" are rather atomistic, and, as any student or rabbinic literature knows, interchangeable, modifiable, combinable – in short, not part of an overall exegesis at all* I do not see a single passage in the brief sample of Sifra we have reviewed, which is interchangeable with any other, let alone "modifiable" or "combinable" with any other, outside of its concrete context. The "certain patterns" of our sample of Sifra govern the whole. They are two, and they dictate the character of the details – if not, in the nature of things, the content.

VII
The Debate with James Kugel

1. Kugel's "Two Introductions" and the Documentary Facts

We have found difficulty in locating evidence in support of Kugel's propositions. Indeed, the preponderance of evidence pointed to precisely the opposite conclusions. Since Kugel clearly has worked hard on the study of midrash-exegeses, readily invoking what everybody knows as proof for his premises or positions *("as any student of rabbinic literature knows")*, we must conclude that – as in the case of all mortals – his strength is his weakness. What he knows he knows in one way, rather than in some other. Having spent a great deal of effort to explain how a given verse has precipitated a received exegesis, he quite reasonably concluded that exegeses begin with the problems of verses. Having reached that position, furthermore, he appears not to have spent a great deal of time in the analysis of rhetoric, on the one side, or in the inquiry into the principles of logical cogency and intelligible discourse, on the other. This has further discouraged him from asking whether a document as a whole proposes to make a point or to register a syllogism or a set of syllogisms. I suppose that, if one works in a pickle factory all day long, everything for supper will taste like pickles.

And yet, I think there is a deeper premise than the one defined by scholarly habits, both bad and good. The clue lies in Kugel's explicit recognition of the category of canon: "there simply is no boundary encountered beyond that of the verse until one comes to the borders of the canon itself." That is another way of saying that the Torah is one and seamless, or that Judaism is Judaism. And so it is – at the end.

But the problem of how diverse documents, with their premises and their distinct syllogisms, fit together is not solved merely by saying it is solved. Precisely how the diverse documents constitute a canon, where, when, and why a given document and its message made its way into the canon – these are questions Kugel and those he represents do not address. They treat as the premise of their literary critical reading of midrash-exegeses what in fact defines the most profound and difficult problem in the reading of all of the documents that, today, after the fact, constitute the canon, or the Torah.

2. The Propositions

A very brief reprise suffices to state the upshot of this example of the results of sustained study of documents and their properties. In italics I quote state what I conceive to be the premise of Kugel's words, which follow, also in italics:

A. *Midrash is precipitated by the character of the verse subject to exegesis:*

   ...midrash's precise focus is most often what one might call surface irregularities in the text: a good deal of the time, it is concerned with...problems.[6]

In detail, Kugel may well be right. That is to say, once an exegete has chosen the verse and knows what he wishes, in general, to prove, then a set of the properties of a given verse may attract attention. Why one type of property,

---

[6]P. 92.

rather than some other, why one issue, not another – these are questions to which the discrete exegesis of a verse on its own does not respond. But I do not register a one-sided disagreement with the position represented by Kugel that the traits of a given verse register in the formation of an exegesis of that verse. I am certain that the received exegetical literature, the thousand-year tradition of reading the midrash-exegeses precisely the way Kugel and others wish to read them, enjoys ample proof in result in detail. But it begs the question to conclude *post hoc, ergo propter hoc*, as Kugel and his friends do.

B.   *Midrash is an exegesis of biblical verses, not of books:*

> *...midrash is an exegesis of biblical verses, not of books. The basic unit of the Bible for the midrashist is the verse: this is what he seeks to expound, and it might be said that there simply is no boundary encountered beyond that of the verse until one comes to the borders of the canon itself.*[7]

It is simply false to claim that there is no boundary between midrash-exegesis of a single verse and the entirety of the canon of Judaism. The opposite is the fact.

And yet here too, Kugel is not completely wrong. Some materials do travel freely from document to document, though apart from verses of Scripture, nothing known to me appears in every document of the dual Torah in its repertoire of late antiquity, through the Talmud of Babylonia. Hyman's *Torah hekketubah vehammesurah*, which lists pretty much all places in the corpus in which a given verse comes under discussion, sustains that judgment, as a rapid survey will show. Nonetheless, the peripatetic sayings and stories do journey hither and yon. So Kugel is talking about facts, if not (in proportion to the whole) a great many, and if not (in weight of evidence) probative ones.

But why they are accepted here and not there, what a given authorship has chosen to accomplish through citing a passage they have found in an earlier document, we cannot explain for the documents of late antiquity merely by saying things move from here to there. If a document's authorship exhibits a cogent program, then we should be able to explain why they have used a peripatetic saying or story or exegesis of a verse of Scripture in the way they have. Or, we should be able to state, we do not know what, if anything, they proposed to accomplish in resorting to the passage at hand. Or we should ask about the history of a composite unit of materials prior to the authorship's selecting it, for at least some travelling materials were composed into a larger conglomerate prior to their insertion in some of the several documents in which they occur. So the reason a given midrash-exegesis recurs may well be found in the history of the larger composite of which it forms a part. That proposition is fairly easy to demonstrate, as a matter of fact. And it calls into question the

---

[7] P. 93.

notion that authorships compose their documents essentially through free association.[8]

C. *The components of midrash-compositions are interchangeable:*

Our midrashic compilations are in this sense potentially deceiving, since they seem to treat the whole text bit by bit; but with the exception of certain patterns, these "'bits" are rather atomistic, and, as any student or rabbinic literature knows, interchangeable, modifiable, combinable – in short, not part of an overall exegesis at all.[9]

Kugel is wrong. He does not demonstrate that the components of midrash-exegesis are mere atoms, readily interchanged, modified, combined in diverse ways. In his defense, I point to what I said at the third proposition. Some (few) midrash-exegeses do occur in a number of passages. Characterizing all of them as Kugel does, however, violates the facts of something on the order of 80-90% of the midrash-exegeses in the documents that I have examined in detail, in the model of what I have done here with Sifra.

But there is another line of argument in support of Kugel's contention. The midrash-documents of medieval times are highly imitative, borrowing and arranging and rearranging whole tracts of received materials. The authorships intervene in various ways, in some cases making up exegeses and assigning them to named authorities of a thousand years earlier. They succeed because of their power of imitation. Now if Kugel wishes to propose that the pseudepigraphic character of the midrash-compilations of medieval and early modern times – the making of collections/*yalquts* continued into the nineteenth century! – demonstrates the interchangeable character of the received materials, I believe he can make a solid case. But that case testifies to the taste of the imitators and pseudepigraphs, rather than to the historical setting and point of origin of the earlier documents. Usefulness to later authorships tells us about the enduring appeal of the creations of earlier ones. It does not tell us that everything is everywhere interchangeable – unless as our premise we take the facticity of attributions, on the one side,[10] and the fundamental irrelevance of

---

[8]The conception that authorships play an active role in the formation of what they include in their documents is not new to me or particular to my school. It is in fact a routine inquiry, one that has produced interesting results for diverse scholars. I call attention, for example, to Steven Fraade, "Sifré Deuteronomy 26 (ad Deut. 3:23): How Conscious the Composition," *Hebrew Union College Annual* 1983, 54:245-302. Despite his certainty on these matters, I can find in Kugel's notes no reference to, or argument with, Fraade. My own debate with Fraade is in my *Religious Study of Judaism. Description, Analysis, and Interpretation* (Lanham, 1986: University Press of America *Studies in Judaism* series) I:93-128, in particular, pp. 104-108, "Fraade vs. Fraade." But Fraade in his HUCA paper is certainly on the right track.

[9]P. 95

[10]I shall refer to Kugel's history of midrash in a moment.

context and circumstance of the original formation of the document, on the other. But, as a matter of fact, Kugel and his friends build on both of these premises.

D. *Midrash is erudite joking*

> *Forever after, one cannot think of the verse or hear it recited without also recalling the solution to its problematic irritant–indeed, remembering it in the study-house or synagogue, one would certainly pass it along to others present, and together appreciate its cleverness and erudition. And so midrashic explications of individual verses no doubt circulated on their own, independent of any larger exegetical context. Perhaps in this sense it would not be inappropriate to compare their manner of circulating to that of jokes in modern society; indeed, they were a kind of joking, a learned and sophisticated play about the biblical text, and like jokes they were passed on, modified, and improved as they went, until a great many of them eventually entered into the common inheritance of every Jew, passed on in learning with the text of the Bible itself.[11]*

Kugel does not prove that "every Jew" has received this "common inheritance," though as a matter of religious faith he may hold that every Jew should accept it. He does not demonstrate that we deal with "a kind of joking," and nothing in the propositions and syllogisms I have outlined justifies his rather jejune characterization of this literature. How this literary judgment, which I regard as unproved and probably groundless, accords with the theological position at hand I cannot say.

What I find stunning in the midrash-compilations as well as in their contents, the midrash-exegeses is the urgency and immediacy of matters, not the cleverness and erudition demonstrated therein. Israel, the people of God, turned to with deep anxieties about salvation to Genesis, Leviticus, and the sacred calendar in Genesis Rabbah, Leviticus Rabbah, and Pesiqta deRab Kahana, respectively.[12] I find nothing amusing, merely clever, or particularly erudite in what the sages found there. In my description, analysis, and interpretation of the midrash-compilations, I find messages of self-evident truth in response to questions of life and death. In this judgment of Kugel's I find no merit, since it treats as trivial and merely personal what is in fact a monumental theological statement of the founders of Judaism. Our sages were not scholars, mere clever erudites. They were holy men and they gave God's judgment, through the Torah,

---

[11]P. 95.

[12]I have retranslated each of these documents and conducted systematic studies of them, along the lines shown here, demonstrating the limited repertoire of rhetorical initiatives and the cogent character of logical modes of argument in behalf of a limited and powerful program of topical propositions.

oral and written, to suffering Israel – then and now. I cannot find redeeming arguments in behalf of Kugel's amazing judgment, which turns the Judaic exegetes of Scripture into erudite college professors of literary criticism.

VIII

From Mishmash to Midrash

Taking *midrash-meaning-exegesis* out of its documentary context, that is, *midrash-meaning-a-document* that organizes and presents midrash turns *midrash* into *mishmash*. That is not because of errors of judgment about trivialities, let alone because he does not know what he is talking about, but because of a fundamental error in the reading of the literature. Since, as I said, Kugel has evidently read the documents atomistically, he claims that they are made up only of atoms. When he works his way through complete compilations of midrash-exegeses and gives us his judgment on whether or not they form mere scrapbooks or purposely statements, documents of integrity, as I have done, for one example among many, in my work on the Mishnah, tractate Avot, the Sifra, Sifré to Numbers, the Tosefta, the Yerushalmi, the Bavli, Genesis Rabbah, Leviticus Rabbah, the Fathers According to Rabbi Nathan, Pesiqta deRab Kahana, and other documents, as typified in my *The Integrity of Leviticus Rabbah*, we shall see whether or not he maintains the view he announces in the statements under discussion here. I am inclined not to anticipate that he will, once he has done his homework.

Chapter Two

The Literary Structure of Pesiqta Rabbati

I

Introduction

The description of a document goes forward in diverse ways. In this second exercise of documentary analysis, I wish to show how we may define the rhetorical character of a cogent piece of writing by analyzing its literary structures and demonstrating their conventional and definitive character. In this way what we have seen in respect to Sifra's remarkable literary cogency will be shown to be routine and not idiosyncratic for the canon of Judaism.

A literary structure is a set of rules that dictate to an authorship recurrent conventions of expression, organization, or proportion that are *extrinsic* to the message of the author or authorship. The conventions at hand bear none of the particular burden of the author's personal and particular message, so they are not idiosyncratic. They convey in their context the larger world-view expressed within the writing in which they are used, so they prove systemic and public. That is because a literary structure conforms to rules that impose upon the individual writer a limited set of choices about how he will convey whatever message he has in mind. Or the formal convention will limit an editor or redactor to an equally circumscribed set of alternatives about how to arrange received materials. These conventions then form a substrate of the literary culture that preserves and expresses the world-view and way of life of the system at hand.

A structure in literature thus will dictate the way in which diverse topics or ideas come to verbal expression. It follows that we cannot know that we have a structure if the text under analysis does not repeatedly resort to the presentation of its message through that disciplined syntactic pattern (or other structure that organizes fixed components of discourse, e.g., materials taken from some other and prior document), external to its message on any given point. And, it follows, quite self-evidently, that we do know that we have a structure when the text in hand repeatedly follows recurrent conventions of expression, organization, or proportion *extrinsic* to the message of the author. The adjective "recurrent" therefore constitutes a redundancy when joined to the noun "structure." For a structure – in our context, a persistent syntactic pattern, rhetorical preference, logical composition – by definition recurs and characterizes a variety of passages.

Like Pesiqta deRab Kahana, Pesiqta Rabbati comprises large-scale literary structures.

How do we know that fact? It is because, when we divide up the undifferentiated columns of words and sentences and point to the boundaries that separate one completed unit of thought or discourse from the next such completed composition, we produce rather sizable statements conforming to a single set of syntactic and other formal patterns. On the basis of what merely appears to us to be patterned or extrinsic to particular meaning and so entirely formal, we cannot allege that we have in hand a fixed, literary structure. Such a judgment would prove subjective. Nor shall we benefit from bringing to the text at hand recurrent syntactic or grammatical patterns shown in other texts, even of the same canon of literature, to define conventions for communicating ideas in those other texts. Quite to the contrary, we find guidance in a simple principle:

A text has to define its own structures for us.

Its authors do so by repeatedly resorting to a given set of linguistic patterns and literary conventions – and no others. On the basis of a survey of recurrent choices, we may account for the "why this, not that" of literary forms. On that same basis of inductive evidence alone we test the thesis that the authors at hand adhere to a fixed canon of literary forms. If demonstrably present, we may conclude that these forms will present an author or editor with a few choices on how ideas are to be organized and expressed in intelligible – again, therefore, public – compositions. When, as in the present exercise, we draw together and compare two distinct documents, each one to begin with has to supply us with evidence on its own literary structures.

So we look for large-scale patterns and point to such unusually sizable compositions as characteristic. Why? Because they recur and define discourse, *pisqa* by *pisqa*. Indeed, as we shall now see, a given *pisqa* is made up of a large-scale literary structure, which in a moment I shall describe in detail. In all, what I mean when I claim that Pesiqta Rabbati, like Pesiqta deRab Kahana, is made up of large-scale literary structures is simple. When we divide a given *pisqa*, or chapter, of Pesiqta Rabbati into its sub-divisions, we find these sub-divisions stylistically cogent and well-composed, always conforming to the rules of one out of three possible formal patterns. To identify the structures of the document before us, we had best move first to the analysis of a single *pisqa*. We seek, within that *pisqa*, to identify what holds the whole together. The second step then is to see whether we have identified something exemplary, or what is not an example of a fixed and formal pattern, but a phenomenon that occurs in fact only once or at random. For the first exercise, we take up *Pisqa* One, and for the second, Two through Five, then Fifteen. I give the complete text of Pisqa One. A bird's eye view of the whole of Pesiqta Rabbati shows it to be a formally uniform document, so that sample suffices for the purposes of working out the argument of this article.

II
Pesiqta Rabbati Pisqa One

The verse that recurs throughout derives from the prophetic lection that is read in the synagogue when the New Moon coincides with the Sabbath:

> [For as the new heavens and the new earth which I am making shall endure in my sight, says the Lord, so shall your race and your name endure;] and month by month at the new moon, week by week on the Sabbath, all mankind shall come to bow down before me, says the Lord; [and they shall come out and see the dead bodies of those who have rebelled against me; their worm shall not die nor their fire be quenched; and they shall be abhorred by all mankind] (Is. 66:22-24).

I:I

1. A. May our master instruct us:
    B. In the case of an Israelite who said the blessing for food on the New Moon but forgot and did not make mention of the New Moon [in the recitation of the grace after meals], what does one have to do?
    C. Our masters have taught us:
    D   If one has forgotten and not made mention of the New Moon, but, once he has completed reciting the Grace after Meals, remembered on the spot, still having in mind the blessing that he has recited, one does not have to go back to the beginning. But he concludes with a brief blessing at the end, which is as follows: "Blessed are you, Lord, our God, king of the world, who has assigned New Moons to Israel, his people. Blessed are you, Lord, who sanctifies both Israel and the New Moons."

2. A. Simeon b. Abba in the name of R. Yohanan said, "And in reference to the New Moon [in the Grace] one has to say, 'And bestow upon us, Lord our God [the blessing of the festival season].'"
    B. Lo, we learn, the New Moons are equivalent to festivals.
    C. For it is said, On the day of your rejoicing, and on your festivals, and on your new moons (Num. 10:10).
    D. And are New Moons equivalent even to the Sabbath?
    E. You may state [the proof of that proposition] as follows:
    F. New Moons are equivalent to festivals and the Sabbath. And how do we know that they are, in fact, equivalent to Sabbaths?
    G. It is on the basis of what the complementary reading of the prophetic writings [for the New Moon that coincides with the Sabbath] states: ...and month by month at the new moon, week by week on the Sabbath, all mankind shall come to bow down before me (Is. 66:23). [The New Moon is treated as equivalent in importance to the Sabbath.]

The thematic principle of composition is shown by the simple fact that No. 2 has no bearing upon No. 1. The opening unit is autonomous and presents a simple legal question. The liturgical reply does not include a proof-text of any kind. No. 2 then pursues its theological question, on the equivalent importance of the New Moon to the Sabbath. Since no rule of conduct is adduced, the issue is theoretical. Then proof derives from the base-text at hand.

I:II

1. A.   Thus did R. Tanhuma commence discourse [citing a Psalm that express sorrow that one cannot go to the Temple on a pilgrim festival]: *[As a hind longs for the running streams, so do I long for you, O God.] With my whole being I thirst for God, the living God. When shall I come to God and appear in his presence? [Day and night, tears are my food; Where is your God?' they ask me all day long. As I pour out my soul in distress, I call to mind how I marched in the ranks of the great to the house of God, among exultant shouts of praise, the clamor of the pilgrims]* (Ps. 42:1-4).

    B.   In respect to this inaugural discourse, [what follows] is the materials that occur at the beginning of the discussion of the passage, *After the death of the two sons of Aaron* (Lev. 16:1ff).

2. A.   Another matter: *With my whole being I thirst for God,*

    B.   specifically [I thirst for the time] when you mete out justice upon the nations of the world,

    C.   in line with the verse, *You shall not curse God* [meaning, judges] (Ex. 22:27).

3. A.   Another matter: *With my whole being I thirst for God:*

    B.   [I thirst for God specifically, for the time] when you will restore that divinity which you formed of me at Sinai:

    C.   *I said, You are God* (Ps. 82:6).

4. A..   Another matter: *[With my whole being]I thirst for God:*

    B.   [I thirst for God specifically, for the time] [Mandelbaum:] when You will be cloaked with the power of divinity as You were cloaked in divinity at Sinai]. [Following Braude: I thirst for God specifically for the time when you cloak me in divinity as you cloaked me in divinity at Sinai.]

    C.   Draw near the end-time and make one alone your divinity in your world: *The Lord will be king over the entire earth* (Zech. 14:9).

    D.   That is in line with the exegesis of the statement concerning Jacob: *So may God give you dew* (Gen. 27:28), [which may be interpreted, May he give you the power of divinity and you take it,] when [therefore] he accepts the power of divinity. [This sustains Braude's reading.]

5. A..   Another matter: *With my whole being I thirst for God:*

    B.   who lives and endures for ever and ever.

6. A..   Another matter: *With my whole being I thirst for God:*

    B.   who watches over our lives, bringing down rain in its season, and calling up due in its time, for the sake of our lives.

7. A.   Another matter: *[With my whole being I thirst for God,] the living God.*

    B.   The living God, who lives and endures by his word.

    C.   Said R. Phineas the priest, son of Hama, "Even though those who carried the promises among the prophets have died, God, who made the promises, lives and endures."

8. A.   *With my whole being I thirst for God, the living God. When shall I come to God and appear in his presence?*

    B.   Said Israel to him, "Lord of the world, When will you restore to us the glory that we should go up [to the Temple [on the three pilgrim festivals and see the face of the Presence of God?"

C. Said R. Isaac, "Just as they came to see, so they came to be seen, for it is said, 'When shall I come to God and appear in his presence? '"

9. A. **Said R. Joshua b. Levi, "Why did they call it 'the Rejoicing of the Place of the Water Drawing'? Because from there they drink of the Holy Spirit"** [Gen. R. LXX:VIII.3.E].

10. A. They said, "When will you restore us to that glory!

B. "Lo, how much time has passed since the house of our life [the Temple] was destroyed! Lo, a septennate, lo, a jubilee, lo, seven hundred seventy-seven years [have gone by], and now it is one thousand one hundred and fifty one years [since then]. [Braude, p. 39, n. 19: "The first year referred to is 847, the next, 1221. Both dates I regard as copyists' glosses. Neither date is mentioned in Parma MS, which lacks Section 2 of this Piska."]

11. A. *When shall I come to God and appear in his presence?*

B. He said to them, "My children, in this age how many times a year did you go up for the pilgrim festivals [in each year]? Was it not merely three times a year? But when the end will come, I shall build it, and you will come up not merely three times a year, but every single month [at the new moon], and every Sabbath you will come up."

C. That is in line with this verse: *and month by month at the new moon, week by week on the Sabbath, all mankind shall come to bow down before me, says the Lord* (Is. 66:22-24). [That is to say, not only on the festivals but on the New Moon and the Sabbath people will bow down before God, just as, at Nos. 8-9, we have said people do on the pilgrim festivals.]

No. 1 is not articulated, but the important contribution is not to be missed. The intersecting-verse, which will be fully expounded before being drawn into contact with the base-verse, is introduced. The relevance of the intersecting-verse cannot be missed. It speaks of the yearning to go to the Temple on a pilgrim festival, and at the end the promise is made that, when the end comes, Israel will go to the Temple not only for pilgrim festivals, but also for the New Moon and the Sabbath. That eschatological reading of the New Moon, in particular, then is fully articlated in the exposition of the intersecting-verse. Nos. 2, 3, 4 speak of the I, Israel, yearning to gain that union with divinity that it once enjoyed. No. 5, 6 then speak of God, and No. 7 underlines the continuing validity of the promises made to Israel by the prophets. The prophets are no more, but God will keep the promises announced through them. This leads us directly to Nos. 8, 10-11, which come to the point of the compositor of the whole. Specifically, the New Moon will enter the status of a pilgrim festival – and that fundamental proposition certainly has the support of the intersecting-verse as we have already expounded it. So the whole forms a cogent and stunning statement. Only No. 9 is borrowed, verbatim.

I:III

1. A. Another interpretation of the verse *...and month by month at the new moon, week by week on the Sabbath, all mankind shall come to bow down before me, says the Lord* (Is. 66:22-24):

   B. How is it possible that all mankind will be able to come to Jerusalem every month and every Sabbath?

   C. Said R. Levi, "Jerusalem is going to become equivalent to the Land of Israel, and the Land of Israel equivalent to the entire world.

   D. And how will people come every New Month and Sabbath from the end of the world?

   E. Clouds will come and carry them and bring them to Jerusalem, where they will say their morning prayers.

   D. That is in line with what the prophet says in praise: *Who are those, who fly like a cloud* (Is. 60:8).

2. A. Another interpretation of the verse *...and month by month at the new moon, week by week on the Sabbath, all mankind shall come to bow down before me, says the Lord* (Is. 66:22-24):

   B. Now lo if the New Moon coincided with the Sabbath, and Scripture has said, Another interpretation of the verse *...and month by month at the new moon, week by week on the Sabbath,* how [is it possible to do so once on the New Moon and once on the Sabbath, for on the occasion on which the two coincide, they can do it only once, not twice]?

   C. Said R. Phineas, the priest, son of Hama, in the name of R. Reuben, "They will come twice, once for the purposes of the Sabbath, the other time for the purposes of the New Moon. The clouds will carry them early in the morning and bring them to Jerusalem, where they will recite the morning-prayer, and they will then bring them home.

   D. *"Who are those, who fly like a cloud* (Is. 60:8) refers to the trip in the morning.

   E. *"And as the doves to the dovecots* (Is. 60:8) refers to the trip in the evening."

3. A. What the verse says is not *Israel,* but rather *all mankind [shall come to bow down before me, says the Lord]* (Is. 66:22-24).

   B. Said R. Phineas, "What is the meaning of *all mankind* [Hebrew: *all flesh ,* BSR]?

   C. "Whoever has restrained [BSR] his desire in this age will have the merit of seeing the face of the Presence of God.

   D. "For it is written, *He who closes his eyes from gazing upon evil* (Is. 33:15).

   E. "And what follows? *The king in his beauty will your eyes behold* (Is. 33:17).

4. A. Another interpretation of the verse *all mankind [shall come to bow down before me, says the Lord]* (Is. 66:22-24):

   B. Does this apply to all the idolators?

   C. Rather, only those who did not subjugate Israel will the Messiah accept.

We proceed to the clause by clause exposition of our base-verse, asking questions that point toward the eschatological theme the compositor wishes to underline. The first question, No. 1, is a practical one. But, we see, the proof-text, Is. 60:8, is then drawn in for further service at No. 2. No. 3 proceeds to the issue of all flesh/mankind, of the base-verse, and No. 4 pursues that same matter – in all, a cogent and well composed discourse.

I:IV.

1. A. On account of what merit will Israel enjoy all of this glory?
    B. It is on account of the merit of dwelling in the Land of Israel.
    C. For the Israelites lived in distress among the nations in this world.
    D. And so you find concerning the patriarchs of the world without end: concerning what did they go to much trouble? Concerning burial in the Land of Israel.

2. A. Said R. Hanina, "All references to shekels that are made in the Torah are to *selas*, in the Prophets are to *litras*, in the Writings are to *centenarii*."
    B. R. Abba bar Yudan in the name of R. Judah bar Simon: "Except for the shekels that Abraham weighed out for Ephron for the burial ground that he purchased from him, which were centenarii [(Mandelbaum:) the word shekel has the same numerical value as *centenarii*]: *The piece of land cost four hundred silver shekels* (Gen,. 23:15).
    C. "Now take note that he paid for hundred silver centenarii for a burial plot.
    D. "So in the case of Jacob, all the gold that he had ever acquired and all the money that he had been given he handed over to Esau in exchange for his right of burial, so that he should not be buried in it.
    E. "For it is said, *[Joseph spoke to the household of Pharaoh saying, If now I have found favor in your eyes, speak, I pray you, in the ears of Pharaoh, saying, My father made me swearing, saying, I am about to die,] in my tomb which I hewed out for myself in the land of Canaan, there shall you bury me* (Gen. 50:4-5).
    F. "And so you find that, when he was departing this earth, he imposed on Joseph an oath, saying to him, Do not, I pray you, bury me in Egypt (Gen. 47:29)."
    G. Why so?
    H. R. Hanina says, "There is a sound reason."
    I. R. Yose says, ""There is a sound reason."
    J. Said R. Simeon b. Laqish in the name of R. Eleazar Haqqappar, "It is because the dead [of the Land of Israel] will live in the time of the Messiah, as David has said, *I shall go before the Lord in the land of the living* (Ps. 116:9).
    K. "Now [can his meaning be that people do not die there, and] is it really the case that in the Land of Israel people live [and do not die]? But do people not die there? And is it not the case that outside of the Land of Israel is the land where people live?
    L. "But as to the Land of Israel, the corpses are commonly found there, and when David said, *In the land of the living,* he meant that the dead there will live in the days of the Messiah."

The connection to the foregoing is rather tenuous. The compositor simply introduces the systematic discussion of the value of living in the land by referring obliquely to what has gone before at 1.A-2, and then proceeding to collect materials on the importance to the patriarchs and to David and the Messiah of living in the land. No. 2 is an autonomous entry, parachuted in for good reasons, and these are spelled out. The dead buried in the Land will live again. Discourse continues in **I:V**, as we now see.

I:V

1. A. R. Yose asked R. Simeon b. Laqish, "Even will such as Jeroboam son of Nabat rise [from the grave when the Messiah comes]?"

    B. He said to him, "Brimstone and salt [will be his fate]."

    C. R. Helbo asked R. Ammi, "Even will such as Jeroboam son of Nabat rise [from the grave when the Messiah comes]?"

    D. He said to him, "I asked R. Simeon b. Laqish, and he said to me, 'Brimstone and salt [will be his fate].'"

    E. R. Berekhiah asked R. Helbo, "Even will such as Jeroboam son of Nabat rise [from the grave when the Messiah comes]?"

    F. He said to him, "I asked R. Ammi, and he said to me, 'I asked R. Simeon b. Laqish, and he said to me, "Brimstone and salt [will be his fate]."'"

    G. Said R. Berekhiah, "Should we wish to state the mystery, what is the sense of his reply to him, 'Brimstone'?

    H. "Is it not the case that the Holy One, blessed be He, is going to exact punishment of the wicked in Gehenna only with brimstone and salt! But the Temple has been destroyed [with brimstone and salt, which therefore have already been inflicted on those buried in the land, inclusive of Jeroboam, who, having received his punishment, along with the others, therefore will rise from the dead]."

2. A. Said R. Judah b. R. Ilai, "For seven years the Land of Israel was burning with brimstone and fire, in line with this verse: *The whole land thereof is brimstone and salt and a burning* (Deut. 29:22).

3. A. Said R. Yose b. Halafta, "For fifty-two years after the destruction of the Temple, no one passed through the Land of Israel,

    B. "in line with this verse, *For the mountains will I take a weeping and a wailing...because they are burned up, so that none passes through..both the fowl of the heavens and the beast are fled and gone* (Jer. 9:9).

    C. "Why is this the case? Because it was burning with the fire that had been poured out on it in line with this verse, *From on high has he sent fire into my bones* (Lam. 1:13)."

4. A. Why was this [done] by God? It was to exact punishment from Jeroboam son of Nabat and his fellows through those seven years during which the Land of Israel was burning with fire.

    B. It follows that even Jeroboam ben Nabat and his fellows will live in the time of the Messiah.

    C. And what was it that saved them from the judgment of Gehenna and to live [in the resurrection of the dead]?

    D. It was the fact that they were buried in the Land of Israel, as it is said, *His land will make expiation for his people* (Dt. 32:43).

The foregoing is concluded here, a distinct essay on Jeroboam, which makes the point introduced in **I:V** that there is distinct merit in living in the Land of

Israel. Nos. 2, 3 are separates that have been inserted because they contain facts important for the unfolding argument. No. 4 carries forward the matter begun at No. 1 and underlines the main point.

I:VI

1. A. Said R. Huna the priest, son of Abin, in the name of R. Abba b. Yamina, "R. Helbo and R. Hama bar Hanina [differed].

   B. "R. Helbo said, 'He who dies overseas and is buried overseas is subject to distress on two counts, distress because of death, distress because of burial.

   C. "'Why? For it is written in connection with Pashhur, *And you, Pashhur, and all those who well in your house shall go into captivity, and you shall to Babylonia and there you shall die and there you shall be buried* (Jer. 20:6).'

   D. "And R. Hama bar Hanina said, 'He who dies overseas, if he comes from overseas and is buried in the land, is subject to distress only by reason of death alone.'"

   E. Then how does R. Hama bar Hanina interpret the verse, *...here you shall die and there you shall be buried* (Jer. 20:6)?

   G. Burial in the Land of Israel achieves atonement for him.

2. A. R. Beroqia and R. Eleazar b. Pedat were walking in a grove [Braude, p. 45], and biers came from abroad. Said R. Beroqia to R. Eleazar, "What good have these accomplished? When they were alive, they abandoned [the Land] and now in death they have come back!"

   B. Said R. Eleazar b. Pedat to him, "No, that is not the case. Since they are buried in the Land of Israel, and a clump of earth of the Land of Israel is given over to them, it effects atonement for them,

   C. "as it is said, *And his land shall make expiation for his people* (Deut. 32:43)."

3. A. If that is the case, then have the righteous who are overseas lost out?

   B. No. Why not?

   C. Said R. Eleazar in the name of R. Simai, "God makes for them tunnels in the earth, and they roll like skins and come to the Land of Israel.

   D. "And when they have come to the Land of Israel, God restores their breath to them.

   E. "For it is said, *He who gives breath to the people upon it and spirit to them that go through it* (Is. 42:5)."

   F. "And there is, furthermore, an explicit verse of Scripture in Ezekiel that makes that point: *You shall know that I am the Lord when I open your graves and bring you to the Land of Israel* (Ez. 37:13).

   G. "Then: *I shall put my spirit in you and you shall live* (Ex. 37:14)."

4. A. Thus you have learned that [1] those who die in the Land of Israel live in the days of the Messiah, and [2] the righteous who die overseas come to it and live in it.

   B. If that is the case, then will the gentiles who are buried in the Land also live?

   C. No, Isaiah has said, *The neighbor shall not say, I too have suffered pain. The people who dwell therein shall be forgiven their sin* (Is. 33:24).

D. The sense is, "My evil neighbors are not going to say, "We have been mixed up [with Israel and will share their fate, so] we too shall live with them."

E. But that one that was the people dwelling therein [is the one that will live,] and what is that people? It is the people that has been forgiven its sin, namely, those concerning whom it is said, *Who is God like you, who forgives sin and passes over transgression for the remnant of his inheritance* (Mic. 7:18) [which can only be Israel].

The established topic continues its course; the compositor has introduced further materials on the theme of living and dying in the Land of Israel. The discourse seems continuous; there is no interest in the base-text and no intersecting-text appears. It is a sustained essay on a topic.

I:VII

1. A. How long are the days of the Messiah?

B. R. Aqiba says, "Forty years, in line with this verse: *And he afflicted you and allowed you to hunger* (Deut. 8:3), and it is written, *Make us glad according to the days in which you afflicted us* (Ps. 90:15). Just as the affliction lasted forty years in the wilderness, so the affliction here is forty years [with the result that the glad time is the same forty years]."

C. Said R. Abin, "What verse of Scripture further supports the position of R. Aqiba? *As in the days of your coming forth from the land of Egypt I will show him marvelous things* (Mic. 7:15)."

D. R. Eliezer says, "Four hundred years, as it is written, *And they shall enslave them and torment them for four hundred years* (Gen. 15:13), and further it is written, *Make us glad according to the days in which you afflicted us* (Ps. 90:15)."

E. R. Berekhiah in the name of R. Dosa the Elder says, "Six hundred years, as it is written, *As the days of a tree shall be the days of my people* (Is. 65:22).

F. "How long are the days of a tree? A sycamore lasts for six hundred years."

G. R. Eliezer b. R. Yose the Galilean says, "A thousand years, as it is written, *For a thousand years in your sight are but as yesterday when it has passed* (Ps. 90:40), and it is written, *The day of vengeance as in my heart but now my year of redemption is come* (Is. 63:4).

H. "The day of the Holy One, blessed be He, is the same as a thousand years for a mortal."

I. R. Joshua says, "Two thousand years, *according to the days in which you afflicted us* (Ps. 90:15).

J. "For there are no fewer *days* [as in the cited verse] than two, and the day of the Holy One, blessed be He, is the same as a thousand years for a mortal."

K. R. Abbahu says, "Seven thousand years, as it is said, As a bridegroom rejoices over his bride will your God rejoice over you (Is. 62:5), and how long does a groom rejoice over his bride? It is seven days,

L. "and the day of the Holy One, blessed be He, is the same as a thousand years for a mortal."

M. Rabbi says, "You cannot count it: *For the day of vengeance that was in my heart and my year of redemption have come* (Is. 63:4)."

N. How long are the days of the Messiah? Three hundred and sixty-five thousand years will be the length of the days of the Messiah.

2. A. Then the dead of the Land of Israel who are Israelites will live and derive benefit from them, and all the righteous who are overseas will come through tunnels.

B. And when they reach the land, the Holy One, blessed be He, will restore their breath, and they will rise and derive benefit from the days of the Messiah along with them [already in the land].

C. For it is said, *He who spread forth the the earth and its offspring gives breath to the people on it* (Is. 42:5).

3. A. When will the royal Messiah come?

B. Said R. Eleazar, "Near to the Messiah's days, ten places will be swallowed up, ten places will be overturned, ten places will be wiped out."

C. And R. Hiyya bar Abba said, "The royal Messiah will come only to a generation the leaders of which are like dogs."

D. R. Eleazar says, "It will be in the time of a generation that is worthy of annihilation that the royal Messiah will come."

E. R. Levi said, "Near the time of the days of the Messiah a great event will take place in the world."

The final issue in the messianic essay concerns the time that the days of the Messiah will last. (Braude's translation, p. 46, "How long to the days of the Messiah," is certainly wrong, as the discussion that follows in No. 3, which does raise that question, indicates.) The several theories, along with their proof-texts, are laid out in a clear way. No. 2 then reviews familiar ideas. No. 3 then goes over another aspect of the matter. None of this composite has been made up for the purposes of our document.

III
The Literary Structures of Pesiqta Rabbati Pisqa One

1. Pesiqta Rabbati Pisqa One I:I

"May our master teach us" – *yelammedenu rabbenu* – introduces a discourse on a matter of law, following a highly conventional and restrictive form: question with the formal introduction, followed by our masters have taught us, with a legal formulation, and then a secondary thematic development. No. 1 presents us with the colloquy, *May our master instruct us...our masters have taught us...*, followed at No. 2 by a secondary point not generated by the primary colloquy. We note that the theme of the pisqa as a whole, the New Moon, does not generate in the legal component of the pisqa a thesis that will dominate discourse later on. There is no correlation whatsoever between the legal problem and the thematic exposition that follows. No. 3 likewise pursues its own interests, without intersecting with any point that will follow.

2. Pesiqta Rabbati Pisqa One I:II

We should expect to have an intersecting-verse fully expounded and then brought into relationship with a base-verse. But that anticipated form is not realized. We do have a brief feint in that direction at No. 1, for No. 1 intends to draw into juxtaposition Ps. 42:1-4 and Lev. 16:1ff. We have an allusion to the matter, in that the two verses – intersecting, base – are cited. But then the authorship refers us to another discourse, without copying that other discourse. In a fully realized execution of the intersecting-verse/base-verse construction, we should have not only an exposition of the intersecting-verse, which we do have here, but also an explicit introduction, at the outset, of the base-verse, which should be Is. 66:22-24. That verse does occur at the end, but no preparation has announced that it is going to be the centerpiece of discussion. The result is an exceedingly defective exercise in which base-verse is ignored, even though a powerful message concerning its ultimate meaning is exposed by the intersecting-verse.

Nos. 3, 4, 5, 6, 7, 8 cite the intersecting-verse, With my whole being I thirst for God, and impute meanings to that verse. Hence the form is simple: citation of a verse, statement of the meaning or application of that verse. No. 9 is tacked on to No. 8 because of thematic reasons. No. 10 continues No. 9. No. 11 pursues the same program of exegesis of what we call the intersecting-verse. Then No. 11 brings us back to the lection for the Sabbath that coincides with the New Moon. But that lection has not been cited, so we cannot imagine that we have a sizable exposition of an intersecting-verse and then its juxtaposition with a base-verse, simply because the "base-verse" in this case is cited only at the end. The theme of a yearning of Israel to union with God is a rather general one. There is no sustained exposition of a proposition that opens the base-verse in a fresh way. True, there is a powerful proposition, which is that in the end of time the New Moon will enter the status of a pilgrim festival. But it is difficult for me to see how the formal characteristics of the composition match the cogency of the programmatic intent. The one formal possibility is that I:I is intended to introduce the base-verse, the presence of which is then taken for granted in the execution of I:II. But I find no evidence in the document before us that that is the intent. There is no continuity in either form or program between I:I and I:II.

Later on we shall contrast this execution of the intersecting-verse/base-verse form with the execution of that same form in Leviticus Rabbah and Pesiqta deRab Kahana. Overall, it suffices to note that in Leviticus Rabbah there will be a full and sustained inquiry into the many and diverse meanings of the intersecting-verse, and only then the base-verse comes into view and its meaning is revised by the intersection. In Pesiqta deRab Kahana, by contrast, the intersecting-verse always focuses upon a single point, the point that the authorship wishes to make with reference to the base-verse. So the articulation is intellectually economical and disciplined, by contrast to the intellectually promiscuous character of the use of the form in Leviticus Rabbah. In our document, the formal discipline is lost altogether; there is neither a systematic treatment of the intersecting-verse nor a highly purposeful intersection, making a single stunning point, such as we note in the two prior compilations, respectively.

3. Pesiqta Rabbati Pisqa One I:III

We have now an exposition of the base-verse, which is Is. 66:22-24. Formally, we find precisely the formal plan characteristic of the foregoing: citation of a verse, a few words that impute meaning to that verse. Once more we shall notice how our authorship contrasts with that of Pesiqta deRab Kahana. For the exegetical form employed in Pesiqta deRab Kahana, in its syntactic traits identical to the one before us, yields a single message, an implicit syllogism repeated many times over. In our document (as in Leviticus Rabbah), by contrast, the exegetical form permits an authorship to say pretty much whatever it wants on a given theme, and does not impose the requirement to state in yet another, new way an established syllogism. These distinctions become important in Chapter Eleven.

4. Pesiqta Rabbati Pisqa One I:IV

I:IV.1-2 seem to me to continue the preceding, that is, I:III.4.

5. Pesiqta Rabbati Pisqa One I:V

This subdivision continues the foregoing.

6. Pesiqta Rabbati Pisqa One I:VI

This subdivision continues the established theme, the importance of living in the Land of Israel.

7. Pesiqta Rabbati Pisqa One I:VII

What I said just now applies here.

IV

The Forms of Pesiqta Rabbati Pisqa One

We may now review the results of the form-analysis. We have defined the following formal preferences:

1. Legal colloquy

May our master instruct us...our masters have taught us..., followed by a secondary lesson.

2. Exegesis of a verse

A verse is cited and then given a secondary or imputed meaning, e.g., Another matter + verse + a few words that state the meaning of that verse or its concrete application.

3. Intersecting-verse/Base-verse (hypothetical)

We should expect to find a base-verse, e.g., Is. 66:22-24, cited, then an intersecting-verse, e.g., Ps. 42:1-4, used to impute to the former some more profound meaning than is obvious at the surface. This form, not realized here, is suggested and of course elsewhere validated as a routine option. That is why it must take its place within the formal repertoire, even though our sample does not present us with an instance in which it is used.

V

The Thematic Program and Proposition of Pesiqta Rabbati Pisqa One: Syllogism, Collage, or Scrapbook?

Before proceeding to test our form-analytical hypothesis, we have now to ask whether the *pisqa* at hand presents a cogent statement of its own, or whether it constitutes a collection of thematically joined but syllogistically distinct statements. Let us review the propositions of our pisqa:

I:I: If one forgot to include a reference to the New Moon in the Grace after Meals. Other rules about the Grace after Meals for the New Moon. The New Moon is equivalent to a festival.

I:II: Israel thirsts for God, who bestows blessings of a natural order and also will bring salvation. Leading to 8.B: When will you restore the glory of going up on the three pilgrim festivals to see the face of God. Ultimately the New Moon will be equivalent to a pilgrim festival.

I:III: Interpretation of Is. 66:22-24: can people really come to Jerusalem every New Moon and every Sabbath? Other problems in that same framework.

I:IV: On what account will Israel enjoy all this glory? Because of the merit of dwelling in the Land of Israel. The resurrection of those who are buried in the Land.

I:V: More on the resurrection of those who are buried in the Land.

I:VI: More on the resurrection of those who are buried in the Land.

I:VII: Secondary expansion of a detail in the foregoing. More on the resurrection of those who are buried in the Land. When will the Messiah come.

We may now ask whether our pisqa forms a highly cogent syllogism, with a proposition systematically proven by each of the components; whether it forms a collage, in which diverse materials seen all together form a cogent statement; or whether it constitutes a scrapbook in which thematically contiguous materials make essentially individual statements of their own.

Among these three choices, the second seems to me, in balance, to apply to Pisqa One. We certainly do not find a single cogent statement, an implicit syllogism repeated over and over in the several components of the pisqa. But we do have more than a mere scrapbook on a common theme. For the basic point, the equivalence of the New Moon to a pilgrim festival, is made both at the legal passage, I:I, and the exegetical one, I:II-III. I:IV-VII then form a mere appendix, tacked on without much good reason. So we may judge our pisqa to be an imperfectly executed collage, one that, in the aggregate, really does make its point.

VI

The Order of the Forms of Pisqa One

The legal colloquy appears first of all, at **I:I**. If **I:II** had worked out an intersecting-verse/base-verse composition, then that would have constituted the form to appear second in sequence. **I:III** presents an exegesis of the base-verse on its own terms. It follows that as a matter of hypothesis, we should expect the order of types of forms to be, first, a legal colloquy, which will introduce the theme and possibly also the thesis; second, the intersecting-verse/base-verse form, which will allow the theme, and possibly the thesis, to come to expression in exegetical, rather than legal terms; and, third, the exegetical form, which allows the base-verse to be spelled out on its own. Miscellanies then will come at the end. So there would appear to be a preferred order of types of units of discourse. But a large-scale test of a sizable sample is now needed.

VII

Testing the Form-Analytical Hypothesis: Five Experiments

1. Introduction

My hypothesis is in three parts. First, I propose to test the proposition that Pesiqta Rabbati in the main, though not wholly, comprises four recurrent literary structures, **I.** legal colloquy, **II.** base-verse/intersecting-verse, **III.** exegetical, and, as we shall see in a moment, **IV.** syllogistic argument for a proposition through the composition of a list of facts, all of them sustained by proofs of Scripture. Second, it would appear that the pisqa of Pesiqta Rabbati, while not a closely argued and cogent syllogistic statement, also is not a mere scrapbook, but does, in the aggregate if not in detail, point toward a distinctive conclusion. Third, the ideal order would place the legal colloquy first, the intersecting-verse/base-verse second, then the exegetical form third, followed by whatever supplementary materials seemed required for a complete statement.

That three-part hypothesis now requires testing. For that purpose we turn to the other four *pisqaot* that I have translated and undertake exactly the same procedure that produced our original hypothesis. If the proposed formal repertoire and program of cogent discourse encompasses the bulk of what is before us, then we find justification to postulate the same formal character for the entirety of the document. My comments on the selected *pisqaot* focus upon form-analytical issues: why do I think a given unit of thought falls into one of the three classifications adduced to date. The upshot of what is to follow had best be stated at the outset. We shall see that our original hypothesis does encompass most of the materials of the sample of five *pisqaot* under study.

2. Pesiqta Rabbati Pisqa Two

1. Legal Colloquy

II:I: when is one obligated to kindle the lamp in celebration of Hanukkah? Where; use of light; why one does so; why recite the Hallel-psalms.

2. Exegesis of a Verse

II:III-IV: Ps. 149:5 + in what glory will they exult + Is. 57:2, 21. My best sense is that we deal with an exegesis of Ps. 149:5. **II:IV** continues the foregoing. At the end Ps. 30:1 makes a minor point in connection with the foregoing. It is not central to the exegetical program concerning Ps. 149:5.

II:V works on the conflict between 2 Sam. 7:5 and 1 Chr. 17:4 to make the point that David did not build the Temple, but Solomon did. The reason for that fact is then made clear. What is explained is how the Psalm can refer to the house of David, when Solomon built it.

II:VI goes over the same ground. David is credited with the Temple, so Ps. 30:1.

3. Intersecting-verse/Base-verse (hypothetical)

I see no instance of this form in Pisqa II.

4. Proposition proved by a list of verses

This is a form not noted earlier. We have a proposition, proved by the facts amassed in a list of facts provided by verses. Thus: **II:II**: How many occasions for rededication through the kindling of lights are there: seven; so too **II:VII**, which goes over the same ground. The list ends with its own point of emphasis.

5. The Thematic Program and Proposition of Pesiqta Rabbati Pisqa Two: The Pisqa as Syllogism, Collage, or Scrapbook

II:I presents no clear hypothesis. The principle of aggregation is merely thematic. I see no hypothesis. **II:II-II:IV** present an exegesis of Ps. 149:5. The return to Ps. 30:1 makes no basic point. The basic point is that when deceased, the righteous endure and praise God. That hypothesis, though not everywhere present, does take pride of place. **II:V** includes David in the credit for the building of the Temple. This is not wholly out of phase with **II:IV**. **II:VI** pursues precisely the same matter. **II:VII** lists seven acts of dedication, going over the ground of **II:II**. The dedication of the world to come will involve a kindling of lights. It is difficult to see the pisqa as a whole as a cogent statement, although the central theme of David's getting credit for the house that Solomon built should not be missed. But the correspondence of the legal inquiry, **II:I**, with the syllogism to follow, **II:IIff.**, is hardly so striking as in Pisqa One. Yet the eschatological interest of **II:I.3.H** should not be missed, and that does recur at **II:II**, **II:VII**. In the balance, however, it is difficult to regard Pisqa II as a collage, which, through the aggregation of diverse materials, creates a single powerful effect. That does not seem to me to be the case. We have something more than a scrapbook but considerably less than a collage, and, in any event, nothing remotely approaching a cogent syllogistic statement.

6. The Order of Types of Units of Discourse

Our final question is whether the types of units of discourse follow a fixed order.

II:I   =   legal syllogism/Type I

II:II   =   list proving a proposition/Type IV

II:III   =   exegesis of verse/Type III

II:IV   =   exegesis of verse/Type III

II:V   =   exegesis of verses/Type III

II:VI   =   exegesis of verse/Type III

II:VII =   list proving a proposition/Type IV

The answer is that – so far as I can see – they do not. We seem to have no instance of Type II, and the order of Types III and IV is not regular.

3. Pesiqta Rabbati Pisqa Three

1. Legal Colloquy

III:I: What do we do with leftover oil of a Hanukkah-lamp? The answer derives from a decree of elders. The outcome is that one should obey the decree of elders. Even God is bound by the decree of elders. This is illustrated by Num. 7:54, which has Ephraim first, then Manasseh. Thus the younger brought prior to the elder, just as the younger was blessed before the elder.

2. Exegesis of a Verse

While we have numerous exegeses of specific verses, e.g., Gen. 13:1ff., 20:1ff., in regard to Lot, at **III:III**, Gen. 48:1ff., in regard to Jacob and Joseph and the blessing of his sons, at **III:IV**, the thrust of the whole is to clarify the important point of the base-verse, the placing of the younger first, the elder second. And that, for its part, serves to illustrate the power of the decree of the sage, in this case, Jacob. So while the Pisqa contains its share of exegeses of verses, its principal building blocks make use of these exegeses in the larger enterprise of spelling out the meaning of the intersection of the intersecting-verse and the base-verse.

3. Intersecting-verse/Base-verse

III:II: Qoh. 12:11/Num. 7:54 goes over precisely the point important at **III:I**. The decree of the elders is primary: *The words of the wise are as goads.* The intersecting-verse and its language are spelled out with care. The climactic statement is that the words of Torah and the words of scribes enjoy the same authority. **III:III** continues the exposition of the intersecting-verse, then shifts into an exposition of the theme of Abraham and Lot, which has no clear point of contact with our verse. But the important point is that Lot and the woman of Zarephath made the same statement, which is that *the words of sages are like goads* – and that is the point that is important. This then yields, at **III:IV**, the important point, which is that Jacob decreed that the younger was to come first. That is the issue of our base-verse, which places the younger first, then the elder son of Joseph.

III:V: Here we have a systematic exposition of the base-verse, Num. 7:54ff., in its own terms.

4. Proposition proved by a list of verses

I see no example of this form in the present pisqa.

5. The Thematic Program and Proposition of Pesiqta Rabbati Pisqa Two: The Pisqa as Syllogism, Collage, or Scrapbook

III:I, II make the same point, and do so very cogently: the words of Torah and the words of scribes enjoy the same authority. **III:III, IV** go over precisely the same ground and prove the same point of other cases. III:IV brings us back to Jacob with Manasseh and Ephraim, which is where we began. So far as the parts are meant to point toward a single, whole proposition, which is that the younger precedes the elder, and that there are lessons to be learned from that fact, Pisqa Three constitutes a highly cogent statement of an implicit syllogism.

6. The Order of Types of Units of Discourse

Our final question is whether the types of units of discourse follow a fixed order.

III:I   = legal syllogism/Type I

III:II = intersecting-verse/base-verse/Type II

III:III = intersecting-verse/base-verse/Type II

III:IV = intersecting-verse/base-verse/Type II

III:V   = exegesis of verses/Type III

The answer is that – so far as I can see – they do: type I, II, and III – in that order. Everything now works: disciplined forms, following the "right" order, and making a single point in a number of different ways. The contrast to the foregoing is striking.

4. Pesiqta Rabbati Pisqa Four

1. Legal Colloquy

IV:I: Does one make mention of Hanukkah in the Prayer-service covering Additional Offerings? Indeed so. Where does one do so? In the Prayer of Thanksgiving. All the wonders God has done were on account of the merit of the tribal progenitors, including the building of the house. This ends with the base-verse, which is 1 Kgs. 18:30-32: the twelve stones that Elijah took for his altar.

2. Exegesis of a Verse

I see no component of the composition that focuses upon the exegesis of a verse, though, of course, many of the large-scale statements draw upon exegeses of Scripture.

3. Intersecting-verse/Base-verse

IV:III: Is. 66:1-2 is drawn into juxtaposition with 1 Kgs. 18:30-32. The main point is that the tribal progenitors' merit stands behind the good things that are discussed here.

4. Proposition proved by a list of verses

IV:II: Hos. 12:14 refers to Moses, Elijah. They were alike in all regards. That includes the one important here, which is that both Moses and Elijah built altars of twelve stones, corresponding to the number of tribal progenitors. While this composition ends with our base-verse, in fact it is a sustained list of facts, of which our base-verse constitutes one. We cannot regard this sizable list as an instance of the intersecting-verse/base-verse construction, and it certainly does not constitute merely a sequence of exegesis of verses of Scripture.

5. The Thematic Program and Proposition of Pesiqta Rabbati Pisqa Two: The Pisqa as Syllogism, Collage, or Scrapbook

The main point is that the merit of the tribal progenitors accounts for all of the good things that have happened to Israel, and that will happen. While that point is stated at **IV:I:3**, the legal question does not relate to it. The correspondence or equivalency of Moses and Elijah, **IV:II**, while drawing upon the fact contributed by the base-verse as a pertinent fact, does not restate the proposition. That composition makes its own, distinctive point. IV:III works on the base-verse and its exposition, and it also alludes, at **IV:III.1.S** to the proposition, the focus is on the exposition of the history of the destruction of the Temple, not upon the centrality of the merit of the twelve tribal progenitors. So, in all, we have not even a collage but a scrapbook. And that is despite the repeated allusions to the proposition that the compositor of the whole has clearly wished to establish.

6. The Order of Types of Units of Discourse

Our final question is whether the types of units of discourse follow a fixed order.

IV:I   =   legal syllogism/Type I

IV:II   =   list proving a proposition/Type IV

IV:III =   intersecting-verse/base-verse/Type II

The answer is that – so far as I can see – they do not. Still, where there is a list, it does intervene between the legal colloquy and the exegetical form that finds a place in the whole, just as is the case above. Seen as a whole Pisqa Four shows us the opposite of Pisqa Three: where nothing works, nothing works.

5. Pesiqta Rabbati Pisqa Five

1. Legal Colloquy

V:I raises the question of the procedure of presenting the lection in both Hebrew and Aramaic translation. May the one who does the one do the other too? No, that may not be done. The final proof-text, Hos. 8:12, leads to **V:II**, which introduces our theme, the setting up of the tabernacle. What follows is that the legal colloquy does not contribute a dominant proposition or even a theme. The whole thing has been included only because of the connection to **V:II** at Hos. 8:12 (V:I2.H connecting to **V:III.1.A**, Another interpretation of the verse.... And that passage has been introduced because in its propositional list, it makes reference, among other matters, to the setting up of the tabernacle. Its point is that if one is prepared to give his life for something, then that thing will be credited to him.

2. Exegesis of a Verse

V:IV works on the exegesis of Song 4:16. I do not see how that verse serves as an intersecting-verse for Num. 7:1. The sole point of contact is thematic, as the exegesis unfolds, and the allusion to the altar at Num. 7:1 accounts for the inclusion in our pisqa of the entire construction. **V:V** goes its own way in interpreting Song 5:1. Only at **V:V.6** do we come back to our base-verse, and then the intersection is a solid and important one. While at No. 1 **V:VII** interprets some of the language of the base-verse, in fact we have a syllogism demonstrated by a long list of facts/proof-texts. **V:X** presents a fine interpretation of the juxtaposition of two verses, Num. 7:1 and Num. 6:24. The meaning of each is clarified in light of the other.

3. Intersecting-verse/Base-verse

V:III weaves Prov. 30:4 together with Num. 7:1. The point of contact is at the ascent of Moses to heaven. Intersecting-verse is applied to Moses, Elijah, and to God. The composition, however, does not seem to me to make any single point, and the way in which the base-verse is recast by its encounter with the intersecting-verse so as to yield an important new proposition is hardly self-evident to me. The main point is that Moses has established the tabernacle as God's residence, but that point is submerged among many others. **V:IV-V** ends with the intersection of Song 4:16 and Num. 7:1. Then the point is that the union of bride, Israel, and groom, God, took place when Moses finished the tabernacle, focussing upon the dual sense of the word KLH as finish and also as bride. But this point is tacked on and hardly the centerpiece of interest. It is as though the redactor has made use of the sizable exegesis of Song 4:16ff. not because that exegesis has imposed its sense or meaning or even theme on the base-verse, but only because of the adventitious occurrence of the base-verse in the other composition. Still, that is a matter of judgment. **V:VI** makes better use of this form to contrast Qoh. 2:21 with Num. 7:1. It makes the point that while Bezallel made the tabernacle, Moses got credit for it. But no reason is given or lesson adduced. So the potential of the form is hardly realized. **V:IX** invokes Song 3:11 along with Num. 7:1, but does not spell out the lessons it wishes to impart; then proceeds to Ps. 85:9, now going over the ground of how the tabernacle reconciled God and Israel. That point is repeated in the unfolding of the pericope.

4. Proposition proved by a list of verses

V:II rests on the point that God credited Moses with those things for which he was prepared to give his life, including the setting up of the tabernacle. **V:VII-VIII-IX** work out a sequence of examples for the proof of the proposition that a certain construction bears a specified meaning. This philological inquiry does not provide the exegesis of any one text, nor do the appearances of a variety of texts yield a fresh meaning for any one or even the lot of them. The centerpiece of discourse is an inquiry into the meaning of words, as diverse examples of a given type prove that meaning. The reason for the insertion of the whole, which comes at **V:IX.7**, the building of the tabernacle caused the nations to say, "Woe," should not be confused with the principle of cogency of the entire composition, which derives from the word-study.

5. The Thematic Program and Proposition of Pesiqta Rabbati Pisqa Five: The Pisqa as Syllogism, Collage, or Scrapbook

V:I makes the point that what is particular to Israel is the Oral Torah meaning in particular the Mishnah. **V:II** stresses that Moses got credit for those matters for which he was ready to give his life. Moses established God's residence on earth when he set up the tabernacle, **V:III**. **V:IV** pursues its own theme, which is the diversity of offerings on the altar. **V:V** presents its exegesis of Song 5:1, never making a point pertinent to what has gone before. Only at the end does V:V allude to our base-verse, making the point that with the setting up of the altar Israel married God. **V:VI** points out that Bezalel did the work but Moses got the credit. It does not say why. **V:VII-IX** take up the meaning of the words, *and it came to pass*. The important point of intersection comes at the end: the building of the tabernacle brought woe to the nations. **V:X** explains why the blessings of Num. 6:24 are juxtaposed with the building of the tabernacle, Num. 7:1. The tabernacle is the source of various blessings for Israel. **V:XI** underlines this same point again and again. While a number of the compositions make the same point – e.g., the tabernacle as a source of blessings – the pisqa as a whole constitutes not a collage but a scrapbook, joined only by the theme of the tabernacle, but presenting no cogent proposition or even a coherent statement of any kind.

6. The Order of Types of Units of Discourse

Our final question is whether the types of units of discourse follow a fixed order.

V:I   = legal syllogism/Type I

V:II   = list proving a proposition/Type IV

V:III = Intersecting-verse/base-verse/Type II

V:IV   = exegesis of verse/Type III

V:V   = exegesis of verses/Type III [but, for reasons already given, one may wish to classify V:IV-V as a massive statement in the form of the intersecting-verse/base-verse/Type II]

V:VI   = Intersecting-verse/base-verse/Type II

V:VII = list proving a proposition/Type IV

V:VIII = list proving a proposition/Type IV

V:IX   = list proving a proposition/Type IV

V:X   = exegesis of verse/Type III

V:XI   = Intersecting-verse/base-verse/Type II

The answer is that – so far as I can see – they do not. Once more: where nothing works, nothing works.

6. Literary Structures of a Pisqa Shared by Pesiqta Rabbati with Pesiqta deRab Kahana: Pesiqta Rabbati Pisqa Fifteen

Let us now conduct the same inquiry of our example of the shared pisqa. We wish to know whether a pisqa that appears in both Pesiqta Rabbati and Pesiqta deRab Kahana exhibits traits of formal preference – types of units of discourse, order of the types – and logical cogency (or lack of the same) characteristic, also, of the pisqaot that occur only in Pesiqta Rabbati. I follow the numbering system of Pesiqta deRab Kahana.

1. Legal Colloquy

None.

2. Exegesis of a Verse

V:XI is the point at which we begin the exegesis of the base-verse in its own terms. The redemption will be through an unusual means. V:XII works on Ex. 12:1 in its own way. V:XIII interprets Ex. 12:2 in a different way, specifically, Israel is in charge of the calendar and is the authority over the moon's seasons. V:XIV interprets the base-verse in its own way. V:XV deals with the base-verse. V:XVI goes over the word for month, meaning, innovation. V:XVII turns to a later clause in the base-verse. V:XVIII deals with the base-verse once more, again with interest in the word for month/new. **V:XIX** goes on to a later part of the base-verse, but only to make the established point.

3. Intersecting-verse/Base-verse

V:I introduces Ps. 104:19 to underline the use of the lunar calendar on the part of Israel. **V:II** invokes Prov. 40:5 and makes the point that Israel is in charge of the lunar calendar. **V:III** appeals to Prov. 13:12-14 on hope deferred/desired fulfilled to make the point that *This month*, Ex. 12:1-2, marked the end of hope deferred and the beginning of desired fulfilled. **V:VII** presents an exegesis of Ex. 12:1 in line with Song 2:8-10, making the point that Israel will be redeemed in Nisan. **V:VIII-X** continue the same exercise.

4. Proposition proved by a list of verses

I am inclined to find in the redemption-in-*This month*-sequence, **V:IV-VI**, a list pointing to a single proposition, which is that redemption will take place in Nisan. The exegesis of the diverse verses that are adduced otherwise has no bearing upon the base-verse, and we cannot see these entries as examples of the intersecting-verse/base-verse construction. For the intersecting-verse never reaches the base-verse and imposes no fresh meaning or perspective upon it. Rather, it makes its own point, which, at the end, serves the larger proposition at hand: redemption in Nisan. The formal trait of the entire sequence is the tacking on of *When did this take place? In this month + Ex. 12:2*. That is a redactional flourish, but it does justify including the item in the present sequence and makes of the whole simply a list of proofs for the proposition at hand.

5. The Thematic Program and Proposition of Pesiqta Rabbati Pisqa Fifteen: The Pisqa as Syllogism, Collage, or Scrapbook

Pisqa Fifteen is not a composite on a comme, e.g., a collage, but presents a tight syllogism, which is repeated in one way or another, n every component of the pisqa. Israel's special status is underlined by the use of the lunar calendar, over which Israel has control, **V:I, II**. The hope deferred, **V:III,** was for redemption, which began to be fulfilled in the month under discussion. *This month*, Nisan, will be the month in which redemption will take place, as it did in Egypt, **V:IV-VI**. **V:VII** maintains that Nisan is the month of redemption, but that Israel has to be patient. **V:VIII** works out a messianic theme on its own, without reverting to the base-verse. **V:IX-X** continue the foregoing. The redemption will be an innovation in some way, so **V:XI**. The waxing and the waning of the moon stand, **V:XII**, for Israel's fortunes. **V:XIII** stresses that it is Israel that is in charge of the lunar calendar. Israel appeals to the moon, the nations to the sun, **V:XIV**, and ultimately Israel will be in charge. **V:XV** goes over the same point. **V:XVI** goes over the familiar point that Israel's coming redemption will represent an innovation. **V:XVII** goes over the theme of redemption, though the proposition at hand goes its own way and emphasizes the atonement for sins that is involved in the daily whole-offering. **V:XVIII** reverts to the proposition that the renewal of the month of Nisan marks redemption. **V:XIX** compares the first redemption in Nisan with the coming redemption in Nisan. This time it will not be in haste. I cannot imagine within the genre at hand a more cogent and single-minded statement of one basic point.

6.   The Order of Types of Units of Discourse

Our final question is whether the types of units of discourse follow a fixed order.

V/XV:I	=	Intersecting-verse/base-verse/Type II
V/XV:II	=	Intersecting-verse/base-verse/Type II
V/XV:III	=	Intersecting-verse/base-verse/Type II
V/XV:IV	=	list proving a proposition/Type IV
V/XV:V	=	list proving a proposition/Type IV
V/XV:VI	=	list proving a proposition/Type IV
V/XV:VII	=	Intersecting-verse/base-verse/Type II
V/XV:VIII	=	Intersecting-verse/base-verse/Type II
V/XV:IX	=	Intersecting-verse/base-verse/Type II
V/XV:X	=	Intersecting-verse/base-verse/Type II
V/XV:XI	=	Exegesis of verse/Type III
V/XV:XII	=	Exegesis of verse/Type III
V/XV:XIII	=	Exegesis of verse/Type III
V/XV:XIV	=	Exegesis of verse/Type III
V/XV:XV	=	Exegesis of verse/Type III
V/XV:XVI	=	Exegesis of verse/Type III
V/XV:XVII	=	Exegesis of verse/Type III
V/XV:XVIII	=	Exegesis of verse/Type III
V/XV:XIX	=	Exegesis of verse/Type III

The answer is that – so far as I can see – the order is absolutely fixed: first type II, then type III. As we shall see in the next chapter, that is the formal preference of the redactors of Pesiqta deRab Kahana. We cannot demonstrate that that same preference characteristically appealed to the framers of Pesiqta Rabbati. Now, where everything synchronizes, the whole works with facility: rhetorical form and logical cogency joining to register with great force a single implicit syllogism.

VIII

Summary: Recurrent Literary Structures: Types of Units of Discourse, their Order, and their Cogency

We may classify all the large-scale compositions of Pesiqta Rabbati within four literary structures. These are the legal colloquy, which itself follows a fairly restrictive pattern in that the form opens with a narrowly legal question, which moves toward a broader, propositional conclusion; the intersecting-verse/base-verse construction, the exegetical form, and the propositional list. The intersecting-verse/base-verse construction itself is copmosed of a variety of clearly formalized units, e.g., exegesis of verses of Scripture and the like. The exegetical form, for its part, is remarkably simple, since it invariably consists of the citation of a verse of Scripture followed by a few words that impute to that verse a given meaning; this constant beginning may then be followed by a variety of secondary accretions which themselves exhibit no persistent formal traits. The propositional list is remarkably cogent in both its formal traits and its principle of cogency.

It goes without saying that the order of the types of forms is not fixed. In Pesiqta Rabbati we find one fixed order: the legal colloquy always comes first. But even that form serves diverse purposes, since, as we noted, in some pisqaot it announces a proposition which will be spelled out and restated in exegetical form as well, while in others the legal colloquy introduces a theme but no proposition in connection with that theme. From that point we may find anything and its opposite: propositional lists, then, intersecting-verse/base-verse-compositions, then exegetical statements, or any other arrangement. The significance of that fact emerges in the sharply disciplined order of the types of forms in Pesiqta deRab Kahana Pisqa Five/Pesiqta Rabbati Pisqa Fifteen. I have already demonstrated that that fixed order characterized the first of the two Pesiqtas throughout.

The matter of cogency invokes a somewhat more subjective judgment. Yet I find it difficult to discover as a general or indicative trait of Pesiqta Rabbati a sustained effort at making a cogent and single statement. That – as we shall shortly see – indeed does mark Pesiqta de Rab Kahana beginning to end. That fact is suggested by our survey of the cogency of the pisqaot of Pesiqta Rabbati that we have reviewed. Among the three analogies which I proposed – syllogism, collage, or scrapbook – we could invoke all three. That means that the authorship of the document as a whole found itself contented with a variety of types of logical discourse. Some of the pisqaot appeared to treat a single topic, but only in a miscellaneous way. The propositions associated with that topic would scarcely cohere to form a single cogent statement. In that case I found we had a scrapbook. Other pisqaot seemed to wish to draw a variety of statements into juxtaposition so that, while not coherent, when viewed all together, those statements would form a single significant judgment upon a theme, hence, a collage. While I cannot demonstrate beyond a doubt the

correctness of my assignment of a given pisqa to a given classification, I think
that, overall, we are on firm ground in making these assignments: Pisqa I,
collage; Pisqa II, scrapbook on a single theme; Pisqa III, syllogism; Pisqa IV,
scrapbook; Pisqa Five, scrapbook. So we find everything and its opposite. The
contrast to Pesiqta Rabbati Pisqa XV=Pesiqta deRab Kahana Pisqa V is then
stunning: there we see what a pisqa looks like when the authorship has made not
merely a composite but a single and uniform composition. In a moment we
shall see that the entirety of Pesiqta deRab Kahana follows suit.

The conclusion may be stated very briefly. The authorship of Pesiqta
Rabbati has made use of a fixed and limited repertoire of large-scale literary
structures – four in all. These it has ordered in diverse ways, so the authorship
found no important message to be delivered through the sequence in which the
types of forms would be utilized. The same authorship pursued a variety of
modes of cogent discourse, sometimes appealing to the theme to hold together
whatever materials they chose to display, sometimes delivering a rather general
message in connection with that theme, and, on occasion, choosing to lay down
a very specific syllogism in connection with a theme. These traits revealed by
our survey take on significance when we – in a different setting – compare
Midrash to Midrash, that is to say, Pesiqta Rabbati to Pesiqta deRab Kahana.
For it is now self-evident that, confronted with a pisqa lacking all identification,
we could readily and easily distinguish a pisqa particular to Pesiqta Rabbati from
one shared with Pesiqta deRab Kahana, and that on more than a single basis.
And, it goes without saying, we should have no difficulty whatsoever in picking
out a pisqa that may fit into either of the two Pesiqtas from a pisqa that would
belong to Sifra, Sifré to Numbers, Genesis Rabbah, Leviticus Rabbah, The
Fathers According to Rabbi Nathan, the Tosefta, the Mishnah, the Yerushalmi,
or the Bavli. Each document exhibits its distinctive and definitive traits of
rhetoric and logic.

Chapter Three

Oral Tradition in Judaism: The Issue of Mnemonics

Judaism maintains that when Moses received the Torah from God at Mount Sinai, it came to him in two media. One was the Torah in writing. The other was the *Torah shebeal peh*, ordinarily translated as "oral Torah." But the Hebrew words mean "that which is memorized," hence, "the memorized Torah." The Mishnah, ca. A.D. 200, is the first document of that part of the Torah that in Judaic myth came to Israel in the medium of memory, "the memorized Torah." Here I ask about memorizing the memorized Torah, that is to say, the mnemonic system revealed through the medium of oral formulation and oral transmission by means of memorization. Specifically, if the Mishnah is a book formulated and transmitted by means of memorization, exactly how does the formulation of the document facilitate remembering its exact words?

The Mishnah, a law code based on philosophical principles current in its age, ca. A.D. 200, frames its ideas in syllogistic patterns. The smallest whole units of discourse (cognitive units), defined as groups of sentences that make a point completely and entirely on their own, become intelligible on three bases: logical, topical, and rhetorical. What I prove here is simple: It is the confluence of logic, topic, and rhetoric that generates at the deepest structure of the Mishnah's language a set of mnemonic patterns. These mnemonics serve by definition to facilitate the easy memorization of the text of the Mishnah. Scholars interested in oral tradition will find the inner traits of a memorized document instructive, for we shall see the complexity and richness of the mnemonic structure – rhetorical, logical, topical alike – that sustains an oral document.

I

Protasis and Apodosis: The Two Components of the Mishnah-Pericope

As I shall presently spell out in detail, the Mishnah is divided into tractates, each defined by a given subject. The tractates are subdivided into what I call intermediate units of tradition ("chapters"), and the intermediate units are comprised of the smallest whole units of discourse or cognitive units. What marks the smallest whole unit of discourse – a handful of sentences? It is that the several sentences of which it is composed are unintelligible or not wholly intelligible by themselves but are entirely intelligible when seen as a group. The smallest whole unit of discourse in the Mishnah invariably constitutes a syllogism, that is, a statement of a proposition, in which a condition or question, constituting a protasis, finds resolution in a rule or answer, the apodosis: If such and such is the case, then so and so is the rule – that is the characteristic cognitive structure of the Mishnah's smallest whole unit of thought or discourse. Even if that statement were made up of two or three or even five declarative sentences, it is only when the proposition is fully exposed, both protasis and apodosis, that the declarative sentences reach the level of full and complete expression, that is, sense and intelligibility.

What is of interest here is that the principles by which the apodosis and protasis of the Mishnah's smallest whole units of discourse are framed follow formal, mnemonic patterns. The patterns of language, e.g., syntactic structures, follow a few simple rules. These rules, once known, apply nearly everywhere. They permit anyone to reconstruct, out of a few key phrases, an entire cognitive unit, and, more important, as we shall see, complete intermediate units of discourse. Let me unpack this critical claim. An intermediate unit of discourse serves to make a single point, that is, to present a given logical proposition. The logical proposition (for example, a general or encompassing rule) rarely comes to articulate expression. Rather, it will be given a set of concrete exemplifications. Three or five or more cases will make the point in detail. Put together, they turn out to express, through examples, a logical proposition. That is what I mean in referring to logic and topic. The underlying logic ordinarily is expressed only in topical form, through concrete instances of what only seldom is stated in so many words.

What is the place of rhetoric? A single rhetorical pattern will govern the whole set of topical instances of a logical proposition. When the logical-topical program changes, the rhetorical pattern will change too. So, as I said, the mnemonics of the Mishnah rest on the confluence of (1) deep logic, (2) articulated topic, and (3) manifest rhetoric. Working downward from the surface, anyone can penetrate into the deeper layers of meaning of the Mishnah. Then and at the same time, while discovering the principle behind the cases, one can easily memorize the whole by mastering the recurrent rhetorical pattern dictating the expression of the cogent set of cases. For it is easy to note the shift from one rhetorical pattern to another and to follow the repeated cases, articulated in the new pattern downward to its logical substrate. So syllogistic propositions, in the Mishnah's authors' hands, come to full expression not only in what people wish to state but also in how they choose to say it. The limits of rhetoric define the arena of topical articulation. Once we ask what three or five joined topical propositions have in common, we state the logic shared among them all.

In discourse such as this, aesthetics, of which mnemonics constitutes a subdivision, joins to topic and logic in the expression of philosophy. True, the gifted author, Plato, as represented in The Dialogues, finds guidance in an aesthetics more immediately accessible than the one at hand. At issue in what Socrates and Plato say, likewise, are matters anyone can find important, even urgent. And yet the arcane and tedious detail of the Mishnah too comprises a set of statements on a program of philosophy and metaphysics, ethics and politics. That program proves no less philosophical, no less pertinent to the life of the people, than the Dialogues, on the one side, and the Republic, on the other. In the age of the Second Sophistic the backcountry philosophers of Galilee in the later second century worried about being and becoming, the potential and the actual, the nature of mixtures, the good life, and the ideal state. Their program of reflection will not have surprised the metropolitan figures, the street-corner preachers with their sizable followings, the philosophers of note and fame. True, the raw materials sages used for the expression of their program will have astounded their contemporaries, in the Second Sophistic, if, to begin with, they had known the topical program at hand. But the sole difference between Stoic physicists, the philosophers who spoke about mixtures, and the Mishnah's physicists, the philosophers who spoke about rennet and cheese, gravy, mixed seeds, and linen and wool, lies not in logic but in topic and, obviously, in rhetoric. What I propose to accomplish here is simply the statement of certain mnemonic principles I have discovered. A complete repertoire of references to the texts in which I discovered them is presented in my *The Memorized Torah* (Atlanta, 1985: Scholars Press for Brown Judaic Studies).

II

Topic and Rhetoric in the Mnemonic Program of the Mishnah

The Mishnah, a philosophical law-code that reached closure at ca. A.D. 200, is divided into tractates, chapters, and paragraphs. We know when a tractate begins and ends because tractates are organized by subject matter. "Chapters" by contrast constitute conventions of printers. There is little internal evidence that the framers of the document broke up the tractates along the lines followed by the copyists and printers of medieval and early modern times. What we have within tractates are subunits on problems or themes presented by the basic topic of the tractate. These subunits or themes are characterized by the confluence of formal and substantive traits. That is to say, a given formal pattern characterizes discourse on a given substantive problem. When the topic or problem changes, the formal pattern also will be altered. What establishes the formal pattern will be three or more recurrences of a given arrangement of words, ordinarily in accord with a distinctive syntactic structure. Fewer than three such occurrences, e.g., of a given mode of formulating a thought, were not found by the framers to suffice to impart that patterned formulation that they proposed to use.

Very commonly in the Division of Purities, which supplied the data on the basis of which the principles of mnemonics spelled out here are worked out, the formulary or syntactic pattern will recur in groups of three or five, or multiples of three or five, examples. Obviously, the resort to highly formalized language patterns facilitates memorization of materials. In so stating, I do not impose my own concerns of the framers or impute to them intentions I cannot demonstrate they held. We know, as a matter of fact, that the Mishnah was received and transmitted principally through the memories of professional tradition-memorizers, "people who repeat," or Tannas (the Aramaic word for repeat, TN', corresponding to the Hebrew, SNH). Accordingly, the patterns I shall here demonstrate to have characterized the formulation of the Mishnah assuredly served as mnemonics, though I should not wish to claim that that is the sole purpose behind the formal speech-patterns of the document. A routine glance at the other principal documents of the rabbinic canon will show that equivalent mnemonic considerations rarely characterize entire compositions, though patterned language will make an appearance in small units of completed discourse, e.g., occasional sayings or stories. The Tosefta, for its part, in no way follows the highly formalized and rigidly disciplined pattern of language characteristic of the Mishnah.

Since I claim that we recognize the subunits, or intermediate units of discourse, of tractates by reference to patterned language corresponding to and marking off consideration of distinctive topics, the focus of inquiry is clear. I have to take up those dimensions of linguistic patterning characteristic of already constituted units of discourse, I mean, the intermediate ones. I have also to deal with the smallest units of discourse and demonstrate that these too are patterned. Only by showing that both the intermediate and the smallest units of completed thought conform to syntactic or other linguistic rules shall I succeed in making my case.

When we come to the irreducible minima of discourse, those smallest possible units of discourse or cognitive units, that join words into intelligible sentences and sentences into intelligible propositions, we ordinarily deal with a brief paragraph made up of two parts, a protasis, which spells out a condition or a question, and an apodosis, which presents the rule governing the condition or the answer to the question. That is to say, the Mishnah is made up of many thousands of syllogisms, and sentences come together into meaningful propositions – small paragraphs – because they present in a systematic way logical propositions, ordinarily susceptible to reduction to a simple statement: If..., then..., or its equivalent.

I first noticed the highly disciplined patterns dictating the way in which thoughts will come to expression as formal propositions (that is, as intelligible sentences) when I worked on the units of discourse in the Mishnah, and in other compositions of the rabbinic canon, in which names of authorities before 70 occur. These I called "the rabbinic traditions about the Pharisees." What I found was that, when I focused upon the smallest whole units of thought, sentences that comprised paragraphs (in simple language) or syllogisms that were whole and complete, a few rules governed. These rules, once memorized, made it exceedingly easy to reconstruct part of the whole units of thought, whatever their content. At that state in my work, I dealt only with the apodosis of the whole units of thought, that is, the "then..." of the "if..., then...,"-construction. What I found was the statement of a condition or a problem, in which, at that time, I discerned no pattern, followed by X says..., Y says.... The attributives, just now cited, would very regularly be followed by words that would recur many times over, always as matched opposites, e.g., "unclean/clean," "prohibited/permitted," and the like. Seeing the same pattern hundreds of times, I realized that I could construct in memory, simply knowing a handful of basic rules, pretty much any dispute in the corpus of materials attributed to the authorities before 70, and, without exception, any dispute assigned to the names of the Houses of Shammai and Hillel. Of course I was by no means the first to recognize the existence of such fixed patterns, since the framers of the Talmuds themselves noticed them and asked why the House of Shammai (nearly) always takes precedence, in reports of disputes, over the House of Hillel. But in a great many details, and in the grasp of the whole, I believe I was the person who first understood the working of the system.

It was one thing to perceive something so superficial as fixed patterns in apodoses, since these are few, brief, highly formal, and commonplace. So I saw little difficulty in focusing upon the apodosis as a focus of mnemonic patterning. I was puzzled by the much more difficult problem of the protasis of the syllogistic statements of the Mishnah. I simply did not grasp where and how the statement of the condition or problem to be disposed of exhibited a parallel set of mnemonic patterns. The reason, I now recognize, was that I was working, in connection with the *Rabbinic Traditions about the Pharisees* (Leiden, 1971: E. J. Brill) I-III, and, for two years more, with *Eliezer ben Hyrcanus. The Tradition and the Man* (Leiden, 1973: E. J. Brill) I-II, only with bits and pieces of intermediate units of discourse ("chapters"). That is to say, because I followed the lines indicated by the occurrences of named authorities, I violated the lines of formal structure of the Mishnah as a whole. I neglected the formally definitive patterns of the intermediate units of discourse. I could never have recognized those patterns, at least, on the basis of systematic and detailed inquiry, by working as I did.

The recognition of intermediate units of discourse, how they found distinct definition in patterned language used in fixed and repetitive statements of a principle or rule in a single syntactic structure, came exactly where it should. When I turned from studies of individual names pursued across the boundaries of the components of the rabbinic canon, I took up studies of individual documents, following the boundaries of a single composition within the canon. Then, and only then, was I able to perceive the syntactic patterns as they repeated themselves, on the one side, and shifted with a change in the topical program, on the other. What I perceived was interplay of rhetorical and topical programs. How so? The logic of a syllogism reached the surface through its recurrent topical expression. The rhetoric utilized in that expression would, in context, prove distinctive to that distinct logical-topical construct. When I had penetrated into that deep structure of discourse in which logic generated topic and topic dictated rhetoric, I also had reached to the center of the mnemonic structure of the Mishnah's intermediate building blocks, that is, the components of the tractates that constitute the principal ones.

III

The Apodosis and its Mnemonic Traits

The smallest whole unit of discourse is made up of fixed, recurrent formulas, clichés, patterns, or little phrases, out of which whole pericopae, or large elements in pericopae, e.g. complete sayings, are constructed. Small units of tradition, while constitutive of pericopae, do not generate new sayings or legal problems, as do apophthegmatic formulae. That is, MRBH – MRBH – produces numerous sayings; *say unclean – say clean* – does not; rather, it merely serves as apodosis for a random protasis.

An example of part of a pericope composed primarily of recurrent formulas is as follows:

> *A basket of fruit intended for the Sabbath.*
> House of Shammai declare exempt.
> And the House of Hillel declare liable.

The italicized words are not fixed formulas. *And* is redactional; the formulation of the statement of the problem does not follow a pattern. The Houses-sentences, by contrast, are formed of fixed, recurrent phrases, which occur in numerous pericopae. Similarly:

> House of Shammai say ... House of Hillel say ...

are fixed small units, whether or not the predicate matches; when it balances, we have a larger unit of tradition composed of two small units:

1.	House of Shammai say,	2.	BKY YTN
3.	House of Hillel say,	4.	Not BKY YTN.

In this pericope, only the statement of the problem or protasis, not given, would constitute other than a fixed unit; House of Shammai/Hillel + say are complete units, and the opinions in the apodosis are others – thus, as I said, a pericope, the apodosis of which is composed entirely of fixed, small units of tradition. By definition these small formulas cannot be random, or they would not constitute formulas. Such small units are whole words, not syntactical or grammatical particles. They also are not mere redactional devices used to join together discrete pericopae in the later processes of collection and organization, such as ma'aseh, SN'MR, 'LYK HKTWB'WMR, and similar connecting-words, editorial conventions, formulaic introductions to Scriptures, and other redactional clichés.

The most important fixed formula is: X says. Now it may seem that so routine a phrase cannot be regarded as a formula. But its form, sense and function here are absent in all other Jewish literature. It obviously is not the only or best possible way of introducing a quotation of a named master. The use of the present tense participle with regard to a named master is anti-historical. We find X says, but not X does, X writes, X decrees, X rules.

Unlike the noun-epithet formula found by Milman Parry in the Iliad and the Odyssey ("Studies in the Epic Technique of Oral Verse-Making. I. Homer and Homeric Style," *Harvard Studies in Classical Philology* 41, 1930, pp. 73-148; and "II. The Homeric Language as the Language of an Oral Poetry," *ibid.*, 43, 1932, pp. 1-50), the formulas before us seldom exhibit a meter, nor is any fixed metrical value often an obvious formal consideration (except in Houses-pericopae), because of the plain fact that at the time of the rabbis people no longer used metric speech for prosaic purposes. But the Houses' syzygy supplies for the apodosis or predicate of the Houses' pericopae the same sort of balanced, therefore easy to memorize, elements. Parry's description applies without qualification: "Unless the language itself stands in the way, the poet ... of the Homeric poems has ... a noun-epithet formula to meet every regularly recurring need. And what is equally striking, there is usually only one such formula." Likewise, the tradent of the Houses' pericopae has a standard syzygy available for the apodosis of every regularly recurring legal problem and sometimes even uses an available syzygy where it does not closely fit the facts of the case. Organization of materials for each memorization says nothing about what lies in the historical background of the materials, only about what was intended for the future: from redaction onward, it may well have been planned that they would be learned by heart, therefore to begin with should be constructed to facilitate easy memorization. The syzygous construction of the Houses' apodosis is a literary convention of written materials. It constitutes a "fixed formula" in literature available to us only in written form. More than this cannot be granted as fact.

Whether or not the redacted pericopae derive from originally oral materials is a question that obviously cannot be settled, one way or the other, by the character of materials which we have only in written form. The later theory of a dual Torah by itself is not pertinent. The Essene community at Qumran, for one, had such a corpus of revealed materials external to Scriptures, and they wrote down at least part of those materials. But even if various sects had traditions, and if those traditions were oral, it would not solve the problem, unless it can be shown that in behalf of such traditions was claimed not merely essential accuracy but exact verbal correspondence with what was originally stated by the authority standing behind them.

Such a claim to exact verbal correspondence is laid down in behalf of the Mishnah. The data we have examined, as well as those to come, show us the basis for the claim. *That is, the text is so formulated as to be relatively easy to memorize.* Saul Lieberman describes the process of formulating and transmitting the Mishnah in "The Publication of the Mishnah" (*Hellenism in Jewish Palestine. Studies in the Literary Transmission, Beliefs, and Manners of Palestine in the I Century B.C.E. – IV Century C.E.* [N.Y., 1950], pp. 83-99). He asks, Was the Mishnah published? That is, either did professional copyists hear it dictated and write it down? Or did an authentic original take written form, and was it then deposited in an archive? Some Jewish books were published in the second way, that is, they were written and deposited. However, Lieberman notes, "Since in the entire Talmudic literature we do not find that a book of the Mishnah was ever consulted in case of controversies or doubt concerning a particular reading, we may safely conclude that the compilation was not published in writing." Rabbis did possess written halakhot and comments, but they were private notes without legal authority, with no more authority than an oral assertion (p. 87). The Mishnah was published in a different way:

> A regular oral ... edition of the Mishnah was in existence, a fixed text recited by the Tannaim of the college. The Tanna (repeater, reciter) committed to memory the text of certain portions of the Mishnah, which he subsequently recited in the college in the presence of the great masters of the Law ... When the Mishnah was committed to memory and the Tannaim recited it in the college it was thereby published ...

The authority of the college-Tanna ("a word apparently first used for college-reciter in the time of Aqiba," Lieberman, p. 88, n. 39) was that of a "published book" (p. 89). What was the nature of that living book? "How was the mass of diverse material arranged and systematized before it was delivered to the Tanna, before he memorized it?" (p. 90) At the time of Aqiba, the body of the Mishnah comprised only the opinions of the representatives of the Houses of Shammai and Hillel and their predecessors (p. 93). Aqiba organized matters, sifting through the whole and crystalizing it in an exact and definite shape. His work resulted in the compilation of a new Mishnah (p. 93). Then the procedure was as follows: "The Master taught the new Mishnah to the first Tanna; afterwards he taught it to the second Tanna" and so on. After the Mishnah was systematized and the Tannaim knew it thoroughly be heart, they repeated it in the college in the presence of the master, who supervised the recitation and corrected it and gave it its final form (p. 93). The materials we have catalogued provide evidence in favor of the theory of the publication of the Mishnah advanced by Lieberman.

IV

The Protasis

[1] Intermediate Divisions of the Mishnah

We consider the protasis and its mnemonic characteristics in two parts. Internal evidence proves that the arrangement of the Order of Purities into twelve principal divisions is fundamental to the redaction of the Mishnah. Once a primary theme shifts, we know that the redactors have completed their treatment of one subject and commenced that of another. We shall now ask whether the dissection, into intermediate divisions, of these same principal divisions is shown by internal evidence to be equivalently fundamental to the redaction of the document.

Since we seek to discern the boundary-lines within the principal divisions of the Mishnah for which the redactors of the Mishnah bear responsibility, we ask for internal evidence about the aggregation of materials into intermediate divisions. We now know that if the Division of Purities were before us in undifferentiated columns of words, or were written in a single immense scroll, without any sort of divisions and subdivisions, we should readily discern twelve principal divisions simply by observing the shift from one primary theme or subject to another. Within the twelve divisions, what internal evidence permits us to differentiate the intermediate divisions, or sizable aggregations of completed cognitive units? What criteria, specifically, will emerge out of the fundamental character itself?

The first of two criteria derives from the nature of the principal divisions themselves: theme. That is, it is along thematic lines that the redactors organized vast corpora of materials into principal divisions, tractates. These fundamental themes themselves were subdivided into smaller conceptual units. The principal divisions, I have shown at great length, treat their themes in units indicated by the sequential unfolding of their inner logical structure. Accordingly, one established criterion for the deliberation of an aggregate of materials from some other, fore or aft, will be a shift in the theme, or predominant and characteristic concern, of a sequence of materials. The second fundamental criterion is the literary character, syntactical and grammatical pattern, which differentiates and characterizes a sequence of primitive units of thought. Normally, when the subject changes, the mode of expression – the formal or formulary character, the patterning of language – will change as well. These two matters, theme and form, therefore must be asked to delineate for us the main lines of the intermediate or subdivisions of the Mishnah's principal divisions, the "chapters." There are therefore four logical possibilities for the application of the two stated criteria, +A, +B, +A-B, -A+B, -A-B:

1. coherent themes expressed through coherent formulary patterns;
2. coherent themes lacking coherent formulary patterns;

3. coherent formulary patterns lacking coherent themes;

4. incoherent themes and incoherent formulary patterns.

In this case the only reason to imagine that we deal with a subdivision is that before and after said set of materials, which lacks coherence of theme and form, are sets which do exhibit traits of coherent theme and/or form, that is, subdivisions demarcated by one of the first possible combinations.

We distinguish to begin with between two kinds of formulary patterns. First is the pattern which is internal to the idea which is expressed and which predominates in the formulation of that idea, its linguistic formalization. If this pattern recurs for two or more cognitive units, then we have a formulary trait internal to the pattern of language of each element in a subdivision. Each and every cognitive unit within said subdivision will express its particular concept or thought in conformity with this common pattern, which therefore is to be designated as internal to the whole. The recurrent pattern of syntax or language is both tradental and redactional, in that what is to be expressed is the work of those responsible for both the formulary and formalized character and the cognitive substance of the subdivision in all of its parts and as a whole. Second is the pattern which is external to the idea which is expressed and superficial, and which occurs chiefly at the outset of a cognitive unit. The arrangement of words of said unit will ignore this external formulary trait. What is to be said can be, and is, stated without regard to the superficial trait shared among several cognitive units. Indeed, we may readily discern that the formulary trait of a series of cognitive units is external to the formulation of all of them, simply because each cognitive unit goes its own way, stating its ideas in its own form or formulary pattern, without any regard whatsoever for the formal traits of other units to which it is joined. The joining – the shared language or formulary or formal pattern – is therefore external to the several units. The present distinction, between internally-unitary formulary traits characteristic of a sequence of cognitive units, and externally-unitary formulary traits shared by a sequence of cognitive units, explains why the first of our four logical possibilities, +A+B (coherent themes, coherent forms), yields two analytical categories. The second logical possibility, +A-B, requires no refinement. We observe that some clearcut sequences of cognitive units talk about the same distinctive subject, but make no effort to conform to a discernible pattern of language. Occasionally we discern subdivisions which are differentiated by formulary patterns but which go over many legal themes, that is, -A+B.

Apart from the grouping of cognitive units in accord with theme and formulary or formal traits, there is one further aspect of the subdivision which is noteworthy. This is the pronounced tendency of the intermediate division to be formed in aggregations of three and multiples of three, or five and multiples of five, cognitive units. The following catalogues enumerate components of 190 intermediate divisions. The result is as follows:

Threes and multiples of three	91	48%
Fives and multiples of five	73	38%
Other	26	14%
	190	100%

Since in any random sequence, one third of the numbers will be multiples of three, and one fifth, equivalently, multiples of five, these are noteworthy disproportions. In the organization of intermediate divisions, the redactors paid considerable attention to the number of cognitive units strung together therein and tended to arrange matters so that sequences of threes and fives would characterize their organization of materials.

V

The Protasis

[2]   The Mishnah's Smallest Components.

Cognitive Units and their Mnemonic Systematization

The Mishnah's internal evidence reveals that primary to the organization and redaction of the document are principal divisions, tractates, and intermediate divisions, "chapters." It also is clear from the earlier inquiries that these intermediate divisions are composed of still smaller units, which are now to be defined. These units to begin with are distinguished from one another by the same criteria as separate one intermediate unit from another, namely, both thematic and formal traits. Sentences or small groups of sentences, exhibiting recurrent traits of stereotype formulation, cover a single problem, issue, or principle, supply opinions assigned to a single authority, or in some other way convey a single rule, idea, or thought on a given subject. Each such unit of thought – hence, cognitive unit or "smallest whole unit of discourse" – is the result of careful formulation. Each one, moreover, represents the formal result of a single cogent process of cognition, that is, analysis of a situation and statement of a rule pertaining to it, observation of a recurrent phenomenon and provision of a generalization covering all observations, reflection upon basic rules and their generation of, or application to, secondary and tertiary details or situations – in all, again, the product of an act of thought. The definition of the Mishnah's smallest whole and irreducible literary-conceptual units as the end-result of an act of thought proceeds along lines by now familiar. We specify distinctive literary forms and formulary patterns and isolate their occurrences, then examine the ways in which said forms and patterns contain and convey whole, complete, and irreducible ideas, rules, opinions – the results of a single sequence of cognition on a single matter.

The Mishnah's language is like ours in morphology and syntax, with a verb which produces statements of past-completed, present-continuing, and future action in both indicative and subjunctive moods, a sentence-structure which normally consists of subject and predicate, and a reasonably full repertoire of devices by which ideas may be expressed in ways fundamentally the same as those by which we convey ideas. That is why we can translate the Mishnah in a literal, word-for-word way and thereby produce in English or German a clear sense of the order and meaning of the Hebrew words. That also is why we cannot take for granted the far from random, and far from broad, range of formal-linguistic possibilities explored by the formulators of the Mishnah. In fact they express their ideas in accord with a remarkably limited repertoire of forms and formulary patterns. Forms, words which function in, but bear no meaning distinctive to, a particular cognitive unit, and formulary patterns, grammatical arrangements of words distinctive to their subject but in fixed syntactical patterns serviceable for a wide range of subjects, are remarkable for their discipline. Outside of the dialogue in stories and narratives (which are rare in the Mishnah), formalization and stereotype patterns of language characterize the whole of the Mishnah. Whatever ideas people had therefore are shaped to conform to a readily discerned set of literary conventions, grammatical patterns applicable to thoughts on any subject and accessible to all of the Mishnah's themes. We already have noticed, for example, that the eleven themes of our Order's twelve principal divisions produce exactly the same sorts of intermediate divisions, to be analyzed and dissected in accord with a single limited literary-thematic (not solely thematic) criterion. The same observation derives from the examination of the thousands of individual cognitive units. The Mishnah is a public and anonymous corpus, in which the contribution of individuals is limited to formalized expression of distinctive conceptions, and which entirely excludes particular ways of stating said conceptions. All cognitive units are forced to conform to a severely limited range of conventions of formulation and form.

This brings us to the question of whether in fact the omnipresent, declarative sentences are as a whole differentiable in terms of recurrent syntactical patterns. In order to spell out the character and distribution of declarative sentences of various sorts, I have taken each stich of the apodosis of a dispute and treated it as if it were a complete sentence. I thus add the protasis to one of the two (or more) stichs of the apodosis. Since we already know that the attributive, X says, is a form independent of what is expressed and external to the formulary pattern in which it appears, I delete the attributive:

A chicken which is cooked for two hours (the House of Shammai say) is uncooked.

This procedure allows us to see the traits of the several cognitive units which, in theory, serve as primary components of the dispute. It further shows us how the dispute's composite character preserves the syntactical traits of its (prior) units and how such traits conform to their tradental-redactional setting.

The decisive formulary traits occur in the protasis, that is, the opening element of a cognitive unit. They may or may not continue throughout the unit. In apocopation, for example, we find the striking disjunctures of components of the subject in particular at the inaugural sentence of a cognitive unit, while declarative sentences may follow until the problem and solution of the unit have been expressed. The differentiating formulary characteristics are thus to be discovered in the commencement of the unit. These traits will be revealed, in that opening sentence, either in the subject or in the predicate. The decisive differentiation is exhibited in the connection – the interface – between the subject and the predicate.

One sort of sentence flows smoothly from subject to verb to complement or predicate. The verb refers to the subject and is completed at the complement or predicate. This sort of sentence is characterized as the simple declarative sentence. In another sort, the subject of the sentence is duplicated, but then leads directly into the predicate. Sometimes this is effected through a shift in word order, e.g., *chickens – when are they fully cooked in the pot?* That is, the topic, chickens, is placed before the interrogative, when. This pattern would not seem peculiar at all, were it not for the numerous instances in which the word order yields nothing like the duplicated protasis, e.g., *A chicken which is cooked for three hours is fully boiled.* There is only one construction in which the formulary peculiarity is exhibited in the apodosis, and this is the contrastive complex, in which we have clearcut balance between the predicate of one sentence, normally a brief one, and that which follows, e.g., *X/unclean, Y/clean* . Two further complex constructions complete our taxonomy, both of them exhibiting apocopation, the one mild, the other severe, and both affecting the subject of the sentence or its protasis (in the case of the latter). What is cut off, or apocopated, is the subject of the sentence, which is disconnected from the verb of the same sentence. When we have a complete disjuncture between the opening unit(s) and the predicate, so that the latter refers to, and depends upon, nothing in the former, then we have the extreme apocopation which is so striking a formulary pattern in our order. Mild apocopation, by contrast, normally begins he who (or, that which), and the predicate, while not referring to the subject of he who/that which, does join up to an element of the inaugural clause, e.g., to the implied or stated object of he who or that which, or to the consequence of what he who does has done. The extreme apocopation, as I said, is made extreme because none of the stichs are the subject of the sentence, and they may be many or few, refers to the predicate. These definitions of formulary patterns exhaust the large-scale categories of syntactical-grammatical types among which all declarative sentences may be divided.

Coherent formulary patterns do characterize sizable sequences of cognitive units on a single theme. These traits, common to a series of distinct cognitive units, are redactional, because they are imposed at that point at which someone intended to join together discrete (finished) units on a given theme. The varieties of traits particular to the discrete units and the diversity of authorities cited therein, including masters of two or three or even four strata from the turn of the first century to the end of the second, make it highly improbable that the several units were formulated in a common pattern and then preserved, until, later on, still further units, on the same theme and in the same pattern, were worked out and added. The entire indifference, moreover, to historical order of authorities and concentration on the logical unfolding of a given theme or problem without reference to the sequence of authorities, confirm the supposition that the work of formulation and that of redaction go forward together.

When we have sizable constructions of cognitive units, all of them conforming to a single, highly distinctive formulary pattern, which itself is internal to the expression of the ideas stated therein, we have no reason whatsoever to doubt that the whole was both made up and put together by one and the same hand. In such constructions the tradental and redactional work is coincident. The other, and principal, sort of intermediate division, that in which an externally-unitary formulary pattern is applied to a single theme or problem, has now to be reconsidered. Having a clear notion of the gross formulary pattern which characterize all of those many intermediate divisions distinguished by a common theme and a common formulary pattern consisting of "simple declarative sentences," we now refine our earlier results. The bulk of the work of giving expression to the cognitive units therefore is carried out in the processes of redaction which resulted in the formation – patterning and aggregation – of the intermediate divisions of the several tractates – in their formulation, and, it is obvious, in their organization and thematic arrangement. I state with heavy emphasis: *The Mishnah is the work of tradent-redactors. The mnemonic consists of the confluence of topic and rhetoric at the level of deep logic.*

VI

From Mnemonics to Meaning in the Mishnah

Let me now offer some generalizations of broader interest. The dominant stylistic trait of the Mishnah is the acute formalization of its syntactical structure, specifically, its intermediate divisions, so organized that the limits of a theme correspond to those of a formulary pattern. The balance and order of the Mishnah are particular to the Mishnah. Documents produced later on do not sustainedly reveal equivalent traits. Since the Mishnah is so very distinctive a document, we now investigate the intentions of the people who made it. About whom does it speak? And why, in particular, have its authorities distinctively shaped language, which in a later document such as the Tosefta does not speak in rhymes and balanced, matched declarative sentences, imposing, upon the conceptual, factual prose of the law, a peculiar kind of poetry? Why do they create rhythmic order, grammatically balanced sentences containing discrete laws, laid out in what seem to be carefully enumerated sequences, and the like? Language not only contains culture, which could not exist without it. Language – in our case, linguistic and syntactical style and stylization – expresses a world-view and ethos. Whose world-view is contained and expressed in the Mishnah's formalized rhetoric?

In the discussion which follows I make no reference whatsoever to the similarly stylized and formalized modes of expression in other documents of law or religion, in ancient times and later on. Self-evidently, the traits of stylization to which I allude are not distinctive to the Mishnah, except in its own context. Davis Mellinkoff, *The Language of Law* (Boston, 1963) points to many traits of legal language which will be familiar to readers of this work, e.g., distinctive use of a common language for a particular purpose, the presence of mannerisms of various kinds, formal words and expressions, and the like. Literary traits of documents much closer to the Mishnah in time upon examination appear to be not distant from the Mishnah's. Remarkably reminiscent of Sifra, the Pahlavi *Nirangestan*, for example, presents citations of Avesta followed by something very like pericopae in dispute-form, a statement of a problem, with diverse opinions, in the names of authorities + *guft* (= 'WMR) + balanced and matched opinions.

My interpretation of the relationship between Mishnaic rhetorical patterns and the reality contained and expressed therein and of the larger meaning of that rhetoric is directed wholly and completely to the document at hand and to the system of which it is a principal expression. It is by no means meant to exclude the possibility that similar literary preferences in other systems and their literature generate exactly the same approach to the interpretation of the meaning of those preferences, or the possibility that exactly the same literary traits bear wholly other meanings in other systems. My claim in all that follows is that Mishnaic redactional and formal traits are to be interpreted, in this context, as expressions of the Mishnaic world and testimonies to its conceptions of reality. Systemic interpretation is all that is attempted here. A more wide-ranging and comparative approach certainly is of interest. But since exactly the same phenomenon may, in diverse systems, bear quite various meanings, the comparative approach must be to systems, not to matters of detail. The problem of undertaking the requisite comparison for me is that I know no work equivalent to mine in the systematic exposition of the laws, system, and language of rules of uncleanness, e.g., of the Pahlavi code.

If we asked the tradental-redactional authorities behind the Mishnah the immediate purpose of their formalization, their answer would be, to facilitate memorization. For that is the proximate effect of the acute formalization of their document. Much in its character can be seen as mnemonic. The Mishnah was not published in writing, Lieberman (cited above) maintains: "Since in the entire Talmudic literature we do not find that a book of the Mishnah was ever consulted in the case of controversies or doubt concerning a particular reading, we may safely conclude that the compilation was not published in writing, that a written ekdosis [edition] of the Mishnah did not exist." As I pointed out in an earlier context, the Mishnah was published in a different way: "A regular oral ekdosis, edition, of the Mishnah was in existence, a fixed text recited by the Tannaim of the college. The Tanna ("repeater," reciter) committed to memory the text of certain portions of the Mishnah which he subsequently recited in the college in the presence of the great masters of the Law. Those Tannaim were pupils chosen for their extraordinary memory, although they were not always endowed with due intelligence ... When the Mishnah was committed to memory and the Tannaim recited it in the college, it was thereby published and possessed all the traits and features of a written ekdosis ... Once the Mishnah was accepted among the college Tannaim (reciters) it was difficult to cancel it." Lieberman's evidence for these conclusions is drawn from two sources, first, sayings within the rabbinical corpus and stories about how diverse problems of transmission of materials were worked out, second, parallels, some of them germane but none of them probative, drawn from Greco-Roman procedures of literary transmission.

Considerably more compelling evidence of the same proposition derives from the internal character of the Mishnah itself. But if stylization and formalization testify to a mnemonic program, then absence of the same traits must mean that some materials were not intended to be memorized. The Mishnah, and the the Mishnah alone, was the corpus to be formulated for memorization and transmitted through "living books," Tannaim, to the coming generations. The Tosefta cannot have been formulated along the same lines. Accordingly, the Mishnah is given a special place and role by those who stand behind it. We have seen the marks of a remarkably coherent, cogent, and exceedingly limited corpus of literary-formulaic devices and redactional conventions. We have been wholly unable to point to significant divergence from a single norm of agglutination: reliance upon distinctive formulary traits which are imposed on a sequence of sentences, and upon distinctive thematic substance, expressed by these same patterned sentences. That is now intermediate units were put together and accounts also for the formalization of small ones – without reference to the diversity of authorities cited therein. As I said, four distinctive syntactical patterns characterize all, with the fifth, the "simple declarative sentence" itself so shaped as to yield its own distinctive traits. If there are traces of diverse theories of formulation and redaction of materials in our division, which would reflect the individual preferences and styles of diverse circles over two hundred years, we have not found them. Those who maintain that the Mishnah as we know it not merely contains ideas from successive generations but also preserves the language and whole sequences of pericopae made up by these successive generations will want to specify the criteria for the recognition of the diverse literary results of those divergent groups.

The unified and cogent formal character of the Mishnah testifies in particular to that of its ultimate tradent-redactors. We learn in the Mishnah about the intention of that last generation of Mishnaic authorities, who gave us the document as we have it. It is their way of saying things which we know for certain. From this we hope to learn something about them and their world-view. One certain fact is that they choose to hand on important materials in such a form as facilitated memorization. The second, which follows closely, is that the document is meant to be memorized. Whether or not it also was copied and transmitted in writing, and whether or not such copies were deemed authoritative, are not questions we can answer on the basis of the Mishnah's internal evidence. The Tosefta certainly suggests that the Mishnah-pericopae were copied and glossed, but its evidence does not pertain to these larger issues.

VII
Mnemonic Rhetoric and Reality

It follows that the system of grammar and syntax distinctive to the Mishnah expresses rules and conventions intelligible to members of a particular community, that which stands behind the Mishnah. It certainly is a peculiar kind of formalized language. It is formed to facilitate a principal function, memorization and transmission of special rules. The language of the Mishnah therefore does not relate those who made and used it to one another or to the world in which they lived. It is not a functional instrument of neutral communication. Rather, it distinguishes its users from that ordinary world, and sets apart one aspect of their interrelationships, the one defined in the Mishnah, from such other aspects as do not require speech in a few patterns and in a kind of poetry. Accordingly, while the language represented in part by the Mishnah may or may not have been used for other purposes than those defined by the Mishnah, the way in which that language is used in the Mishnah bespeaks a limited and circumscribed circumstance. How things were said can have been grasped primarily by the people instructed in saying and hearing things in just that way. In this sense formalized language sets the Mishnah apart from its larger linguistic context, for Middle Hebrew was a language utilized outside of rabbinical circles.

The Mishnah's is language for an occasion. The occasion is particular: formation and transmission of special sorts of conceptions in a special way. The predominant, referential function of language, which is to give verbal structure to the message itself, is secondary in our document. The expressive function, to convey the speaker's attitude toward what he is talking about, the conative function, to focus upon who is being addressed, and other ritualized functions of language come to the fore. The Mishnah's language, as I said, therefore is special, meant as an expression of a non-referential function (Farb, *Word Play*, pp. 23-24). So far as the Mishnah was meant to be memorized by a particular group of people for a distinctive purpose, it is language which includes few and excludes many, unites those who use it and sets them apart from others who do not.

The formal rhetoric of the Mishnah is empty of content, which is proved by the fact that pretty much all themes and conceptions can be reduced to these same few formal patterns. These patterns, I have shown, are established by syntactical recurrences, as distinct from repetition of sounds. The same words do not recur, except in the case of the few forms we have specified, or key-words in a few contexts. These forms have to be excised from the formulary patterns in which they occur, e.g., 'WMR, M'SH, the dispute, so that we may discern the operative and expressive patterns themselves. On the other hand, long sequences of sentences fail to repeat the same words – that is, syllabic balance, rhythm, or sound – yet they do establish a powerful claim to order and formulary sophistication and perfection. That is why we could name a pattern, he-who ... it is ...-apocopation: The arrangement of the words, as a grammatical pattern, not their substance, is indicative of pattern. Accordingly, while we have a document composed along what clearly are mnemonic lines, the document's susceptibility to memorization rests principally upon the utter abstraction of recurrent syntactical patterns, rather than on the concrete repetition of particular words, rhythms, syllabic counts, or sounds.

A sense for the deep, inner logic of word patterns, of grammar and syntax, rather than for their external similarities, governs the Mishnaic mnemonic. Even though the Mishnah is to be memorized and handed on orally, it expresses a mode of thought attuned to abstract relationships, rather than concrete and substantive forms. The formulaic, not the formal, character of Mishnaic rhetoric yields a picture of a subculture which speaks of immaterial and not material things. In this subculture the relationship, rather than the thing or person which is related, is primary and constitutes the principle of reality. The thing in itself is less than the thing in cathexis with other things, so too the person. The repetition of form creates form. But what here is repeated is not form, but formulary pattern, a pattern effected through persistent grammatical or syntactical relationships and affecting an infinite range of diverse objects and topics. Form and structure emerge not from concrete, formal things but from abstract and unstated, but ubiquitous and powerful relationships.

This fact – the creation of pattern through grammatical relationship of syntactical elements, more than through concrete sounds – tells us that the people who memorized conceptions reduced to these particular forms were capable of extraordinarily abstract perception. Hearing peculiarities of word order in quite diverse cognitive contexts, their ears and minds perceived regularities of grammatical arrangement, repeated functional variations of utilization of diverse words, grasping from such subtleties syntactical patterns not imposed or expressed by recurrent external phenomena and autonomous of particular meanings. What they heard, it is clear, not only were abstract relationships, but also principles conveyed along with and through these relationships. For what was memorized, as I have said, was a fundamental notion, expressed in diverse examples but in recurrent rhetorical-syntactical patterns. Accordingly, what they could and did hear was what lay far beneath the surface of the rule: both the unstated principle and the unsounded pattern. This means, I stress, that their mode of thought was attuned to what lay beneath the surface, their mind and their ears perceived what was not said behind what was said, and how it was said. Social interrelationships within the community of Israel are left behind in the ritual speech of the Mishnah, just as, within the laws, natural realities are made to give form and expression to supernatural or metaphysical regularities. The Mishnah speaks of Israel, but the speakers are a group apart. The Mishnah talks of this-worldly things, but the things stand for and evoke another world entirely.

Who is the personna, serving as the Mishnah's voice? The Mishnah is remarkably indifferent to the identification and establishment of the character of the person who speaks. It not only is formally anonymous, in that it does not bear a signature or a single first-person identification. It also is substantively anonymous, in that it does not permit variation of patterns of formulation to accord with the traits of individuals or even to suggest that individuals who do occur have distinctive traits of speech, word choice, or, in the final analysis, even generative conception. This absence of individuation should not suggest that the Mishnah to our Division is essentially neutral as to the imposition of a highly distinctive mode of discourse. The contrary is the case. Green *(Biography)* states this matter as follows:

> These documents appear to be not accidental, inchoate collections, but carefully and deliberately constructed compilations. Each document has its own ideological and theological agendum, and it is axiomatic that the agendum of any document, though shaped to a degree by inherited materials, ultimately is the creation of the authorities, most of whom are anonymous, who produced the document itself. They have determined the focus, selected the materials, and provided the framework that unites the discrete pericopae and gives the document its internal consistency and coherence. The features of these documents suggest that their agenda transcend the teaching of any single master.

First, rabbinic documents contain a substantial amount of unattributed material. This gives them an atemporal quality, and creates the sense that the document, or the tradition, is speaking for itself, independent of any individual mind. Second, rabbinic documents are not constructed around the sayings of any individual, but follow either a thematic, formal, topical, or scriptural arrangement in which the teachings of opinions of various masters are gathered together to address a single issue or to interpret a particular verse of scripture. This sort of arrangement points to a process of selection in which the teachings of individuals have been made subservient to the goals of the documents. Indeed, within the documents the comments of the masters and their disagreements with each other almost always focus on matters of detail. The larger conceptions which inform the documents themselves are never called into question. Third, although every teaching in rabbinic literature originated in the mind of an individual, the continued vitality of those teachings depended on the rabbinic circles and communities who preserved and transmitted them. The chain of tradents, only occasionally mentioned by name, the redactors and the editors who stand behind the present form of both discrete pericopae and entire documents substantively revised, embellished and defined received materials, and sometimes invented new ones, to suit their various agenda.

All of this means that we know about early rabbinic figures what the various authorities behind the documents want us to know, and we know it in the way they wanted us to know it. Consequently, the historical context, the primary locus of interpretation for any saying attributed to a given master or story about him is the document in which the passage appears, not the period in which he is alleged to have lived. What does the rhetoric of the Mishnah leave unstated? The first thing we never are told is who is speaking, where we are, and the purpose for which discourse is undertaken. These may be taken for granted, but nothing in the Mishnah of our Division and little enough in the Tosefta cares to tell us about the societal or concrete context of rhetoric. If this is a mode of communication, then to whom is communication addressed? Who, we ask again, is the speaker, and who the listener?

The sole evidence of the speaker is the use of the invariable attributive. 'WMR, which bears no meaning particular to a saying and homogenizes all sayings. 'WMR states only that what follows bears the name of an authority and therefore is claimed to be authoritative. 'WMR is all we are told about the setting of a saying, where it was said, for what purpose, and, in all, in what social, spatial, temporal, and intellectual context. To put matters simply, 'WMR obscures all data of particularity and human circumstance. Yet 'WMR generally, though not always, is intellectually partitive. That is, once we have the presence of 'WMR, we know that a private authority, not the anonymous and unanimous consensus of the corpus represented by the speaker – the document – is at hand. The use of 'WMR establishes that the conception now to be stated is private. No claim is to be made for the consensus of the community for what is to be said. It follows that the silence of the Mishnah on the authority behind a saying means to claim the consensus of the community (to speak in solely secular terms) for the stated proposition.

But is what is stated to be interpreted as transactional, in that relationships between speaker, listener, and topic are presupposed? The Mishnah is remarkably reticent on that very matter. Its language invariably is descriptive, in the continuous participle. Its claim, through formal rhetoric, is that such-and-so is the way things are, describes and establishes the norms and forms of being. There is no speaker nor person-spoken-to, in the sense that a single individual to some other gives private expression to what is said (whether it reflects consensus of private opinion) or private context to what is heard. The acute formalization of all things detaches from the private person any claim that he alone says, in his own way, a particular opinion. It imposes upon all sayings the authority of the document as a whole (again, to use secular and descriptive language). The absence of differentiation among, and description of, the audience to what is said bears the same implication. This is how things are, without regard to the situation to which they are addressed, the condition, let alone opinion, of the people by whom they are heard. The abstraction of thought is carried over into the nuanced situation of the people by whom and to whom thought is conveyed.

In this sense, therefore, the language of the Mishnah and its grammatically formalized rhetoric create a world of discourse quite separate from the concrete realities of a given time, place, or society. The exceedingly limited repertoire of grammatical patterns by which all things on all matters are said gives symbolic expression to the notion that beneath the accidents of life are a few, comprehensive relationships: unchanging and enduring patterns lie deep in the inner structure of reality and impose structure upon the accidents of the world. This means, as I have implied, that reality for the Mishnaic rhetoric consists in the grammar and syntax of language, consistent and enduring patterns of relationship among diverse and changing concrete things or persons. What lasts is not the concrete thing but the abstract interplay governing any and all sorts of concrete things. There is, therefore a congruence between rhetorical patterns of speech, on the one side, and the framework of discourse established by these same patterns, on the other. Just as we accomplish memorization by perceiving not what is said but how what is said is persistently arranged, so we speak to, undertake to address and describe, a world in which what is concrete and material is secondary. The mode of expression in all contexts is principal.

The Mishnah's ideas are shaped, in particular, as gnomic expressions. They deal with basic truths, make use of devices to create a pattern (if not one of sound). The vocabulary is invariably impersonal, they do or one does or he who. And the verb nearly always is in the present tense, and always is in the present tense for descriptive rules. This too enhances the aura of universal application. So too, "Constructions such as parallelism, symmetry, and reversal of the elements in the expression are common" (Farb, *Word Play*, p. 118). Farb states, "These characteristics combine to produce a strategy of language manipulation for the particular purposes of teaching, conveying wisdom, and expressing a philosophy" (Farb, p. 118). But all of this is attained, as we have seen, through formalization of syntax at its deep levels.

The skill of the formulators of the Mishnah is to manipulate the raw materials of everyday speech. What they have done is so to structure language as to make it strange and alien, to impose a fresh perception upon what to others – and what in the Tosefta – are merely unpatterned and ordinary ways of saying things. What is said in the Mishnah is simple. How it is said is arcane. Ordinary folk cannot have had much difficulty understanding the words, which refer to ordinary actions and objects. How long it must have taken to grasp the meaning of the patterns into which the words are arranged, how hard it was and is to do so, is suggested by the necessity for the creation of Tosefta, the two Talmuds, and the commentaries in the long centuries since the Mishnah came into being. In this sense, the Mishnah speaks openly about public matters, yet its deep substructure of syntax and grammatical forms shapes what is said into an essentially ritualistic language. It takes many years to master the difficult argot, though only a few minutes to memorize the simple patterns. That paradox reflects the situation of the creators of the Mishnah.

Up to now I have said only a little about tense structure. The reason is that the Mishnah exhibits remarkable indifference to the potentialities of meaning inherent therein. Its persistent preference for the plural participle, thus the descriptive present tense, is matched by its capacity to accept the mixture of past, present, and future tenses, which can be jumbled together in a single sentence and, even more commonly, in a single pericope. It follows that the Mishnah is remarkably uninterested in differentiation of time-sequences. This fact is most clearly shown by the gemisch of the extreme-apocopated sentence, with its capacity to support something like the following: *"He who does so and so ... the rain came and wet it down ... if he was happy ... it [is] Under the law, If water be put."* Clearly, the matter of tense, past, present, future, is simply not relevant to the purpose of the speaker. If tense is irrelevant, however, then we find ourselves in the undifferentiated present. What is said is meant to bear no relationship whatever to the circumstance or particular time or context in which what is said applies. The absence of a powerful and recurrent system of tense differentiation is strong evidence in favor of our conception that the Mishnah describes a world detached from time.

The temporal and worldly authority of the Mishnah's unspecified "speaker" likewise is curiously unspecified. What is omitted is any reference to a system of institutional enforcement, political, or supernatural. At no point in our division is there an effort to give nuance to language to be used for one setting, as against some other, in the home as distinct from the Temple, the court, the school, or the street. The homogenization of thought and its expression in a limited and uniform rhetorical pattern impose the conception that the norms are axiomatic for, and expose the logic of, all situations in general, but pertain to none in particular. This once again brings to the surface the notion, implicit in the way the Mishnah says things, that the Mishnah describes how things are, whether or not material reality conforms. The absence of descriptive reference to a speaker and his role reinforces the conception that this-worldly details of identified authorities, with circumscribed and concrete authority, are not pertinent. The reason is that what comes under description does not depend upon the details of this-worldly institutions. That is why the document is so strikingly indifferent to the differentiation of rhetoric. Diverse ideational materials are reduced to a single rhetoric. The various contexts to which what is said is applicable are never given specific definition in the choice of words or rhetorical patterns. In the profoundly conventional discourse of the Mishnah, the one thing left untouched by the affect of convention is the concrete world, which is to conform, whether in fact it does or does not conform.

It scarcely needs saying that this sameness of rhetoric hardly is functional to the situation of ordinary people. If the language of the Mishnah serves a small group, its intent is quite the opposite: to encompass and describe all things. We have therefore to distinguish between the effects of formalization of thought, which produce a private framework of discourse among specialists, and the function thereof, which is to make discourse among individuals public and general and abstract it from the ordinary life. The Mishnah lacks abundant ways to speak in grammatical utterances, reducing to its handful of possibilities all truths about all things pertinent to Purities (not to exclude the other five divisions). A level of address has been chosen, and, it is clear, is severely imposed upon all themes and all contexts. It is not possible for that aesthetic-mnemonic sameness to express the diverse things which need saying in ordinary circumstances.

In this sense the Mishnaic rhetoric, while anti-contextual, creates its own context of meaning. Its indifference to any other setting of discourse but its own is suggested, as I said, by its partitive attributional formula, the same for all sayings of one genre, and also by its single honorific. The Mishnah is remarkably uninterested in diverse honorifics, using the single title, Rabbi, in all circumstances and for nearly all named authorities. The some differentiation effected by the title is to omit from consideration the teachings of people who do not have that title, and this is effected solely in the Tosefta. As I said, the absence of all reference to who is listening imposes an equivalent sameness upon the audience. What is said is said to whom it may concern, and the important parts of what is said are stated by people who are permitted neither individuation nor identification, who talk, as I have emphasized, in the same syntactical patterns about all subjects and in all contexts. In context it is trivial to notice that sexual differences play no role, except as demanded by the setting of a case or rule. Since women do the cooking, cases and examples of rules which deal with kneading dough will use the feminine form. In general, though, in the Mishnah there is neither male nor female, nor is there the slightest suggestion that women speak differently from men. Where a woman is quoted, what she is made to say, hardly surprisingly, is in the familiar rhetoric. The reason is that differences of sex are as irrelevant to the Mishnah's speech-world as differences of context, social status, or institutional circumstance.

Outside of the precedents, the formal characteristics of which are difficult to discern and which in any case occur seldom in the Mishnah, our Order presents remarkably little living dialogue. (X says is not dialogue, nor are disputes and debates dialogical in any natural sense.) Mishnaic syntax is based upon the monologue. Occasionally, as in disputes, two or more monologues are juxtaposed, but scarcely constitute dialogues. The reciter recites. No response is suggested within our document. In this sense, dialogue, a basic form human speech, is noteworthy for its absence. Tosefta makes up for the matter, with its citation of the Mishnah, as if to assume one side of a conversation, and its even more pronounced effort at interchange, its reference to something mentioned by the Mishnah in the form, "What are ...?" or "Under what circumstances ...?" But in the main the document's highly formal character precludes the possibility of dialogue, there being only a few ways of possibly uttering a thought, and these, as we have seen, not only formal but also gnomic.

The extraordinary lack of a context of communication – specification of speaker, hearer – of our document furthermore suggests that for the Mishnah, language is a self-contained formal system used more or less incidentally for communication. It is a system for description of a reality, the reality of which is created and contained by, and exhausted within, the description. The saying of the words, whether heard meaningfully by another or not, is the creation of the world. Speech is action and creation. The speech-community represented by the Mishnah stands strongly not only against nuance but also against change. The imposition of conventional and highly patterned syntax clearly is meant to preserve what is said without change (even though, we know, changes in the wording of traditions were effected for many centuries thereafter). The language is meant to be unshakeable, and its strict rules of rhetoric are meant not only to convey, but also to preserve, equally strict rules of logic, or, more really, equally permanent patterns of relationship. What was at stake in this formation of language in the service of permanence? Clearly, how things were said was intended to secure eternal preservation of what was said. Change affects the accidents and details. It cannot reshape enduring principles, and language will be used to effect their very endurance. What is said, moreover, is not to be subjected to pragmatic experimentation. The unstated but carefully considered principles shape reality and are not shaped and tested by and against reality. Use of pat phrases and syntactical clichés divorced from different thoughts to be said and different ways of thinking testifies to the prevailing notion of unstated, but secure and unchanging, reality behind and beneath the accidents of context and circumstance.

Clearly, so far as Middle Hebrew serves as a secular language, the Mishnah has transformed a common speech to sacred language and has done so through peculiar formalization of syntactical structures in particular. Yet we cannot point to anything intrinsically sacred even in those structures and patterns. For example, there is no use of the divine name, no tendency either to cite, let alone to model sentences after those of, sacred Scripture. Indeed, Scripture is treated with remarkable disinterest. The authorship of the Mishnah overall is remarkably uninterested in Scriptural proofs for its propositions. Accordingly, what serves as the vehicle of sanctification is the imposition upon common speech of fixed, secular patterns of syntax, which functionally transform talk about common things into sacred language through the employment of certain stereotype patterns. What is regular is sacred. These patterns themselves on the surface, as I said, are routine and secular, yet in function accomplish the sanctification of language, its transformation into something other than, and different from, ordinary speech. We should expect distinctive word choices, but I discern none. Who used the Mishnah's language? Clearly, people who memorized the Mishnah used it. To them was accorded significant status in the later schools. But that does not answer the question, Who first used this language and for what purpose? The answer by now is familiar. It was a group which proposed to create a document which would be transmitted by memory and therefore required formulation which would facilitate the mnemonic process.

Two facts have been established. First, the formalization of the Mishnaic thought-units is separate from the utilization of sound and other extrinsic characteristics of word choice. It depends, rather, upon recurrent grammatical patterns independent of the choices of words set forth in strings. The listener or reader has to grasp relations of words, in a given sequence of sentences, quite separate from the substantive character of the words themselves. Accordingly, second, the natural language of Middle Hebrew is not apt to be represented by the highly formal language of the Mishnah. The Mishnaic language constitutes something more than a random sequence of words using routinely to say things. It is meant as a highly formulaic way of expressing a particular set of distinctive conceptions. It is, therefore, erroneous to refer to Mishnaic-language; rather, we deal with the Mishnaic revision of the natural language of Middle Hebrew. And, it is clear, what the Mishnah does to revise that natural language is ultimately settled in the character of the grammar, inclusive of syntax, of the language. Middle Hebrew has a great many more grammatical sequences than does the Mishnaic Hebrew, and, it follows, Mishnaic Hebrew declares ungrammatical – that is, refuses to make use of – constructions which Middle Hebrew will regard as wholly grammatical and entirely acceptable. The single striking trait of the formalization of the Mishnaic language therefore is that it depends upon grammar. And just as, by definition, "Grammar is autonomous and independent of meaning" (Chomsky, p. 17), so in the Mishnah, the formalization of thought into recurrent patterns is beneath the surface and independent of discrete meanings. Yet the Mishnah imposes its own discipline, therefore its own deeper level of unitary meaning, upon everything and anything which actually is said.

To summarize our discussion of Mishnaic rhetoric, let us now ask about the ecology of Mishnaic modes of speech (Haugen, pp. 337-7). What is its classification in relationship to other languages? A variety of Middle Hebrew, it is used in particular by people engaged in the memorization and transmission of teachings on behalf of which is claimed divine revelation. Accordingly, its users are religious specialists. What are the domains of use? So far as we know, the Mishnah's distinctive modes of speech are particular to the Mishnah. But this judgment must be qualified. Even in the Tosefta the same modes do not consistently occur and scarcely serve to characterize intermediate divisions.

Accordingly, what is particular to the Mishnah is not the remarkably distinctive sentence structures we have discerned, but recurrent use of such sentence structures to give expression to sizable groups of cognitive units. That indeed is a limited domain of use. What concurrent languages are employed by the users of this mode of speech? Clearly, we may assume, Middle Hebrew in non-Mishnaic patterns was available to them. Whether in addition they spoke Aramaic or Greek is not equivalently clear, nor do we know that they spoke Middle Hebrew as a language of ordinary use. Accordingly, we do know the dialinguistical data necessary to answer this question.

Does the Mishnah yield evidence of dialect? The answer is clearly that it does not. On the contrary, the speech is decidedly uniform and unnuanced. To what degree has the Mishnaic variety of Middle Hebrew been standardized, unified and codified? Here the answer is clear. We have the highest degree of standardization. What kind of institutional support stands behind the Mishnah? The answer is not wholly clear from the data we have examined. I am inclined to think that, if we take seriously the claim in behalf of the Mishnah that it is Oral Torah, then we have to assign to the Mishnah the claim of an extraordinary sort of Heavenly support for its variety of patterns of speech. But we must answer in secular, not mythic, terms. The Mishnah probably was supported through the activities of those who memorized the language and those who supported them, a wide circle of savants. What are the attitudes of the users toward the language? It certainly is public and ritualistic, not a language of intimacy. Its use assuredly confers upon the user a defined status, leading to personal identification as a Tanna in the schools and and a rabbi outside of them.

Finally, how does the Mishnaic variety of Hebrew relate to other languages? The answer is, of course, that it is not a language at all, but rather, a variety of a language, limited and formalized for special purposes. Its ecology will then share the profile of cultic languages in general, with the qualification that, if Middle Hebrew was widely used, it is a revision of a common language into a cultic language. Its relatedness to, and difference from, unpatterned Middle Hebrew serves to shape and express the ethos and world-view of a particular speech-community.

VIII

Mnemonics and Meaning

In the absence of more than episodic evidence, we must speculate about the purpose of the editing of the Mishnah in final form solely by systematically extrapolating from the facts of its redaction insight into the purpose of its redaction. What we learn from the character of the literature about the circle that produced the literature, so far as that character speaks of those who created it, is nothing whatsoever. The people who made the Mishnah do not want us to know them, because, I should imagine, nothing about them was deemed

important in the understanding of what they did. That is why they do not
organize materials around given names of authorities, though as I said, some
such constructions do survive. It is futile to ask whether the redactors were
lawyers, philosophers, wonder workers, teachers, government officials,
preachers, soldiers, holy men, priests, anointed messiahs, or any of the other
things people who produce a holy document such as this might have been. To
ask whether they legislated for themselves or for all Israelites is equally
hopeless, because, as we know, silent as they are on themselves, so reticent are
they about those to whom they seek to speak.

Yet they do take certain things for granted. In order to make sense of what
they do tell us, there are things which we have to know and which are not told to
us by them. But from the perspective of form and rhetoric the catalogue hardly
is a long one. The Mishnah presupposes the existence of Scripture (the "Old
Testament"). It is not possible to make sense of the details of any tractate
without knowledge of Scriptural laws. Yet what, in rhetoric and grammar, is it
about, and in, Scripture that is presupposed? It is not, I have stressed, the style
and language of Scripture. It is necessary to know certain facts of Scripture,
e.g., that a corpse contaminates, that there is a dimension of the clean and the
unclean. The knowledge even of facts of Scripture by themselves cannot, of
course, suffice. The Mishnah has distinctive conceptions even of the meaning of
simple facts, data of Scripture themselves. In the present context, what is
important is that knowledge of Scripture's forms and style in no important way
improves understanding of those of the Mishnah or even is relevant to
interpreting them.

Yet there is a side to Scripture which, I think, is at the very bedrock of the
Mishnah's linguistic character and explains the Mishnah's self-evident
preoccupation with the interplay of theme and form. Scripture speaks of creation
through words, and, we know, it is as much through how things are said as
through what is said that the Mishnah proposes to effect its own creative
purpose. The priestly notion of creation by means of speech is carried through
in the Mishnah's most distinctive and ubiquitous attributive, X 'WMR, one
says, just as at Genesis 1:3, 6, 9, 11, 14, 20, 24, 29, at each of he stages of
creation, God says ('MR) something and it is. The supposition of the Mishnah
that Scripture is known is, while not trivial, obvious.

There is a second, less blatant supposition. It is that the language of the
Mishnah will be understood, its nuances appreciated, its points of stress and
emphasis grasped. Our discussion of the cathectically neutral and indifferent
style of the Mishnah, its failure to speak to some distinct audience in behalf of
some defined speaker, does not obscure the simple fact that the Mishnah is not
gibberish, but a corpus of formed and intensely meaningful statements, the form
of which is meant to bear deep meaning. Accordingly, the gnomic sayings of
the Mishnah, corresponding in their deep, universal grammar to the subterranean
character of reality, permit the inference that the reality so described was to be

grasped and understood by people of mind. Given the unarticulated points at which stress occurs, the level of grammar autonomous of discrete statements and concrete rulings, moreover, we must conclude that the framers of the Mishnah expected to be understood by remarkably keen ears and active minds. Conveying what is fundamental at the level of grammar autonomous of meaning, they manifested confidence that the listener will put many things together and draw the important conclusions for himself or herself. That means that the Mishnah assumes an active intellect, capable of perceiving inferred convention, and a vividly participating audience, capable of following what was said with intense concentration.

This demands, first, memorizing the message, second, perceiving the subtle and unarticulated message of the medium of syntax and, grammar. The hearer, third, is assumed to be capable of putting the two together into the still further insight that the cogent pattern exhibited by diverse statements preserves a substantive cogency among those diverse and delimited statements. Superficially-various rules, stated in sentences unlike one another on the surface and made up of unlike word choices, in fact say a single thing in a single way. None of this is possible, it goes without saying, without anticipating that exegesis of the fixed text will be undertaken by the audience. The Mishnah demands commentary. It takes for granted that the audience is capable of exegesis and proposes to undertake the work. The Mishnah commands a sophisticated and engaged socio-intellectual context within the Israelite world. The Mishnah's lack of specificity on this point should not obscure its quite precise expectation: The thing it does not tell us which we have to know is that the Mishnah will be understood. The process of understanding, the character of the Mishnah's language testifies, is complex and difficult. The Mishnah is a document which compliments its audience.

Language serves the authorities of the Mishnah as an instrument of power, specifically, power to create reality. Wittgenstein (cited by Farb, p. 192) said, "The limits of my language mean the limits of my world." What are the limitations of the Mishnah's formalized modes of speech? What sort of reality is made possible within them and is constructed by them? To what degree, specifically, does Mishnaic language attain new possibilities for the containment and creation of reality precisely by its tendency to avoid explicit generalizations and its perpetual expression of precise but abstract relationships between things only in concrete terms? And, finally, we return to the central and inescapable question, For what purpose was the Mishnah made?

We begin, as we did above, with the gnomic character of the Mishnaic discourse. Clearly, the Mishnah claims to make wise and true statements, statements which, moreover, apply at any time and in any place. It follows, second, that the Mishnah proposes to describe how things truly are. And third, accordingly, the people who made the Mishnah did so in order to put together, in a single document and in encapsulated form, an account of the inner structure of reality, specifically, of that aspect of reality which, in their judgment, is susceptible of encapsulation in formally-patterned words. When, fourth, we recall the exceedingly limited repertoire of ways by which statements are made, we recognize that, to the authorities of the Mishnah, all of the diverse and changing things in the world can be reduced to a few simple, descriptive equations. These fifth, are to be expressed in particular by the inner and deep traits of the interrelationships of words, by persistent patterns of grammar and of syntax, rather than by superficial traits of sound and repetition of concrete thought. The principle is to be derived by the listener's reflection upon any set of diverse rules or statements, his contributed perception of what unites the whole, which will be left unsaid but everywhere deemed obvious.

Relying entirely on the traits of syntax and grammar which are before us, what can we say about the deepest convictions concerning reality characteristic of people who spoke in the ways we have considered? There is a deep sense of balance, of complementarity, of the appropriateness of opposites in the completion of a whole thought. Many times do we hear: if thus, then so, and if not thus, then not so. Mishnaic rhetoric demands, because the Mishnah's creators' sense of grammar requires, the completion of the positive by the negative, and of the negative by the positive. The contrastive complex predicate is testimony to the datum that order consists in completion and wholeness. So, too, the many balanced declarative sentences before us reveal the same inner conviction that in the completion of a pattern, in the working out of its single potentiality through a sequence of diverse actualities, lie that besought order and wholeness. The fact that it is the intermediate division which constitutes the formulary context of the Mishnah needs no further specification. Accidents do require specification and repetition. The Mishnah is scarcely satisfied to give a single instance of a rule, from which we may generalize. It strongly prefers to give us three or six or nine instances, on the basis of which we may then conclude that there is, indeed, an underlying rule. The singleton-case is not the rule solely for itself, nor, all by itself, for all things.

I do not perceive an equivalent meaning in the duplicated subject. When, however, we come to apocopation – beside the sequentially balanced sentence, the Mishnah's other remarkable formulary structure – we once more perceive something from the external expression about the mind, the inner structure of which is subject to articulation. What do we have in apocopation? It is, first of all, a powerful sense of superficial incompleteness and disorder. Apocopated sentences are composed of disjoined phrases. The subject of such sentences generally is made up of two or more such phrases, each of them introducing its own actor and acted-upon, its subject and predicate. What unites the several clauses and imposes meaning upon all of them is the ultimate predicate. This, by itself, cannot always be asked to refer to any single one of the phrases of the subject. But it encompasses the result of all of them, all together. It is, therefore, a construction the meaning of which depends upon a context which is inferred from, but not made explicit by, its constituents. In a profound sense, the apocopated sentence, which we found so distinctive to the Mishnah, expresses that deep sense of a wholeness beneath discrete parts which Mishnaic language presupposes.

For it is the mind of the hearer which makes sense of the phrases and clauses of the subject and perceives the relationship, endowing whole meaning upon the clauses of the subject, required by the predicate. The mind of the hearer is central in the process by which apocopation attains meaning. The capacity for perceiving the rational and orderly sense of things exhibited by that mind is the unstated necessity of apocopation. That, as we have seen in the preceding discussion, is characteristic of Mishnaic modes of expression, therefore also of perception. Hearing discrete rules, applicable to cases related in theme and form, but not in detail and concrete actualities, the hearer puts together two things. First is the repetition of grammatical usages. Second is the repetition of the same principle, the presence of which is implied by the repetition of syntactical patterns in diverse cases. These two, stable principle and disciplined grammar autonomous of meaning, are never stated explicitly but invariably present implicitly.

So there are these two striking traits of mind reflected within Mishnaic rhetoric: first, the perception of order and balance, second, the perception of the mind's centrality in the construction of order and balance, the imposition of wholeness upon discrete cases, in the case of the routine declarative sentence, and upon discrete phrases, in the case of the apocopated one. Both order and balance are contained from within and are imposed from without. The relationships revealed by deep grammatical consistencies internal to a sentence and the implicit regularities revealed by the congruence and cogency of specified cases rarely are stated but always are to be discerned. Accordingly, the one thing which the Mishnah invariably does not make explicit but which always is necessary to know is, I stress, the presence of the active intellect, the participant who is the hearer. It is the hearer who ultimately makes sense of, perceives the sense in, the Mishnah. Once more we are impressed by the Mishnah's expectation of high sophistication and profound sensitivity to order and to form on the part of its impalpable audience.

In this sense the Mishnah serves both as a book of laws and as a book for learners, a law-code and a school-book. But it is in this sense alone. If the Mishnah is a law-code, it is remarkably reticent about punishments for infractions of its rules. It rarely says what one must do, or must not do, if he or she becomes unclean, and hardly even alludes to punishments or rewards consequent upon disobedience or obedience to its laws. "Clean" and "unclean" rhetorically are the end of the story and generate little beyond themselves. If the Mishnah as a school-book, it never informs us about its institutional setting, speaks of its teachers, sets clearcut perceptible educational goals for its students, and, above all, attempts to stand in relationship to some larger curriculum or educational and social structure. Its lack of context and unselfconsciousness framework of discourse hardly support the view that, in a this-worldly and ordinary sense, we have in our hands a major division of a law-code or of a school-book.

Nor is the Mishnah a corpus of traditions which lay claim to authority or to meaning by virtue of the authorities cited therein. That is why the name of an authority rarely serves as a redactional fulcrum. As I have stressed, the tense structure is ahistorical and anti-historical. Sequences of actions generally are stated in the descriptive present tense. Rules attain authority not because of who says them, but because (it would seem) no specific party at a specific time stands behind them. The reason, I think that shortly after the promulgation of the Mishnah, the Mishnah gained for itself the place in the revealed Torah of Moses at Sinai, testifies against its capacity to serve as an essentially historical statement of who said what, when, and for which purpose. The Mishnah, as I have emphasized, is descriptive of how things are. It is indifferent to who has said so, uninterested in the cumulative past behind what it has to say. These are not the traits of a corpus of "traditions." I am inclined to think that law-code, school-book, and corpus of traditions all are not quite to the point of the accurate characterization of the Mishnah.

Yet, if not quite to the point, all nonetheless preserve a measure of proximate relevance to the definition of the Mishnah. The Mishnah does contain descriptive laws. These laws require the active participation of the mind of the hearer, thus are meant to be learned, not merely obeyed, and self-evidently are so shaped as to impart lessons, not merely rules to be kept. The task of the hearer is not solely or primarily to obey, though I think obedience is taken for granted, but to participate in the process of discovering principles and uncovering patterns of meaning. The very form of Mishnaic rhetoric, its formalization and the function of that form testify to the role of the learner and hearer, that is, the student, in the process of definitive and indicative description, not communication, of what is and of what is real. Self-evidently, the Mishnah's citation of authorities makes explicit the claim that some men, now dead, have made their contribution, therefore have given shape and substance to tradition, that which is shaped by one and handed onward by another. So the Mishnah indeed is, and therefore is meant as, a law-code, a school-book, and a corpus of tradition. It follows that the purpose for which the Mishnah was edited into final form was to create such a multi-purpose document, a tripartite goal attained in a single corpus of formed and formal sayings. And yet, it is obvious, the Mishnah is something other than these three things in one. It transcends the three and accomplishes more than the triple goals which on the surface form the constitutive components of its purpose.

To describe that transcendent purpose, we return to Wittgenstein's saying: "The limits of my language mean the limits of my world." The Mishnah's formulaic rhetoric on the one side imposes limits, boundaries, upon the world.

What fits into that rhetoric, can be said by it, constitutes world, world given shape and boundary by the Mishnah. The Mishnah implicitly maintains, therefore, that a wide range of things fall within the territory mapped out by a limited number of linguistic conventions, grammatical sentences. What is grammatical can be said and therefore constitutes part of the reality created by Mishnaic word. What cannot be contained within the grammar of the sentence cannot be said and therefore falls outside of the realm of Mishnaic reality. Mishnaic reality consists in those things which can attain order, balance, and principle. Chaos then lies without. Yet, if we may extrapolate from the capacity of the impoverished repertoire of grammar to serve for all sorts of things, for the eleven topics of our division, for example, then we must concede that all things can be said by formal revision. Everything can be reformed, reduced to the order and balance and exquisite sense for the just match characteristic of the Mishnaic pericope. Anything of which we wish to speak is susceptible of the ordering and patterning of Mishnaic grammar and syntax. That is a fact which is implicit throughout our division. Accordingly, the territory mapped out by Mishnaic language encompasses the whole of the pertinent world under discussion. There are no thematic limitations of Mishnaic formalized speech. Yet reality, the world of clean and unclean in the present context, is forced to surpass itself, to strive for a higher level of order and meaning through its submission to Mishnaic formalization. Implicit in the rhetoric of our document is the notion, now alluded to many times, of deep regularities which in principle unite cases, just as regularities in rhetoric unite cases. What is abstract need not be spelled out and instantiated endlessly because it already is spelled out through recurrent, implicit relationships among words, among cases. In this context we recall Green's statement,

> If the performance of rituals within the Temple exposes the lines of God's revealed reality, then thinking ... about these rituals outside the Temple, even without the possibility of performing all of them, has the same result. The Mishnaic rabbis express their primary cognitive statements, their judgments upon large matters, through ... law, not through myth or theology, neither of which is articulated at all. Early Rabbinism took ritual beyond the realm of practice and transformed it into the object of speculation and the substance of thought. Study, learning, and exposition became ... the basic Rabbinic activity ...

Restating this view in terms of Mishnaic grammatical rhetoric, we may say that the thinking about matters of detail within a particular pattern of cognitive constructions treats speculation and thought as themselves capable of informing and shaping being, not merely expressing its external traits: Language becomes ontology.

Language in the Mishnah replaces cult, formalism of one kind takes the place of formalism of another. The claim that infinitely careful and patterned doing of a particular sort of deeds is *ex opere operato* an expression of the sacred has its counterpart in the implicit character of the Mishnah's language. Its rhetoric is formed with infinite care, according to a finite pattern for speech, about doing deeds for a particular sort. Language now conforms to cult then. The formal cult, once performed in perfect silence, now is given its counterpart in formal speech. Where once men said nothing, but through gesture and movement, in other circumstances quite secular, performed holy deed, now they do nothing, but through equally patterned revision of secular words about secular things perform holy speech. In the cult it is the very context which makes an intrinsically neutral, therefore secular, act into a holy one. Doing the thing right, with precision and studied care, makes the doing holy. Slaughtering an animal, collecting its blood and butchering it, burning incense and pouring wine – these by themselves are things which can be and are done in the home as much as in the cult. But in the cult they are characterized by formality and precision. In the Mishnah, by contrast, there is no spatial context to sanctify the secular act of saying things. The context left, once cult is gone, is solely the cultic mode of formalism, the ritualization of speech, that most neutral and commonplace action. The Mishnah transforms speech into ritual and so creates the surrogate of ritual deed. That which was not present in cult, speech, is all that is present now that the silent cult is gone. And, it follows, it is by the formalization of speech, its limitation to a few patterns, and its perfection through the creation of patterns of relationships in particular, that the old nexus of Heaven and earth, the cult, now is to be replicated in the new and complementary nexus, cultic speech about all things.

What the limitation of Mishnaic language to a few implicit relational realities accomplished, therefore, is the reduction of the world to the limits of language. In ritual-grammar the world therein contained and expressed attains formalization among, and simplification by, the unstated but remarkably few principles contained within, and stated by, the multitudinous cases which correspond to the world. Mishnaic language makes possible the formalization of the whole of the everyday and workaday world. It accomplishes the transformation of all things in accord with that sense for perfect form and unfailing regularity which once were distinctive to the operation of the cult. Mishnaic language explores the possibility of containing and creating a new realm of reality, one which avoids abstractions and expresses all things only through the precision of grammatical patterns, that is, the reality of abstract relationships alone.

Have we come closer to a perception of the purpose for which, according to the internal testimony of our order, the Mishnah was created as a document easy to memorize and probably published not in writing but only orally? In a concrete sense, of course, we have not. Mishnaic rhetoric says nothing explicit about the purpose of the rhetoric. In the simplest sense, as we noted, the proximate purpose of formalization was to facilitate the mnemonic process. Yet it is to beg the question to say that the purpose of facilitating memorization is to help people remember things. The authors of the Mishnah wants their book to be memorized for a reason. The reason transcends the process, pointing, rather, to its purpose. Nor do we stand closer to the inner intentions of the Mishnah's authorities when we raise the polemical purpose of memorization. This was to act out the claim that there are two components of "the one whole Torah which Moses, our rabbi, received from God at Sinai," one transmitted in writing, the other handed on by tradition, in oral form only. True, the claim for the Mishnah, laid down in tractate Abot, ca. A.D. 250, the Mishnah's first and most compelling apologetic, is that the authority of the Mishnah rests upon its status as received tradition of God. It follows that tradition handed on through memory is valid specifically because, while self-evidently not part of the written Torah, which all Israel has in hand, it is essential to the whole Torah. Its mode of tradition through memory verifies and authenticates its authority as tradition begun by God, despite its absence from the written part of Torah. Both these things – the facilitation of memorization, the authentication of the document through its external form – while correct also are post facto. They testify to the result of Mishnaic rhetoric for both educational-tradental and polemical-apologetic purposes. Once we memorize, we accomplish much. But why, to begin with, commit these gnomic sayings to such language as facilitates their memorization?

In a world such as the Mishnah's, in which writing is routine, memorization is special. What happens when we know something by heart which does not happen when we must read it or look for it in a scroll or a book? It is that when we walk in the street and when we sit at home, when we sleep and when we awake, we carry with us, in our everyday perceptions, that memorized gnomic saying. The process of formulation through formalization and the coequal process of memorizing patterned cases to sustain the perception of the underlying principle, uniting the cases just as the pattern unites their language, extend the limits of language to the outer boundaries of experience, the accidents of everyday life itself. Gnomic sayings are routine in all cultures. But the reduction of all truth particularly to gnomic sayings is not.

To impose upon those sayings an underlying and single structure of grammar corresponding to the inner structure of reality is to transform the structure of language into a statement of ontology. Once our minds are trained to perceive principle among cases and pattern within grammatical relationships, we further discern in the concrete events of daily life both principle and underlying autonomous pattern. The form of the Mishnah is meant to correspond to the formalization perceived within, not merely imposed upon, the conduct of concrete affairs, principally, the meaning and character of concrete happenings among things, in the workaday life of people. The matter obviously is not solely ethical, but the ethical component is self-evident. It also has to do with the natural world and the things which break its routine, of which our Division speaks so fully and in such exquisite detail. Here all things are a matter of relationship, circumstance, fixed and recurrent interplay. If X, then Y, if not X, then not Y – that is the datum by which minds are shaped.

The way to shape and educate minds is to impart into the ear, thence into the mind, perpetual awareness that what happens recurs, and what recurs is pattern and order, and, through them, wholeness. How better than to fill the mind with formalized sentences, generative both of meaning for themselves and of significance beyond themselves, in which meaning rests upon the perception of relationship? Pattern is to be discovered in alertness, in the multiplicity of events and happenings, none of which states or articulates pattern. Mind, trained to memorize through what is implicit and beneath the surface, is to be accustomed and taught in such a way as to discern pattern. Order is because order is discovered, first in language, then in life. As the cult in all its precise and obsessive attention to fixed detail effected the perception that from the orderly center flowed lines of meaning to the periphery, so the very language of the Mishnah, in the particular traits which I have specified, also in its precise and obsessive concentration on innate and fixed relationship, effects the perception of order deep within the disorderly world of language, nature, and man. Such is the power of oral tradition, exemplified in this rather odd but interesting case of the Mishnah, Judaism's first document beyond Scripture.

So to conclude: There is a perfect correspondence between what the Mishnah proposes to say and the way in which it says it. An essential part of the ethos of Mishnaic culture is its formal and formulaic sentence, the means by which it makes its cognitive statements and so expresses its world-view. Not only does ethos correspond to world-view, but world-view is expressed in style as much as in substance. In the case of Mishnaic form, the ethos and world-view come together in the very elements of grammatical formalization, which, never made articulate, express the permanence and paramount character of relationship, the revelatory relativity of context and circumstance. Life attains form in structure. It is structure which is most vivid in life. The medium for the expression of the world-view is the ethos. But for the Mishnah, ethos neither appeals to, nor, so far as I can see, expresses, emotion. Just as there is no room for nuance in general in the severe and balanced sentences of the Mishnah, so there is no place for the nuance of emotion of commitment in general. The rhetoric of our document makes no appeal to emotion or to obedience, describing, not invoking, the compelling and ineluctable grounds for assent. This claim that things are such and so, relate in such and such a way, without regard or appeal to how we want them to be, is unyielding. Law is law, despite the accidents of workaday life, and facts are facts. The bearer of facts, the maker of law, is the relationship, the pattern by which diverse things are set into juxtaposition with one another, whether subject and predicate, or dead creeping thing and loaf of Heave-offering. What is definitive is not the thing but the context and the circumstance, the time, the condition, the intention of the actor. In all, all things are relative to all things.

The bridge from ethos to world-view is the form and character of the sentence which transforms the one into the other. The declarative sentence through patterned language takes attitude and turns it into cognition. Mishnaic "religion" – its Judaism as a religion that appeals to a Torah given only orally as well as to another Torah that was given in writing – not only speaks of values. Its mode of speech is testimony to its highest and most enduring, distinctive value. This language does not speak of sacred symbols but of pots and pans, of menstruation and dead creeping things, of ordinary water which, because of the circumstance of its collection and location, possesses extraordinary power, of the commonplace corpse and the ubiquitous diseased person, of genitalia and excrement, toilet-seats and the flux of penises, of stems of pomegranates and stalks of leeks, of rain and earth and clay ovens, wood, metal, glass, and hide. This language is filled with words for neutral things of humble existence. It does not speak of holy things and is not symbolic in its substance. In the Mishnah, Holy Things are merely animals a farmer has designated, in his intention, as holy. The language of the Mishnah speaks of ordinary things, of workaday things which everyone must have known. But because of the peculiar and particular way in which it is formed and formalized, this same language not only adheres to an aesthetic theory but expresses a deeply embedded ontology and methodology of the sacred, specifically of the sacred within the secular, and of the capacity for regulation, therefore for sanctification, within the ordinary.

World-view and ethos are synthesized in language formulated as oral tradition. The synthesis is expressed in grammatical and syntactical regularities. What is woven into some sort of ordered whole is not a cluster of sacred symbols. The religious system is not discerned within symbols at all. Knowledge of the conditions of life is imparted principally through the description of the commonplace facts of life, which symbolize, stand for, nothing beyond themselves and their consequences for the clean and the unclean. That description is effected through the construction of units of meaning, intermediate divisions composed of cognitive elements. The whole is balanced, explicit in detail, but reticent about the whole, balanced in detail but dumb about the character of the balance. What is not said is what is eloquent and compelling as much as what is said. Accordingly, that simple and fundamental congruence between ethos and world-view is to begin with, for the Mishnah, the very language by which the one is given cognitive expression in the other. The medium of patterned speech conveys the meaning of what is said. Oral formulation and oral transmission of teaching does not only preserve tradition. Oral tradition creates tradition.

Chapter Four

From Corpus to Canon: Framing an Issue for Inquiry

I

The Problem of Canonicity

A variety of writings containing statements attributed to sages, or rabbis, came to closure between the editing of the Mishnah, in ca. A.D. 200, and the formation of the Bavli, the Talmud of Babylonia, in ca. A.D. 600. These writings in the history of Judaism have formed not only a literary corpus, exhibiting traits in common, but also a theological and legal canon, making a cogent and authoritative statement in common. Since, in the first two chapters, I have argued that the document – and not the adventitious character of its contents – forms the primary arena for discourse and analysis, I move on to the design of a research program that expresses that premise. Let me spell out the way in which I have been able to define the questions that require an answer and therefore determine the data that demand attention.

Specifically, I want to know how a document makes its part of such a canonical statement, speaking, for its particular subject, in behalf of the entirety of the Judaic system at hand. How, in other words, does the authorship of a canon take up sources and turn them into traditions, in the case of a given topic. I take up a Bavli tractate because, on any given topic, a tractate of the Bavli presents the final and authoritative statement that would emerge from the formative period of the Judaism of the dual Torah. That statement constituted not only an authoritative, but also an encompassing and complete account. That is what I mean by the making of a canonical statement on a subject: transforming whatever lay in hand into a not-merely cogent but fixed and authoritative statement. What I wish to find out is the canonical status of the Bavli, insofar as the authorship of the Bavli transformed its antecedents, its sources, into traditions: the way things had been, are and must continue to be, in any given aspect of the life and world view of Israel, the Jewish people, as the Bavli's authorship understood the composition of that Israel.

II

The Bavli and Canonical Discourse in the Judaism of the Dual Torah

The selection of the Bavli as the beginning of the canonical inquiry presents no puzzle. In the centuries beyond the closure of the Bavli in ca. A.D. 600, people would nearly universally turn to the Bavli as the starting point for all inquiry into any given topic, and rightly so. Since the Bavli made the first and enduringly definitive statement, we impute to the Bavli canonical status. If, therefore, we wish to ask about how a variety of writings turned into a canon, that is to say, about the canonicity of documents of the formative age of the Judaism of the dual Torah, we shall inquire into the standing of a Bavli-tractate as a canonical testimony on its subject within the larger system. What we want to know about that canonical testimony is the nature of the canon as exemplified in a given documentary treatment of a given subject, therefore asking *what constitutes the definition of a canonical statement and how such a statement works.*

This plan of research forms the first in a planned three stage inquiry, into literature, history of ideas, and structure, aimed at spelling out the cogency of the Judaism of the dual Torah, that is, written and oral, which in late antiquity came to its final and complete expression in the Bavli. What I want to describe is the system as a complete and whole composition, with its own points of emphasis and proportion, and, further, I hope to accomplish not only the description, but also the analysis and interpretation, of that same great Judaism, that is, the Judaism of the dual Torah, oral and written, of Moses, our rabbi, that began in the revelation at Sinai. The work begins, as it must, with a problem of description, specifically, of literature as a medium for the delivery of a cogent statement that transcends any single book, then proceeds to an analytical problem, the history of an idea that forms one central component of the encompassing intellectual system at hand, and, finally, moves onward to a still broader exercise of interpretation, which I shall describe in due course. I have in mind a kind of unfolding collage, in which each of the components bears its own integrity and autonomy, yet points toward a larger whole, of which it forms a part. The canvas is empty, except in my mind's eye.

Let me first offer a thumbnail sketch of the literature the canonical status of which concerns us. It is a set of writings produced by sages of Judaism from about 200 to about 600 A.D. These writings rest on two base-documents, the Scriptures of ancient Israel (to Christianity, the Old Testament, to Judaism, the Written Torah), and the Mishnah (in Judaism, the first component of the Oral Torah ultimately encompassing all the literature at hand). All of the writings of Judaism in late antiquity copiously cite Scripture. More important, some of them serve (or are presented and organized) as commentaries on the former, the written Torah, others as amplifications of the latter, the Mishnah as the beginning of the transcription of the oral Torah. Since Judaism treats all of these writings as a single, seamless Torah, the one whole Torah revealed by God to Moses, our rabbi, at Mount Sinai, the received hermeneutic naturally does the same. All of the writings are read in light of all others, and words and phrases are treated as autonomous units of tradition, rather than as components of particular writings, e.g., paragraphs – units of discourse – and books – composite units of sustained and cogent thought.

III

The Issue of Canon as Canonicity Pertains to the Judaism of the Dual Torah

What I want to know, therefore, is what holds the whole together, and how a corpus of writing became a canon of theology and law. From the Talmud of the Land of Israel, Genesis Rabbah, and Leviticus Rabbah, through Pesiqta deRab Kahana, onward to The Fathers According to Rabbi Nathan and the Talmud of Babylonia, a rather cogent set of statements may be discovered to define the premises of one writing after another. Specifically, powerful interest in history and salvation, recurring emphasis on the correspondence between Israel's holy way of life and the salvation of Israel in history, the reading of Scripture as an account of the present and future – these will have struck the compositors of diverse documents as not fresh but traditional, meaning, ineluctable and necessary. These statements comprise one critical component of the Judaism of the dual Torah.

We already have a clear thesis on the historical unfolding of that Torah, and, consequently, the history of literary components of the system and the structure of their relationships seem to me fairly clear. Compositors of writings of the two centuries from the Mishnah to the first of the two Talmuds, specifically, will have found puzzling the theological premises of the literature put together from the fourth century forward. For the authors of the Mishnah, with its close companion in the Tosefta, the compilers of tractate Abot, the author-compilers of Sifra to Leviticus – none of these circles of authorship took so keen an interest in the issue of salvation or in the correspondence between the biblical narrative and contemporary history. I have already offered an account of where, when, how, and why so complete a shift from one consensus to another took place.

But I have yet to describe – let alone analyze and interpret – that fresh consensus that came to full expression after 400 not document by document, but as a cogent statement characteristic, as premise, of them all. The historical study of the unfolding of ideas in the canonical sequence of rabbinical writings, worked out in my *Foundations of Judaism* (Philadelphia, 1983-1985: Fortress), and the comparative study of midrash in the canon of the dual Torah addressed in a variety of writings (spelled out in the preface of my *From Tradition to Imitation: The Plan and Program of Pesiqta Rabbati and Pesiqta deRab Kahana* [Atlanta, 1987: Scholars Press for Brown Judaic Studies] have brought us to the question that clearly transcends the comparative method in the study of documents. That question defines the research problem worked out in this article.

IV

A Metaphorical Framing of the Problem

Let me begin with an analogy. Specifically, I invoke the analogy of the stars. All of them suns of their respective systems, but also parts of larger congeries, and these yet components of still larger ones: the sun, the milky way, the entirety of matter. Seen near at hand, our sun is the only star, so by day. But at night when we see the skies, we realize that ours is not the only sun, but a star like other stars. And, penetrating into deep space, we understand that the whole – our solar system, our galaxy – finds its place in a vast realm indeed. What I want to know therefore is how the individual stars of the firmament of Judaism form a galaxy, specifically, how the particular documents of the Judaism of the dual Torah form thjat single, one whole Torah of Moses, our rabbi, that, all together and all at once, constitute the Torah. I frame the matter in concrete and literary terms, but the issue encompasses the fundamental structure and system of Judaism: that galaxy of all the stars of Sinai.

Hard as it is to come to grips with the whole, seen all at once, so difficult it is to reckon with the textual community of Judaism. And who can chart – let alone navigate – the heavens imagined in the Judaism of the dual Torah! What force, what gravity and matter and anti-matter, holds the whole together? How to know the limits of the textual community, since these are not indicated by the covers of a book or even the sides of a book shelf? Having worked out [1] the description of texts, read one by one, to the present work, [2] the analysis of those same texts seen in relationship to one another, that is, to comparison and contrast among a set of documents, hence to connection, and, ultimately, I proceed – in a series of studies essentially unrelated to one another – [3] to the interpretation of texts under the aspect of continuity, that is to say, eternity.

The specific research problem I wish to define – to come down to earth – is how the Bavli (the Talmud of Babylonia) as exemplified in one tractate relates to its sources, by which I mean, materials it shares with other and by definition earlier documents. The question that defines the problem is how the Bavli has formed *of* available writings (redacted in documents now in hand and otherwise) a single, cogent, and coherent statement presented as summary and authoritative. In what ways does a Bavli-tractate frame a canonical statement out of what its authorship has in hand? Can we discern within the Bavli's treatment of a subject traits of canonicity, that is, laying down a final and experienced judgment for all time? And can we see within the Bavli elements of a program to turn sources into a single tradition, on a given topic? When I can answer that program of questions, I can form a hypothesis, resting on literary facts, concerning the literary and doctrinal canonicity of the rabbinic corpus of late antiquity. That is to say, I can frame a theory on how the Judaism of the dual Torah speaking through the Bavli in conclusion constituted of its received materials a whole and proportioned system – way of life, world view, addressed to a defined Israel – and turned into a systemic statement, that is, a canon, a variety of available writings on any given subject. Let me place this concrete problem into its larger context, and then define the requirements of the research program at hand.

From the remarkable statement of the Judaic system of the dual Torah which is adumbrated in the Yerushalmi (the Talmud of the Land of Israel) and fully exposed by the Bavli (the Talmud of Babylonia), a broad and firm consensus came to expression. It is the consensus that constitutes both the theological component of that system and also the legal, concrete realization in the everyday life of the people of that same system. These two together, the way of life and the world-view, addressed an Israel of the system's own definition. The question before us arises from the fact that that Judaic system – the Judaism of the dual Torah, as authoritatively stated by the Bavli – encompassed also documents, making of the these diverse writings now more than a mere collection of books but a canon, that is (from the system's perspective) a single, whole, homogeneous, cogent and (therefore) authoritative statement. The matter may be expressed in a simple way. I discern three dimensions by which any document of that Judaism may be measured: autonomy, connection, continuity. A book in the canon at hand stands by itself, within its own covers; it also relates to other books of the same canon through specific connections, indicated by intrinsic traits of rhetoric, topic, and logic or by shared materials, common to a number of documents. And it also forms part of an undifferentiated canon, that is, the Torah, or Judaism, through the dimension of complete continuity. Hence among those three dimensions, autonomy, connection, continuity, we now address the third. It follows that the Judaism of the dual Torah transformed a variety of writings from a literary *corpus* into a systemic theological-legal *canon*. The problem of forthcoming research is to take the first step toward the description of that Judaism. I shall begin by turning to the authoritative literature and asking where and how that literature exhibits internal traits of canonicity, I mean, coherence to a broad, systemic composition.

Let me spell out what I conceive to be the problem of canonicity and spell out what is at stake in the problem of literary description with which this sizable exercise commences. Theologians of the canon of Judaism correctly identify as the premise of all exegesis deep connections between one document and the next, so that all documents impose meanings upon each, and each demands a reading in the setting of the whole literature. The position at hand addresses the *entirety* of the writings of the ancient rabbis, all together, all at once, everywhere and all the time. Here I begin to investigate the continuities among all documents, thus a textual community. Issues of the continuity of documents form a first step toward the much larger description of the whole of canonical Judaism: the Judaism of the dual Torah. That is a Judaism that to begin with invokes its canon to define itself: a Judaism of the dual Torah as against a Judaism that appeals to a different symbol altogether from a canonical one, e.g., the Judaic system of the Essenes of Qumran, with its teacher of righteousness as its critical symbolic expression.

Each document in the corpus of the rabbinic writings of late antiquity bears points in common with others. But how do all of them form a canon? There is a necessary but not sufficient answer to that question. The points in common include citing a common Scripture in an essentially uniform way (so it would seem) and more important, addressing a shared program of interest to the common Scriptures. But the more profound fact provides the sufficient response. No document of the Judaism under discussion, that which came to its original expression in the Mishnah, ca. A.D. 200, and reached its full statement, in late antiquity, in the Talmud of Babylonia, stands on its own. All documents reach us as the Torah, that is to say, through the medium and the consensus of the Judaic community of the dual Torah, and all of them join together because of their authority in that community, their standing as statements of the (dual) Torah.

To define still further what I mean by the problem of canonicity, let me invoke the analogy of a library. Books brought together form a library. Each title addresses its own program and makes its own points. Books produced by a cogent community constitute not merely a library but a canon: a set of compositions each of which contributes to a statement that transcends its own pages. The books exhibit intrinsic traits that make of them all *a community of texts*. We should know on the basis of those characteristics that the texts form a community even if we knew nothing more than the texts themselves. But that does not make a canon of them all, only of those components of the corpus that exhibit the requisite traits. A book enjoys its own autonomous standing, but it also situates itself in relationship to other books of the same classification. Each book bears its own statement and purpose, and each relates to others of the same classification. The community of texts therefore encompasses individuals who (singly or collectively) comprise (for the authorships: compose) books. What makes of all books, without regard to indicative traits, is more than that set of facts that indicate how a book does not stand in isolation. Specifically, in the Judaic system of the dual Torah, moreover, all parties concur as premise that the documents at hand form a canon. In the language of Judaism, all of them find a place in – and as part of – the Torah. And that fact defines what to me is the next stage in the problem of the history of Judaism, which, as is clear, I take to be the canonicity of the system.

V

From a Community of Texts to a Textual Community

That is a fact we know on the basis of information deriving from sources other than the texts at hand, which, on their own, do not link each to all and all to every line of each. Extrinsic traits, that is imputed ones, make of the discrete writings a single and continuous, uniform statement: one whole Torah in the mythic language of Judaism. The community of Judaism imputes those traits, sees commonalities, uniformities, deep harmonies: one Torah of one God. In secular language, that community expresses its system – its world view, its way of life, its sense of itself as a society – by these choices, and finds its definition in them. Hence, in the nature of things, the community of Judaism forms *a textual community.* That cogent community that forms a canon out of a selection of books therefore participates in the process of authorship, just as the books exist in at least two dimensions. What I want to know is how the community has accomplished the task of identifying its canon. That is to say, even while recognizing that canonicity is imputed and decided, I wonder whether people looked for one set of qualities, rather than some other, in determining the status of a piece of writing, e.g., presence or absence of a certain set of ideas, relationship to other statements on the same subject, reasons and points of rational decision: the rules of why this, not that, so far as these rules accommodate facts and judge them.

That is a literary question to begin with, and so, to find out the rules of canonicity that lead me into the center and heart of the system at hand, I turn first to a sample of the canonical literature, which I describe as exemplary of a canonical method of exegesis, then, in a later volume, to a central idea, which I analyze as a substantial mode of linkage and union of the canonical system, and, in a third and I hope, final volume, I address the whole all together and all at once. At this point I cannot say how I shall do so, but I know what I must do. I propose to take the measure of the dimension of continuity not between one book and the next but *among* all the books of the canon. What that means is to ask how diverse treatments of a given topic are formed into a single statement, and, for that purpose, I take a Bavli tractate and its disposition of the topic assigned to it.

And yet, even while taking the measure of that dimension, I recognize that we weigh out social, not narrowly literary, extrinsic and adventitious, not intrinsic and cogent and logical qualities. This study through its limited case therefore addresses the whole, seen all together and all at once. For the case at hand it marks off the outer limits of the galaxy of writings – the walls of the library building – that all together form the canon. Drawing upon the analogy of books in canonical relationship, we may say that the third dimension finds its perspective in the larger building that takes in all the books all together. It of course comprises the community that determines what falls within the canon and what does not.

VI

How Documents Relate

Documents – cogent compositions made up of a number of complete units of thought – by definition exist on their own. That is to say, by invoking as part of our definition the trait of cogency of individual units as well as of the entire composite, we complete a definition of what a document is and is not. A document is a cogent composite of cogent statements. But, also by definition, none of these statements is read all by itself. A document forms an artifact of a social culture, and that in diverse dimensions. Cogency depends on shared rhetoric, logic of intelligible discourse, topic and program – all of these traits of mind, of culture. Someone writes a document, someone buys it, an entire society sustains the labor of literature. Hence we place any document into its culture and society. That social context of documents forms a necessary but not sufficient condition of the canonicity of a set of documents. What suffices, beyond the social setting, is the consensus of the group upon a given documentary statement, and to discover the basis of that consensus is to uncover what holds the social group together, its inner agreement on matters the group can scarcely articulate: points of self-evidence, matters of implicit certainty.

Each document therefore exists in both a textual and literary context, and also a social dimension of culture and even of politics. As to the former, documents may form a community whose limits are delineated by shared conventions of thought and expression. Those exhibiting distinctive, even definitive traits, fall within the community, those that do not, remain without. These direct the author to one mode of topic, logic, and rhetoric, and not to some other. So much for intrinsic and literary traits. As to the extrinsic ones, readers – that is, the members of the faith, who constitute in this context the textual community – bring to documents diverse instruments of intelligibility, knowledge of the grammar of not only language but also thought. These social endowments prove decisive. For they explain why people can read one document and not some other. One relationship therefore derives from a literary culture, which forms the authorship of a document, and the other relationship from a social culture. The literary bond links document to document, but it is only the essentially social bond that links reader to document – and also document (through the authorship, individual or collective) to reader. The one relationship is exhibited through intrinsic traits of language and style, logic, rhetoric, and topic, and the other through extrinsic traits of curiosity, acceptance and authority. While documents find their place in their own literary world and also in a larger social one, the two aspects have to remain distinct, the one textual, the other contextual. Moving from the literary characteristics and contents to the social context draws us upward into that structure and system, that Judaism, to which the canon testifies, and which has – by the way – formed, among many other systemic components, the canon too.

It follows that relationships between and among documents also matter for two distinct reasons. The intrinsic relationships, which are formal, guide us to traits of intelligibility, teaching us through our encounter with one document how to read some other of its type or class. If we know how to read a document of one type, we may venture to read another of the same type, but not – without instruction – one of some other type altogether. The extrinsic relationships, which derive from context and are relative to community, direct us to how to understand a document as an artifact of culture and society. Traits not of documents but of doctrines affecting a broad range of documents come into play. The document, whatever its contents, therefore becomes an instrument of social culture, e.g., theology and politics, a community's public policy. A community then expresses itself through its choice of documents, the community's canon forming a principal mode of such self-definition. So, as I said, through intrinsic traits a document places itself within a larger community of texts. Extrinsic traits, imputed to a document by not its authorship but its audience, selects the document as canonical and make of the document a mode of social definition. The community through its mode of defining itself by its canonical choices forms a textual community – as community expressed through the books it reads and values.

One principal issue worked out in establishing a community of texts is hermeneutical, the chief outcome of defining a textual community, social and cultural. The former teaches us how to read the texts on their own. The latter tells us how to interpret texts in context. When we define and classify the relationships between texts, we learn how to read the components – words, cogent thoughts formed of phrases, sentences, paragraphs – of those texts in the broader context defined by shared conventions of intellect: rhetoric, logic, topic. More concretely, hermeneutical principles tell me how, in light of like documents I have seen many times, to approach a document I have never before seenat all. Hermeneutics teaches me the grammar and syntax of thought.

But here the issue is not hermeneutical. At issue is not the reading and interpretation of texts but their social utility, their status as cultural indicators. When I know the choices a community has made for its canon and can explain and interpret the canonicity – the exegesis of exegesis that defines the canon – I can find my way deep into the shared viewpoint of that community, moving from the contents of the texts to the contexts in which those texts bear meaning. And that brings us back to the basic matter: a text exists in diverse contexts, on its own, among other texts, and as part of a much larger social canon, e.g., a library or a court of appeal for authoritative judgments such as proof-texts supply. A text testifies to more than its contents, but also to relationships extrinsic to it, and in situating a text in relationship to its larger context – including the literary context – we gain entry into that textual community, that canonical world, that in describing the Judaism of the dual Torah as a whole, we must enter. It is important now to help us sort out the most basic matters for discussion.

VII
Autonomy, Connection, Continuity

The relationships among the documents produced by the sages of Judaism may take three forms: complete dependence, complete autonomy, intersection in diverse manner and measure. That second dimension provokes considerable debate and presents a remarkably unclear perspective. For while the dimensions of autonomy and continuity take the measure of acknowledged traits – books on their own, books standing in imputed, therefore socially verified, relationships – the matter of connection hardly enjoys the same clear definition. On the one side, intrinsic traits permit us to assess theories of connection. On the other, confusing theological and social judgments of continuities and literary and heuristic ones of connection, people present quite remarkable claims as to the relationships between and among documents, alleging, in fact, that the documents all have to be read as a single continuous document: the Torah. When we can describe the relationships between two documents and among three or more, we shall know what a given group of editors or authorities contributed on its own, and also how that authorship restated or reworked what it received from a prior group. Determining that relationship further guides us to principles of exegesis of documents, allegations and formulations of ideas and rules. If a document depends on some other, prior one, then what we find in the later writing is to be read in light of the earlier (but, of course, never vice versa). If there is no clear evidence of dependence, then the later document demands a reading in essentially its own terms. Determining the relationship of document to document forms the necessary second step Finding out what changed and what remained the same in the unfolding of the system as a whole tells us the history of the system as its canonical writings contain that history.

Seeing the documents as a continuous and final statement, we now want to understand the direction and goal of the history at hand and turn back to see how, from the viewpoint of the end, the system took shape: a history that emerges from a dialectical process of study and restudy. That third dimension takes its perspective from a distance and encompasses all of the documents: the system as a whole. It sees the documents as continuous not from one to the next but all in all, all together, all at once.

VIII
The Bavli and the Coming Research-Program

As I said above, I want to know how the Bavli has formed of available writings (redacted in documents now in hand and otherwise) a single, cogent, and coherent statement. In what ways does a Bavli-tractate frame a canonical statement out of what its authorship has in hand? Let me spell out the information I seek and how I propose to find it. As I said earlier, on any given topic, a tractate of the Bavli presents the final and authoritative statement that emerged from the formative period of the Judaism of the dual Torah. That statement constituted not only an authoritative, but also an encompassing and complete account. In the centuries beyond, people would nearly universally turn to the Bavli as the starting point for all inquiry into any given topic, and rightly so. Since the Bavli made the first and definitive statement, we impute to the Bavli canonical status. If, therefore, we wish to ask about the canonicity of a document of the formative age of the Judaism of the dual Torah, we shall inquire into the standing of a Bavli-tractate *as a canonical testimony* on its subject within the larger system. What we want to know about that canonical testimony is the nature of the canon as exemplified in a given documentary treatment of a given subject, therefore asking *what constitutes the definition of a canonical statement*?

Let me now specify the kinds of factual information that will permit me to frame a reply to that question. My particular concern is the Bavli's relationship to prior treatments of a given subject, with special interest in how the authorship of the Bavli has made use of what it had in hand, and how in its sorting out of available materials it has defined the task of making a full and authoritative statement. In assessing the stance of the Bavli, in making its final statement, vis à vis prior writings on a given topic, I can uncover the rules that guide an authorship in its work of summary and systematization: of systemic statement of the whole, all together and all at once, a given subject. I can conceive of no better way of uncovering how people make a statement we now realize was canonical from the beginning, than situation those people in the setting of what had gone before – and had not attained the canonical status that the Bavli's authorship achieved for their document. So far as canonicity constitutes a literary question concerning rules of how one writes a canonical document, giving the signals to the community that one's writing constitutes a final, authoritative statement, through inductive inquiry into relationships I should be able to answer that question and describe those rules: why this not that. That interest requires me to collect answers to questions deriving from these comparative inquiries:

1. *The topical program* of prior writings on the subject as compared to the topical program of the Bavli on the same subject, with attention to questions such as these: does the Bavli follow the response to the Mishnah characteristic of the authorship of the Tosefta? the Sifra (or Sifré to Numbers or Sifré to Deuteronomy, where relevant) Does the Bavli follow the response to relevant passages of Scripture that have caught the attention of compilers of Midrash-exegeses in Genesis Rabbah, Leviticus Rabbah, Pesiqta deRab Kahana, and other documents generally thought to have come to closure prior to the Bavli?

2. *The Bavli's use or neglect of the available treatments ("sources") in the prior literature*: if the Bavli does make use of available materials, does it impose its own issues upon those materials or does it reproduce those materials as they occur elsewhere? Has the authorship of the Bavli carried forward issues important in prior writings, or has it simply announced and effected its own program of inquiry into the topic at hand?

3. *The traits of the Bavli's canonical statement, that is, derivative and summary at the end, or essentially fresh and imputed retrospectively?* In consequence of the detailed examination of the Bavli's authorship's use of and response to available sources, how may we characterize the statement of the Bavl as a whole in comparison to prior statements? And, since that statement is canonical by the definition of the entire history of Judaism, we ask about the upshot: the shape and character of a canonical statement on a given subject.

IX

The Special Case of the Yerushalmi

In finding answers to the questions at hand, I do not enter into the canonicity of the counterpart Talmud's statement on the chosen topic. The reason for setting the Yerushalmi aside has now to be specified. The Yerushalmi can provide an answer to our question, as much as does the Bavli. But the Bavli, not the Yerushalmi, defined the Judaism of the dual Torah as to both theology and law, and therefore the Yerushalmi, while suggestive and engaging, will not guide us to the definition of the literary traits (if any) of canonicity in the Judaism of the dual Torah. In my *Judaism: The Classical Statement. The Evidence of the Bavli* (Chicago, 1986: University of Chicago Press) I systematically compared the Yerushalmi and the Bavli and showed why the Bavli and not the Yerushalmi served as the medium for the complete and final statement of late antiquity – and was received as such. So it is the qualities of the Bavli, and that document alone, that will guide us to the literary definition of canonicity – so far as there can be a literary definition at all. The relationship of the authorship of the Bavli to the Yerushalmi's treatment of a given aspect of the topic at hand will therefore constitute only a small aspect of our inquiry. The main issue is, as I said at the outset, how to uncover the rules of canonicity as the Bavli reveals those rules. If the question has been properly framed, it should produce illuminating answers.

Part Two

RELIGION

Chapter Five

Constantine, Shapur II and The Jewish-Christian Confrontation in Fourth-Century Iran

In the fourth century, beginning with the conversion of Constantine in 312 and ending with the recognition of Christianity as the religion of the Roman Empire in the Theodosian Code of 387, Christianity reached that position of political and cultural dominance that it would enjoy until the twentieth. In that same fourth century, in response to the triumph of Christianity in the Roman Empire, Judaism as shaped by sages in the Land of Israel defined its doctrines of history, Messiah, and who is Israel. Those doctrines successfully countered the challenge of Christianity from then to the point at which Christianity lost its status as self-evident truth in the West. So the age of Constantine was marked by the interplay of issues as defined in the same way by Judaism and Christianity. What we shall see in the present instance is that, on the Iranian side of the frontier, in the empire of Shapur II (307-379), the confrontation between Judaism and Christianity in the aftermath of the legalization of Christianity in Rome went forward along precisely the lines that guided discourse within Rome itself. When we recall that Constantine had written to Shapur II and had declared himself the protector of Christians within the Sasanian empire, we understand why the Christian party fo the debate, represented by Aphrahat, should have taken his place comfortably within the position outlined on the Roman side of the frontier.

Constantine told Shapur II that it is with "joy" that he heard

> ...tidings so in accordance with my desire, that the fairest districts of Persia are filled with those men on whose behalf alone I am at present speaking, I mean the Christians. I pray therefore that both you and they may enjoy prosperity, and that your blessings and theirs may be in equal measure...I commend these persons to your protection....Cherish them with your wonted humanity....[1]

No wonder, then, that from the viewpoint of Christians in Iran, events in Rome were seen to mark that caesura in time, that validation of the faith, that

---

[1]Trans. Ernest Cushing Richardson in *Select Library of Nicene and Post-nicene Fathers. Second Series* (Grand Rapids, repr. 1961), 1:543-544; see also Georg Bert, *Aphrahat's des persischen Weisen Homilien* (Lepizig, 1888), pp. 69-88, and my *History of the Jews in Babylonia* (Leiden, 1969) 4:21-2.

Christians in Rome itself perceived. In Homily 23, Aphrahat, for his part, despairs of seeing an Iranian Constantine. Seeing Rome as Esau, Aphrahat identified that kingdom with Jesus: "The kingdom of the children of Esau is being kept safe for its giver, doubt not about it, that that kingdom will not be conquered. For a mighty champion whose name is Jesus shall come with power, and bearing as his armor all the power of the kingdom...." When in 337 Shapur II decreed that the Christians pay double the normal head tax, it marked the beginning of a systematic persecution of Christians, which lasted for nearly a half century.

In our setting, we ask whether living in Iran, rather than in Rome, persuaded Aphrahat that the issues separating Judaism from Christianity were to be read in some way other than that of Christian theologians represented, in the time of Constantine, by Eusebius, who found in the conversion of the emperor, then the Roman state, proof for the validity of Christianity. The answer, as we shall now see, negative. While in Iran, Aphrahat saw things precisely as did his counterparts in Rome, and that is shown, as I shall now demonstrate, by his framing of the issues in the received terms of Christianity in Rome, without the slightest revision of matters to accommodate the condition of Christianity in Iran. SInce, when Aphrahat took up other questions than those in the Judaic-Christian confrontation, he found reason to revise the received viewpoint to accommodate the facts of his own time and place, the persistence of the received formulation of the debate becomes suggestive. Specifically, it tells us that once matters had reached theological definition, political circumstances would not greatly affect the framing of issues. Where Aphrahat stood in a line beginning, as we shall see, with Paul, there he repeated, in Iran, viewpoints far more pertinent to the Christian situation in now-Christian Rome than in anti-Christian Zoroastrian Iran.

I

The Issues of the Confrontation in the Age of Constantine and Shapur II

We find in the Judaism of the sages who redacted the principal documents of Judaism that reached closure in the century beyond the conversion of Constantine both a doctrine and an apologetic remarkably relevant to the issues presented to Christianity and Judaism by the crisis of Christianity's worldly triumph. A shared program brought the two religions into protracted confrontation on an intersecting set of questions, a struggle that has continued until our own time – originated in the fact that, to begin with, both religions agreed on almost everything that mattered. They differed on little, so made much of that little. Scripture taught them both that vast changes in the affairs of empires came about because of God's will. History proved principles of theology. In that same Torah prophets promised the coming of the Messiah, who would bring salvation. Who was, and is, that Messiah, and how shall we know? And that same Torah addressed a particular people, Israel, promising that people the expression of God's favor and love. But who is Israel, and who is not Israel? In this way Scripture defined the categories shared in common, enabling Judaism and Christianity to engage, if not in dialogue, then in two monologues on the same topics. The terms of this confrontation continued for centuries because the conditions that precipitated it, – the rise to political dominance of Christianity and the subordination of Judaism, – remained constant for fifteen hundred years.

We know the fourth century as the decisive age in the beginning of the West as Christian. But to people of the time, the outcome uncertain. The vigorous repression of paganism after Julian's apostasy expressed the quite natural fear of Christians that such a thing might happen again. Bickerman states matters in a powerful way:

> Julian was yesterday, the persecutors the day before yesterday. Ambrose knew some magistrates who could boast of having spared Christians. At Antioch the Catholics had just endured the persecution of Valens...and unbelievers of every sort dominated the capital of Syria. The army, composed of peasants and barbarians, could acclaim tomorrow another Julian, another Valens, even another Diocletian. One could not yet, as Chrysostom says somewhere, force [people] to accept the Christian truth; one had to convince them of it.[2]

Although matters remained in doubt, the main fact remains: In the beginning of the fourth century Rome was pagan, in the end, Christian. In the beginning Jews in the Land of Israel administered their own affairs. In the end their institution of self-administration lost the recognition it had formerly enjoyed. In the beginning Judaism enjoyed entirely licit status, and the Jews, the protection of the state. In the end Judaism suffered abridgement of its former liberties, and the Jews of theirs.

From the viewpoint of the Jews, the shift signified by the conversion of Constantine marked, as I said, a *caesura* in history. The meaning of history commencing at Creation pointed for Christians toward Christ's triumph in the person of the Emperor and the institution of the Christian state. To Israel, the Jewish people, what can these same events have meant? The received Scriptures of ancient and recent Israel – both Judaic and Christian – now awaited that same sort of sifting and selection that had followed earlier turnings of a notable order, in 586 B.C., and after 70, for example: which writing had now been proved right, which irrelevant? So Christians asked themselves, as they framed the canon of the Bible, both Old and New Testaments. Then to Israel, the Jewish people, what role and what place for the received Torah of Sinai, in its diversity of scrolls? The dogged faith that Jesus really was Christ, Messiah and King of the world, now found vindication in the events of the hour. What hope endured

---

[2]Cited by Wilken, pp. 32-33.

for the salvationof Israel in the future. In the hour of vindication the new Israel confronted the old, the one after the spirit calling into question the legitimacy of the one after the flesh: what now do you say of Christ? For Israel, the Jewish people, what was there to say in reply, not to Christ but to Christians? These three issues frame our principal concerns: the meaning of history, the realization of salvation, definition one's own group in the encounter with the other. In the case of Aphrahat, it was the matter of the definition of "Israel" that comes to the fore. Elsewhere I present all of the three issues in a systematic way.[3]

II
The Issue:
Who Is Israel

The legacy of ancient Israel consisted not only of Scriptures but also of a paramount social category, Israel, God's people and first love. The Church from its origins in the first century confronted the task of situating itself in relationship to "Israel," and Paul's profound reflections in Romans constitute only one among many exercises in responding to that question. For the society of the Church, like the society of the Jews, required a metaphor by which to account for itself. And revering the Scriptures, each group found in "Israel" the metaphor to account for its existence as a distinct social entity. It follows that within the issue Who is Israel? we discern how two competing groups framed theories, each both of itself and also of the other. We therefore confront issues of the identity of a given corporate society as these were spelled out in debates about salvation. The salvific framing of the issue of social definition – who is Israel today (for Judaism)? what sort of social group is the Church (for Christianity)? – served both parties. We deal with a debate on a single issue. It finds its cogency in the common premise of the debate on who is Israel. The shared supposition concerned God's favor and choice of a given entity, one that was *sui generis*, among the social groups of humanity. Specifically, both parties concurred that God did favor and therefore make use of one group and not another. So they could undertake a meaningful debate on the identity of that group.

The debate gained intensity because of a further peculiarity of the discourse between these two groups but no others of the day. Both concurred that the group chosen by God will bear the name, Israel. God's choice among human societies would settle the question, which nation does God love and favor. Jews, who saw themselves as the Israel today joined in the flesh to the Israel of the scriptural record. Christians explained themselves as the Israel formed just now, in recent memory, even in the personal experience of the living, among those

---

[3]See my *Judaism and Christianity in the Age of Constantine. Issues in the Initial Confrontation* (Chicago, 1987: University of Chicago Press).

saved by faith in God's salvation afforded by the resurrection of Jesus Christ. We therefore must not miss the powerful social and political message conveyed by what appear to be statements of a narrowly theological character about salvation and society. In these statements on who is Israel, the parties to the debate chose to affirm each its own unique legitimacy and to deny the other's right to endure at all as a social and national entity.

But both parties shared common premises as to definitions of issues and facts to settle the question. They could mount a sustained argument between themselves because they talked about the same thing, invoked principles of logic in common, shared the definition of the pertinent facts. They differed only as to the outcome. Let us turn to the articulation of the question at hand. The issue of who is Israel articulated in theological, not political, terms covers several topics: are the Jews today "Israel" of ancient times? Was, and is, Jesus Christ? If so, who are the Christians, both on their own and also in relationship to ancient Israel? These questions scarcely can be kept distinct from one another. And all of them cover the ground we have already traversed concerning the meaning of history and the identity of the Messiah. First, was, and is, Jesus Christ? If so, then the Jews who rejected him enjoyed no share in the salvation at hand. If not, then they do. The Christian challenge comes first. If Jesus was and is Christ, then Israel "after the flesh" no longer enjoys the status of the people who bear salvation. Salvation has come, and Israel "after the flesh" has denied it. If he is Christ, then what is the status of those – whether Jews or gentiles – who did accept him? They have received the promises of salvation and their fulfillment. The promises to Israel have been kept for them. Then there is a new Israel, one that is formed of the saved, as the prophets had said in ancient times that Israel would be saved. A further issue that flowed from the first – the rejection of Jesus as Christ – concerns the status of Israel, the Jewish people, now and in time to come. Israel after the flesh, represented from the Gospels forward as the people that rejected Jesus as Christ and participated in his crucifixion, claims to be the family of Abraham, Isaac, Jacob. Then further questions arise. First, does Israel today continue the Israel of ancient times? Israel maintains that Israel now continues in a physical and spiritual way the life of Israel then. Second, will the promises of the prophets to Israel afford salvation for Israel in time to come? Israel "after the flesh" awaits the fulfillment of the prophetic promise of salvation. Clearly, a broad range of questions demanded sorting out. But the questions flow together into a single issue, faced in common. The Christian position on all these questions came to expression in a single negative: no, Israel today does not continue the Israel of old, no, the ancient promises will not again bear salvation, because they have already been kept, so, no, the Israel that declines to accept Jesus' claim to be the Christ is a no-people.

The response of Israel's sages to these same questions proves equally unequivocal. Yes, the Messiah will come in time to come, and yes, he will come to Israel of today, which indeed continues the Israel of old. So the issue is squarely and fairly joined. Who is Israel raises a question that stands second in line to the Messianic one, with which we have already dealt. And, it must follow, the further question of who are the Christians requires close attention to that same messianic question. So, as is clear, the initial confrontation generated a genuine argument on the status and standing, before God, of Israel "after the flesh," the Jewish people. And that argument took on urgency because of the worldly, political triumph of Christianity in Rome, joined, as the fourth century wore on, by the worldly, political decline in the rights and standing of Israel, the Jewish people.

Before Christianity had addressed the issue of who the Christians were, Paul had already asked what the Jews were not. Christians formed the true people of God.[4] So the old and lasting Israel, the Jewish people, did not. Paul had called into question "Israel's status as God's chosen people," because (in Ruether's words) "Israel had failed in its pursuit of righteousness based on the Torah...had been disobedient...[so that] the privileged relation to God provided by the Mosaic covenant has been permanently revoked". So from its origins, Christianity had called into question Israel's former status, and, as Gager says, held that "Israel's disobedience is not only not accidental to God's plan of salvation, it has become an essential part of its fulfillment." The Christian position on one side of ,the matter of who is Israel, namely, who is not Israel, had reached a conclusion before the other aspect of the matter – the Christians' status as a New Israel – came to full expression.[5]

That matter of status closely follows the issue of salvation, as we have already noted. As soon as Christians coalesced into groups, they asked themselves what *sort* of groups they formed. They in fact maintained several positions. First, they held that they were a people, enjoying the status of the Jewish people, and that, as Harnack says, "furnished adherents of the new faith with a political and historical self-consciousness." So they were part of Israel and continued the Israel of ancient times, not a new group but a very old one. But the further defined themselves as not only a new people, but a new *type* of group, recognizing no taxonomic counterpart in the existing spectrum of human societies, peoples or nations. The claims of the Christians varied according to circumstance, so Harnack summarizes matters in a passage of stunning acuity:

> Was the cry raised, "You are renegade Jews" – the answer came, "We are the community of the Messiah, and therefore the true Israelites." If people said, "You are simply Jews," the reply was, "We are a new creation and a new people." If again they were taxed with their recent origin and told that they were but of yesterday, they retorted, "We only seem to be the younger People; from the beginning we have been latent; we have always existed, previous to any other people; we are the original

---

[4]Ruether, pp. 64ff.

[5]Ruether, pp. 64ff., Gager, pp. 256-8.

people of God." If they were told, "You do not deserve to live" the answer ran, "We would die to live, for we are citizens of the world to come, and sure that we shall rise again."[6]

These reflections on the classification of the new group – superior to the old, *sui generis*, and whatever the occasion of polemic requires the group to be – fill the early Christian writings. In general there were three: Greeks or gentiles, Jews, and the Christians as the new People.

When Christians asked themselves what sort of group they formed, they answered that they constituted a new group, and a group of a new type altogether. They identified with the succession to Israel after the flesh, with Israel after the spirit, with a group lacking all parallel or precedent, with God-fearers and law-keepers before Judaism was given at Sinai. The dilemma comes to expression in Eusebius:

> In the oracles directed to Abraham, Moses himself writes prophetically how in the times to come the descendants of Abraham, not only his Jewish seed but all the tribes and all the nations of the earth, will be deemed worthy of divine praise because of a common manner of worship like that of Abraham.... How could all the nations and tribes of the earth be blessed in Abraham if no relationship of either a spiritual or a physical nature existed between them?...How therefore could men reared amid an animal existence...be able to share in the blessings of the godly, unless they abandoned their savage ways and sought to participate in a life of piety' like that of Abraham?...Now Moses lived after Abraham, and he gave the Jewish race a certain corporate status which was based upon the laws provided by him. If the laws he established were the same as those by which godly men were guided before his time, if they were capable of being adopted by all peoples so that all the tribes and nations of the earth could worship God in accordance with the Mosaic enactments, one could say that the oracles had foretold that because of Mosaic laws men of every nation would worship God and live according to Judaism....However since the Mosaic enactments did not apply to other peoples but to the Jews alone..., a different way, a way distinct from the law of Moses, needed to be established, one by which the nations of all the earth might live as Abraham had so that they could receive an equal share of blessing with him.[7]

Since, with the advent of Constantine, a political dimension served to take the measure of the Christian polity, we have to ask about the political consciousness of the Church in its original formulation. In this matter Harnack points out that the political consciousness of the Church rests on three premises, first, the political element in the Jewish apocalyptic, second, the movement of the gospel to the Greeks, and third, the ruin of Jerusalem and the end of the Jewish state. He says, "The first of these elements stood in antithesis to the

---

[6]Harnack, pp. 241, 244.

[7]*The Proof of the Gospel* I 2:, cited by Luibheid, p. 41.

others, so that in this way the political consciousness of the church came to be defined in opposite directions and had to work itself out of initial contradictions."[8] From early times, Harnack says, the Christians saw Christianity as "the central point of humanity as the field of political history as well as its determining factor." That had been the Jews' view of themselves. With Constantine the corresponding Christian conception matched reality.

Now the Christians formed a new People, a third race. When the change came, with the Christianization of the Empire at the highest levels of government, the new people, the third race, had to frame a position and policy about the old people, enduring Israel "after the flesh." And, for its part, the Jewish people, faced with the Christian *défi* found the necessity to reaffirm its enduring view of itself, now, however, in response to a pressure without precedent in its long past. The claim of the no-people that the now and enduring Israel is the no-people knew no prior equivalent. The age of Constantine marked the turning of the world: all things were upside down. How to deal with a world that (from the perspective of Israel, the Jewish people) had gone mad? Israel's answer, which we shall reach in due course, proves stunningly a propos: right to the issue, in precisely the terms of the issue. But first let us see how a substantial Christian theologian phrases the matter in the polemic at hand.

III

Aphrahat

To show us how a fourth century Christian theologian addressed the question at hand, namely, who is Israel in the light of the salvation of Jesus Christ, we turn to Aphrahat, a Christian monk in Mesopotamia, ca. 300-350, who wrote, in Syriac, a sustained treatise on the relationship of Christianity and Judaism. His demonstrations, written in 337-344, take up issues facing the Syriac speaking Church in the Iranian Empire. The church then was suffering severe persecution on the part of the Government, for the monks and nuns, maintaining they had no property, could not pay taxes. Since at that time Jews enjoyed stable and peaceful relationships with the Iranian government while Christians did not, the contrast between weak Christianity and secure Judaism required attention as well. Aphrahat presents his case on the base of historical facts shared in common by both parties to the debate, Judaism and Christianity, that is, facts of Scripture. He rarely cites the New Testament in his demonstrations on Judaism. Moreover, when he cites the Hebrew Scriptures, he ordinarily refrains from fanciful or allegoristic reading of them. but, like the rabbis with whom Jerome dealt, stressed that his interpretation rested solely on the plain and obvious, factual meaning at hand. His arguments thus invoked rational arguments and historical facts: this is what happened, this is what it

---

[8]Harnack, p. 256-7.

means. Scriptures therefore present facts, on which all parties concur. Then the argument goes forward on a common ground of shared reason and mutually-agreed-upon facts. Still more important, the program of argument – is Israel, the Jewish people, going to be saved in the future, along with the issue of the standing and status of the Christian people – likewise follows points important to both parties.

Here, as I claimed at the outset, we find Judaic and Christian thinkers disagreeing on a common set of propositions: who is Israel? Will Israel be saved in the future, or have the prophetic promises already been kept. We take up Aphrahat's explanation of "the people which is of the peoples," the people "which is no people," and then proceed to his address to Israel after the flesh. The two issues complement one another. Once the new people formed out of the peoples enters the status of Israel, then the old Israel loses that status. And how to express that judgment? By denying the premise of the life of Israel after the flesh, that salvation for the people of God would come in future time. If enduring Israel would never enjoy salvation, then Israel had no reason to exist: that is the premise of the argument framed ion behalf of the people that had found its reason to exist (from its perspective) solely in its salvation by Jesus Christ . So what explained to the Christian community how that community had come into being also accounted, for that same community, for the (anticipated) disappearance of the nation that had rejected that very same nation-creating event.

The church then – ca. 337-345 – was suffering severe persecution on the part of the Government, for the monks and nuns, maintaining they had no property, could not pay taxes. Since at that time Jews enjoyed stable and peaceful relationships with the Iranian government while Christians did not, the contrast between weak Christianity and secure Judaism required attention as well. Aphrahat presents his case on the base of historical facts shared in common by both parties to the debate, Judaism and Christianity, that is, facts of Scripture. He rarely cites the New Testament in his demonstrations on Judaism. Moreover, when he cites the Hebrew Scriptures, he ordinarily refrains from fanciful or allegoristic reading of them, but, like the rabbis with whom Jerome dealt, stressed that his interpretation rested solely on the plain and obvious, factual meaning at hand. His arguments thus invoked rational arguments and historical facts: this is what happened, this is what it means. Scriptures therefore present facts, on which all parties concur. Then the argument goes forward on a common ground of shared reason and mutually-agreed-upon facts. Still more important, the program of argument – is Israel, the Jewish people, going to be saved in the future, along with the issue of the standing and status of the Christian people – likewise follows points important to both parties.

Here, as I claimed at the outset, we find Judaic and Christian thinkers disagreeing on a common set of propositions: who is Israel? Will Israel be saved in the future, or have the prophetic promises already been kept. We take up Aphrahat's explanation of "the people which is of the peoples," the people "which is no people," and then proceed to his address to Israel after the flesh. The two issues complement one another. Once the new people formed out of the peoples enters the status of Israel, then the old Israel loses that status. And how to express that judgment? By denying the premise of the life of Israel after the flesh, that salvation for the people of God would come in future time. If enduring Israel would never enjoy salvation, then Israel had no reason to exist: that is the premise of the argument framed ion behalf of the people that had found its reason to exist (from its perspective) solely in its salvation by Jesus Christ . So what explained to the Christian community how that community had come into being also accounted, for that same community, for the (anticipated) disappearance of the nation that had rejected that very same nation-creating event.

Let me point to Aphrahat's *Demonstration Sixteen, "On the Peoples which are in the Place of the People."* Aphrahat's message is this: "The people Israel was rejected, and the peoples took their place. Israel repeatedly was warned by the prophets, but to no avail, so God abandoned them and replaced them with the gentiles. Scripture frequently referred to the gentiles as "Israel." The vocation of the peoples was prior to that of the people of Israel, and from of old, whoever from among the people was pleasing to God was more justified than Israel: Jethro, the Gibeonites, Rahab, Ebedmelech the Ethiopian, Uriah the Hittite. By means of the gentiles God provoked Israel."

First, Aphrahat maintains,

> The peoples which were of all languages were called first, before Israel, to the inheritance of the Most High, as God said to Abraham, "I have made you the father of a multitude of peoples" (Gen. 17:5). Moses proclaimed, saying, "The peoples will call to the mountain, and there will they offer sacrifices of righteousness" (Deut. 33:19).

Not only so, but God further rejected Israel:

> To his people Jeremiah preached, saying to them, "Stand by the ways and ask the wayfarers, and see which is the good way. Walk in it." But they in their stubbornness answered, saying to him, "We shall not go." Again he said to them, "I established over you watchmen, that you might listen for the sound of the trumpet." But they said to him again, "We shall not hearken." And this openly, publicly did they do in the days of Jeremiah when he preached to them the word of the Lord, and they answered him, saying,"To the word which you have spoken to us in the name of the Lord we shall not hearken. But we shall do our own will and every word which goes out of our mouths, to offer up incense-offerings to other gods" (Jer. 44:16-17).

That is why God turned to the peoples: "When he saw that they would not listen to him, he turned to the peoples, saying to them, 'Hear O peoples, and know, O church which is among them, and hearken, O land, in its fullness' (Jer. 6:18-

19)." So who is now Israel? It is the peoples, no longer the old Israel: "By the name of Jacob [now] are called the people which is of the peoples." That is the key to Aphrahat's case. The people that was a no people, that people that had assembled out of the people, has now replaced Israel.

Like Eusebius, Aphrahat maintained that the peoples had been called to God before the people of Israel:

> See, my beloved, that the vocation of the peoples was recorded before the vocation of the people. But because the time of the peoples had not come, and another was [to be] their redeemer, Moses was not persuaded that a redeemer and a teacher would come for the people which was of the peoples, which was greater and more worthy than the people of Israel.

The people that was a no-people should not regard itself as alien to God:

> If they should say, "Us has he called alien children," they have not been called alien children, but sons and heirs...But the peoples are those who hearken to God and were lamed and kept back from the ways of their sins.

Indeed, the peoples produced believers who were superior in every respect to Israel:

> Even from the old, whoever from among the peoples was pleasing to God was more greatly justified than Israel. Jethro the priest who was of the peoples and his seed were blessed: "Enduring is his dwelling place, and his nest is set on a rock" (Num. 24:21).

Aphrahat hear refers to the Gibeonites, Rahab, and various other gentiles mentioned in the scriptural narrative.

Addressing his Christian hearers, Aphrahat then concludes,

> By us they are provoked. On our account they do not worship idols, so that they will not be shamed by us, for we have abandoned idols and call lies the thing which our fathers left us. They are angry, their hearts are broken, for we have entered and have become heirs in their place. For theirs was this covenant which they had, not to worship other gods, but they did not accept it. By means of us he provoked them, and ours was the light and the life, as he preached, saying when he taught, "I am the light of the world" (John 8:12).

So he concludes,

> This brief memorial I have written to you concerning the peoples, because the Jews take pride and say, "We are the people of God and the children of Abraham. " But we shall listen to John [the Baptist] who, when they took pride [saying], "We are the children of Abraham," then said to them, "You should not boast and say, Abraham is father unto us, for from these very rocks can God raise up children for Abraham" (Matthew 3:9).

In *Demonstration Nineteen, "Against the Jews, on account of their saying that they are destined to be gathered together,"* Aphrahat proceeds to the corollary argument, that the Israel after the flesh has lost its reason to endure as a nation. Why? Because no salvation awaits them in the future. The prophetic promises of salvation have all come to fulfillment in the past, and the climactic salvation for Israel, through the act of Jesus Christ, brought the salvific drama to its conclusion. Hence the Jews' not having a hope of "joining together" at the end of their exile forms a critical part of the entire picture. Here is a summary of the argument:

> The Jews expect to be gathered together by the Messiah, but this expectation is in vain. God was never reconciled to them but has rejected them. The prophetic promises of restoration were all fulfilled in the return from Babylonia. Daniel's prayer was answered, and his vision was realized in the time of Jesus and in the destruction of Jerusalem. It will never be rebuilt.

Aphrahat thus stresses that the Jews' sins caused their own condition, a position which sages accepted: "On account of their sins, which were many, he uprooted and scattered them among every nation, for they did not listen to his prophets, whom he had sent to them." The Jews now maintain that they will see salvation in the future, but they are wrong:

> I have written this to you because even today they hope an empty hope, saying, "It is still certain for Israel to be gathered together," for the prophet thus spoke, "I shall leave none of them among the nations" (Ex. 39:28). But if all of our people is to be gathered together, why are we today scattered among every people?

But, Aphrahat states, "Israel never is going to be gathered together." The reason is that God was never reconciled to Israel:

> I shall write and show you that never did God accept their repentance [through] either Moses or all of the prophets....Further, Jeremiah said, "They are called rejected silver, for the Lord has rejected them (Jer. 6:30). ...See, then, they have never accepted correction in their lives.

Aphrahat presents an array of prophetic proof-texts for the same proposition. Then he turns to the peoples and declares that they have taken the place of the people:

> Concerning the vocation of the peoples Isaiah said, "It shall come to be in the last days that the mountain of the House of the Lord will be established at the head of the mountains and high above the heights. Peoples will come together to it, and many peoples will go and say, Come, let us go up to the mountain of the Lord, to the House of the God of Jacob. He will teach us his ways, and we shall walk in his paths. For from Zion the law will go forth, and the word of the Lord from Jerusalem" (Is. 2:2, 3).

Does Israel not hope for redemption in the future? Indeed so, but they are wrong:

> Two times only did God save Israel: Once from Egypt, the second time from Babylonia; from Egypt by Moses, and from Babylonia by Ezra and by the prophecy of Haggai and Zechariah. Haggai said, "Build this house, and I shall have pleasure in it, and in it I shall be glorified, says the Lord...(Hag. 1:8)." All of these things were said in the days of Zerubbabel, Haggai, and Zechariah. They were exhorting concerning the building of the house.

The house was built – and then destroyed, and it will not be rebuilt (Aphrahat wrote before Julians proposed rebuilding of the temple, so he could not have derived further proof from that disaster).

So much for the challenge of those who held such views as Aphrahat expresses. The case is complete: the people which is no-people, the people which is of the peoples, have taken the place of the people which claims to carry forward the salvific history of ancient Israel.   The reason is in two complementary parts. First, Israel has rejected salvation, so lost its reason to exist, and, second, the no-people have accepted salvation, so gained its reason to exist. So the threads of the dispute link into a tight fabric: the shift in the character of politics, marked by the epochal triumph of Christianity in the state, bears profound meaning for the messianic mission of the Church, and, further, imparts a final judgment on the salvific claim of the competing nations of God: the Church and Israel. What possible answer can sages have proposed to this indictment? Since at the heart of the matter lies the claim that Israel persists in the salvific heritage that has passed to the Christians, sages reaffirm that Israel persists – just as Paul had framed matters – after the flesh, an unconditional and permanent status. For one never ceases to be the son of his mother and his father, and the daughter is always the daughter of her father and her mother. So Israel after the flesh constitutes the family, in the most physical form, of Abraham, Isaac, and Jacob. And, moreover, as that family, Israel inherits the heritage of salvation hand on by the patriarchs and matriarchs.   The spiritualization of "Israel" here finds its opposite and counterpart: the utter and complete "genealogization" of Israel.

IV

The Judaic Response in Leviticus Rabbah

Just as nothing in Aphrahat's case would have struck as alien his Roman-Christian counterparts, so we shall now see that, on the Roman side of the border, the Judaic sages responded just as their counterparts in Iran framed matters. The Judaic position vis a vis Christianity was not affected by political frontiers, even as the Judaic-Christian confrontation had been precipitated by a political event in the conversion of Constantine. Briefly to examine the Judaic side of the issue, we turn to a document framed in what Jews know as the Land of Israel, in the Christian Roman empire of the fifth century, a century beyond the crisis at hand. A cogent and propositional commentary to the book of Leviticus, Leviticus Rabbah, ca. 400-450, reads the laws of the on-going sanctification in nature of the life of Israel as an account of the rules of the one-time salvation in history of the polity of Israel.

To the framers of Leviticus Rabbah, one point of emphasis proved critical: Israel remains Israel, the Jewish people, after the flesh, because Israel today continues the family begun by Abraham, Isaac, Jacob, Joseph and the other tribal founders, and bears the heritage bequeathed by them. That conviction of who is Israel never required articulation. The contrary possibility fell wholly outside of sages' (and all Jews') imagination. To state matters negatively, the people could no more conceive that they were not the daughters and sons of their fathers and mothers than that they were not one large family, that is, the family of Abraham, Isaac, and Jacob: Israel after the flesh. That is what "after the flesh" meant. The powerful stress on the enduring merit of the patriarchs and matriarchs, the social theory that treated Israel as one large, extended family, the actual children of Abraham, Isaac, and Jacob – these metaphors for the fleshly continuity surely met head on the contrary position framed by Paul and restated by Christian theologians from his time onward. In this respect, while Aphrahat did not deny the Israel-ness of Israel, the Jewish people, he did underline the futility of enduring as Israel. Maintaining that Israel would see no future salvation amounted to declaring that Israel, the Jewish people, pursued no worthwhile purpose in continuing to endure. Still, the argument is head-on and concrete: who is Israel? who enjoys salvation? To sages, as we shall see, the nations of the world serve God's purpose in ruling Israel, just as the prophets had said, and Israel, for its part, looks forward to a certain salvation.

The position of the framers of Leviticus Rabbah on the issues at hand emerges in both positive and negative formulation. On the positive side, Israel, the Jewish people, the people of whom Scriptures spoke and to whom, today, sages now speak, is God's first love. That position of course presents no surprises and can have been stated with equal relevance in any circumstances. We in no way can imagine that the authors of Leviticus Rabbah stress the points that they stress in particular because Christians have called them into question. I doubt that that was the case. In fact when we survey the verses important to Aphrahat's case and ask what, in the counterpart writings of sages in all of late antiquity, people say about those same verses, we find remarkably little attention to the florilegium of proof-texts adduced by Aphrahat.[9] While the argument on who is Israel did not take shape on the foundation of a shared program of verses, on which each party entered its position, the issue was one and the same. And the occasion – the political crisis of the fourth century – faced both parties.

---

[9]See my *Aphrahat* and Judaism (Leiden, 1970: E. J. Brill), pp. 150-195).

Sages delivered a message particular to their system. The political context imparted to that message urgency for Israel beyond their small circle. As to confronting the other side, no sage would concede what to us is self-evident. This was the urgency of the issue. For the definition of what was at issue derived from the common argument of the age: Who is the Messiah? Christ or someone else? Here too, while the argument between Christian theologians and Judaic sages on the present status of Israel, the Jewish people, went forward on the same basic issues, it ran along parallel lines. True, lines of argument never intersected at all, just as, in our review of sage's doctrine of the Messiah, we could not find a point of intersection with the Christian position on the Christhood of Jesus. The issue in both topics, however, is what was the same, even though the exposition of arguments on one side's proposition in no way intersected with the other side's.

When Aphrahat denied that God loves Israel any more, and contemporary sages affirmed that God yet loves Israel and always will, we come to a clearcut exchange of views on a common topic. Parallel to Aphrahat's sustained demonstrations on a given theme, the framers of Leviticus Rabbah laid forth thematic exercises, each one serving in a cumulative way to make a given point on a single theme. Therefore in order to describe sages' position, we do well to follow their ideas in their own chosen medium of expression. I can find no more suitable way of recapitulating their reply to the question, Who is Israel? than by a brief survey of one of the sustained essays they present on the subject in Leviticus Rabbah.[10] We proceed to the unfolding, in Leviticus Rabbah Parashah Two, of the theme: Israel is precious. At Lev. R. II:III.2.B, we find an invocation of the genealogical justification for the election of Israel:

> He said to him, "Ephraim, head of the tribe, head of the session, one who is beautiful and exalted above all of my sons will be called by your name: [Samuel, the son of Elkanah, the son of Jeroham,] the son of Tohu, the son of Zuph, an Ephraimite" [1 Sam. 1:1]; "Jerobaom son of Nabat, an Ephraimite" [1 Sam. 11:26]. "And David was an Ephraimite, of Bethlehem in Judah" (1 Sam. 17:12).

Since Ephraim, that is, Israel, had been exiled, the deeper message cannot escape our attention. Whatever happens, God loves Ephraim. However Israel suffers, God's love endures, and God cares. In context, that message brings powerful reassurance. Facing a Rome gone Christian, sages had to begin with to state the obvious – which no longer seemed self-evident at all. What follows spells out this very point: God is especially concerned with Israel.

II:IV

1. A. Returning to the matter (GWPH): "Speak to the children of Israel" (Lev. 1:2).

---

[10]The complete texts are in the Appendix to my *Judaism and Christianity in the Age of Constantine*.

B. R. Yudan in the name of R. Samuel b. R. Nehemiah: "The matter may be compared to the case of a king who had an undergarment, concerning which he instructed his servant, saying to him, 'Fold it, shake it out, and be careful about it!'

C. "He said to him, 'My lord, O king, among all the undergarments that you have, [why] do you give me such instructions only about this one?'

D. "He said to him, 'It is because this is the one that I keep closest to my body.'

E. "So too did Moses say before the Holy One, blessed be He, Lord of the Universe: 'Among the seventy distinct nations that you have in your world, [why] do you give me instructions only concerning Israel? [For instance,] "Command the children of Israel" [Num. 28:2], "Say to the children of Israel" [Ex. 33:5], "Speak to the children of Israel"' [Lev. 1:2].

F. "He said to him, 'The reason is that they stick close to me, in line with the following verse of Scripture: "For as the undergarment cleaves to the loins of a man, so have I caused to cleave unto me the whole house of Israel"'" (Jer. 13:11).

G. Said R. Abin, "[The matter may be compared] to a king who had a purple cloak, concerning which he instructed his servant, saying, 'Fold it, shake it out, and be careful about it!'

H. "He said to him, 'My Lord, O king, among all the purple cloaks that you have, [why] do you give me such instructions only about this one?'

I. "He said to him, 'That is the one that I wore on my coronation day.'

J. "So too did Moses say before the Holy One, blessed be He, Lord of the Universe: 'Among the seventy distinct nations that you have in your world, [why] do you give instructions to me only concerning Israel? [For instance,] "Say to the children of Israel," "Command the children of Israel," "Speak to the children of Israel."'

K. "He said to him, 'They are the ones who at the [Red] Sea declared me to be king, saying, "The Lord will be king"' (Ex. 15:18)."

The point of the passage has to do with Israel's particular relationship to God: Israel cleaves to God, declares God to be king, and accepts God's dominion. Further evidence of God's love for Israel derives from the commandments themselves. God watches over every little thing that Jews do, even caring what they eat for breakfast. The familiar stress on the keeping of the laws of the Torah as a mark of hope finds fulfillment here: the laws testify to God's deep concern for Israel. So there is sound reason for high hope, expressed in particular in keeping the laws of the Torah. Making the matter explicit, Simeon b. Yohai (Lev. R. II:V.1.A-B) translates this fact into a sign of divine favor:

II:V

1. A. Said R. Simeon b. Yohai, "[The matter may be compared] to a king who had an only son. Every day he would give instructions to his steward, saying to him, 'Make sure my son eats, make sure my son drinks, make sure my son goes to school, make sure my son comes home from school.'

B. "So every day the Holy One, blessed be He, gave instructions to Moses, saying, 'Command the children of Israel,' 'Say to the children of Israel,' 'Speak to the children of Israel.'"

We now come to the statement of how Israel wins and retains God's favor. The issue at hand concerns Israel's relationship to the nations before God, which is corollary to what has gone before. It is in two parts. First of all, Israel knows how to serve God in the right way. Second, the nations, though they do what Israel does, do things wrong. First, Israel does things right. Why then is Israel beloved? The following answers that question.

V:VIII

1. A. R. Simeon b. Yohai taught, "How masterful are the Israelites, for they know how to find favor with their creator."

    E. Said R. Hunia [in Aramaic:], "There is a tenant farmer who knows how to borrow things, and there is a tenant farmer who does not know how to borrow. The one who knows how to borrow combs his hair, brushes off his clothes, puts on a good face, and then goes over to the overseer of his work to borrow from him. [The overseer] says to him, 'How's the land doing?' He says to him, 'May you have the merit of being fully satisfied with its [wonderful] produce.' 'How are the oxen doing?' He says to him, 'May you have the merit of being fully satisfied with their fat.' 'How are the goats doing?' 'May you have the merit of being fully satisfied with their young.' 'And what would you like?' Then he says, 'Now if you might have an extra ten denars, would you give them to me?' The overseer replies, 'If you want, take twenty.'

    F. "But the one who does not know how to borrow leaves his hair a mess, his clothes filthy, his face gloomy. He too goes over to the overseer to borrow from him. The overseer says to him, 'How's the land doing?' He replies, 'I hope it will produce at least what [in seed] we put into it.' 'How are the oxen doing?' 'They're scrawny.' 'How are the goats doing?' 'They're scrawny too.' 'And what do you want?' 'Now if you might have an extra ten denars, would you give them to me?' The overseer replies, 'Go, pay me back what you already owe me!'"

If Aphrahat had demanded a direct answer, he could not have received a more explicit one. He claims Israel does nothing right. Sages counter, speaking in their own setting of course, that they do everything right. Sages then turn the tables on the position of Aphrahat – again addressing it head-on. While the nations may do everything Israel does, they do it wrong.

Sages recognized in the world only one counterpart to Israel, and that was Rome. Rome's history formed the counterweight to Israel's. So Rome as a social entity weighed in the balance against Israel. That is why we return to the corollary question: who is Rome? For we can know who is Israel only if we can also explain who is Rome. And, I should maintain, explaining who is Rome takes on urgency at the moment at which Rome presents to Israel problems of an unprecedented character. The matter belongs in any picture of who is Israel. Sages' doctrine of Rome forms the counterpart to Christian theologians' theory on who is Israel. Just as Aphrahat explains both who are the Christians and also who is Israel today, so sages in Leviticus Rabbah develop an important theory on who is Rome. They too propose to account for the way things are, and that means, they have to explain who is this counterpart to Israel. And sages' theory does respond directly to the question raised by the triumph of Christianity in the Roman Empire. For, as we shall see, the characterization of Rome in Leviticus Rabbah bears the burden of their judgment on the definition of the Christian people, as much as the sages' characterization of Rome in Leviticus Rabbah expressed their judgment of the place of Rome in the history of Israel.

To understand that position on the character of Rome, we have to note that it constitutes a radical shift in the characterization of Rome in the unfolding canon of the sages' Judaism. For the treatment of Rome shifts in a remarkable way from the earlier approach to the subject. Rome in the prior writings, the Mishnah (ca. A.D. 200) and the Tosefta (ca. A.D. 300-400), stood for a particular place. We begin, once more, with the view of the Mishnah. For matters show a substantial shift in the characterization of Rome from the earlier to the later writings. Had matters remained pretty much the same from earlier, late second century, to later, fourth and early fifth century, writings, we could not maintain that what is said in the fourth century documents testifies in particular to intellectual events of the fourth century. We should have to hold that, overall, the doctrine was set and endured in its original version. What happened later on would then have no bearing upon the doctrine at hand, and my claim of a confrontation on a vivid issue would not find validation. But the doctrine of Rome does shift from the Mishnah to the fourth-century sages' writings, Leviticus Rabbah, Genesis Rabbah, and the Talmud of the Land of Israel. That fact proves the consequence, in the interpretation of ideas held in the fourth century, of the venue of documents in that time.

We have already seen the adumbration of the position that, in Leviticus Rabbah, would come to remarkably rich expression. Rome now stood for much more than merely a place among other places. Rome took up a place in the unfolding of the empires – Babylonia, Media, Greece, then Rome. Still more important Rome is the penultimate empire on earth. Israel will constitute the ultimate one. That message, seeing the shifts in world history in a pattern and placing at the apex of the shift Israel itself, directly and precisely takes up the issue made urgent just now: the advent of the Christian emperors. Why do I maintain, as I do, that in the characterization of Rome as the fourth and penultimate empire/animal, sages address issues of their own day? Because Rome, among the successive empires, bears special traits, most of which derive from the distinctively Christian character of Rome.

Rome is represented as only Christian Rome can have been represented: it looks kosher but it is unkosher. Pagan Rome cannot ever have looked kosher, but Christian Rome, with its appeal to ancient Israel, could and did and moreover claimed to. It bore some traits that validate, but lacked others that validate – just as Jerome said of Israel. It would be difficult to find a more direct confrontation between two parties to an argument. Now the issue is the same – who is the true Israel? and the proof-texts are the same, and, moreover, the proof-texts are read in precisely the same way. Only the conclusions differ!

The polemic represented in Leviticus Rabbah by the symbolization of Christian Rome makes the simple point that, first, Christians are no different from, and no better than, pagans; they are essentially the same. Christians' claim to form part of Israel then requires no serious attention. Since Christians came to Jews with precisely that claim, the sages' response – they are another Babylonia – bears a powerful polemic charge. But that is not the whole story, as we see. Second, just as Israel had survived Babylonia, Media, Greece, so would they endure to see the end of Rome (whether pagan, whether Christian). But there is a third point. Rome really does differ from the earlier, pagan empires, and that polemic shifts the entire discourse, once we hear its symbolic vocabulary properly. For the new Rome really did differ from the old. Christianity was not merely part of a succession of undifferentiated modes of paganism. The symbols assigned to Rome attributed worse, more dangerous traits than those assigned to the earlier empires. The pig pretends to be clean, just as the Christians give the signs of adherence to the God of Abraham, Isaac, and Jacob. That much the passage concedes. For the pig is not clean, exhibiting some, but not all, of the required indications, and Rome is not Israel, even though it shares Israel's Scripture. That position, denying to Rome, in its Christian form, a place in the family of Israel, forms the counterpart to the view of Aphrahat that Israel today is no longer Israel – again, a confrontation on issues. I present only the critical passage at which the animals that are invoked include one that places Rome at the interstices, partly kosher, partly not, therefore more dangerous than anyone else.

XIII:V

9. A. Moses foresaw what the evil kingdoms would do [to Israel].
   B. "The camel, rock badger, and hare" (Deut. 14:7). [Compare: "Nevertheless, among those that chew the cud or part the hoof, you shall not eat these: the camel, because it chews the cud but does not part the hoof, is unclean to you. The rock badger, because it chews the cud but does not part the hoof, is unclean to you. And the hare, because it chews the cud but does not part the hoof, is unclean to you, and the pig, because it parts the hoof and is cloven-footed, but does not chew the cud, is unclean to you" (Lev. 11:4-8).]
   C. The camel (GML) refers to Babylonia, [in line with the following verse of Scripture: "O daughter of Babylonia, you who are to be devastated!] Happy will be he who requites (GML) you, with what you have done to us" (Ps. 147:8).
   D. "The rock badger" (Deut. 14:7) – this refers to Media.
   E. Rabbis and R. Judah b. R. Simon.

F. Rabbis say, "Just as the rock badger exhibits traits of uncleanness and traits of cleanness, so the kingdom of Media produced both a righteous man and a wicked one."

G. Said R. Judah b. R. Simon, "The last Darius was Esther's son. He was clean on his mother's side and unclean on his father's side."

H. "The hare" (Deut 14:7) – this refers to Greece. The mother of King Ptolemy was named "Hare" [in Greek: lagos].

I. "The pig" (Deut. 14:7) – this refers to Edom [Rome].

J. Moses made mention of the first three in a single verse and the final one in a verse by itself [(Deut. 14:7, 8)]. Why so?

K. R. Yohanan and R. Simeon b. Laqish.

L. R. Yohanan said, "It is because [the pig] is equivalent to the other three."

M. And R. Simeon b. Laqish said, "It is because it outweighs them."

N. R. Yohanan objected to R. Simeon b. Laqish, "'Prophesy, therefore, son of man, clap your hands [and let the sword come down twice, yea thrice]' (Ez. 21:14)."

O. And how does R. Simeon b. Laqish interpret the same passage? He notes that [the threefold sword] is doubled (Ez. 21:14).

In the apocalypticizing of the animals of Lev. 11:4-8/Deut. 14:7, the camel, rock badger, hare, and pig, the pig, standing for Rome, again emerges as different from the others and more threatening than the rest. Just as the pig pretends to be a clean beast by showing the cloven hoof, but in fact is an unclean one, so Rome pretends to be just but in fact governs by thuggery. Edom does not pretend to praise God but only blasphemes. It does not exalt the righteous but kills them. These symbols concede nothing to Christian monotheism and veneration of the Torah of Moses (in its written medium). Of greatest importance, while all the other beasts bring further ones in their wake, the pig does not: "It does not bring another kingdom after it." It will restore the crown to the one who will truly deserve it, Israel. Esau will be judged by Zion, so Obadiah 1:21. Now how has the symbolization delivered an implicit message? It is in the treatment of Rome as distinct, but essentially equivalent to the former kingdoms. This seems to me a stunning way of saying that the now-Christian empire in no way requires differentiation from its pagan predecessors. Nothing has changed, except matters have gotten worse. Beyond Rome, standing in a straight line with the others, lies the true shift in history, the rule of Israel and the cessation of the dominion of the (pagan) nations. To conclude, Leviticus Rabbah came to closure, it is generally agreed, around A.D. 400-450, that is, approximately a century after the Roman Empire in the east had begun to become Christian, and half a century after the last attempt to rebuild the Temple in Jerusalem had failed – a tumultuous age indeed. Accordingly, we have had the chance to see how distinctive and striking are the ways in which, in the text at hand, the symbols of animals that stand for the four successive empires of humanity and point towards the messianic time, serve for the framers' message. Rome in the fourth century became Christian. Sages responded by facing that fact quite squarely and saying, "Indeed, it is as you say, a kind of Israel, an heir of Abraham as your texts explicitly claim. But we remain the sole legitimate Israel, the bearer of the birthright – we and not you. So you are our brother: Esau, Ishmael, Edom." And the rest follows.

Sages framed their political ideas within the metaphor of genealogy, because to begin with they appealed to the fleshly connection, the family, as the rationale for Israel's social existence. A family beginning with Abraham, Isaac, and Jacob, Israel today could best sort out its relationships by drawing into the family other social entities with which it found it had to relate. So Rome became the brother. That affinity came to light only when Rome had turned Christian, and that point marked the need for the extension of the genealogical net. But the conversion to Christianity also justified sages' extending membership in the family to Rome, for Christian Rome shared with Israel the common patrimony of Scripture – and said so. The two facts, the one of the social and political metaphor by which sages interpreted events, the other of the very character of Christianity – account for the striking shift in the treatment of Rome that does appear to have taken place in the formative century represented by work on Leviticus Rabbah.

V

Aphrahat in Iran, Sages in Rome: The Single Issue

The issue is joined, fully, completely, head-on. And well it was. For the stakes, for both sides, were very high. Aphrahat alerts us to the Christians' human problem. They saw themselves as a people without a past, a no-people, a people gathered from the peoples. Then who they can claim to be hardly derives from who they have been. Identifying with ancient Israel – a perfectly natural and correct initiative – admirably accounted for the Christian presence in humanity, provided a past, explained to diverse people what they had in common. One problem from Christians theologians' perspective demanded solution: the existing Israel, the Jewish people, which revered the same Scriptures and claimed descent, after the flesh, from ancient Israel. These – the Jews – traced their connection to ancient Israel, seeing it as natural, and also, supernatural. The family tie, through Abraham, Isaac, Jacob, formed a powerful apologetic indeed. The Jews furthermore pointed to their family record, the Scriptures, to explain whence they come and who they are. So long as the two parties to the debate shared the same subordinated political circumstance, Jewry could quite nicely hold its own in the debate; the pleading tone of Aphrahat's writing opens a window onto the heart of the historical newcomers to salvation, as Christians saw themselves. But with the shift in the politics of the Empire, the terms of debate changed. The parvenu become paramount, the Christian party to the debate invoked its familiar position now with the power of the state in support. Aphrahat's framing of the issue reflects that political fact – even though Aphrahat, living in Shapur II's Iran, did not himself live in a Christian empire. The sages represented by Leviticus Rabbah answered the issues set forth on the agenda represented by Aphrahat, because wherever they lived, they too followed the inner logic of the issue, not the dictates of an ephemeral circumstance, in reflecting on the confrontation with the other Israel.

For Israel what was there to say, but what, in Israel's view, God had said to Israel in the Torah's record of the very beginnings of the world. What now makes that old message matter is simple: the specific context to which, at just this moment, the old words were spoken. That milieu is what imparts meaning to the message: the rise to state recognition and favor of one of the two parties to the dispute of the godly genealogy. And what gives that fact weight for us is the further, equally simple fact that, in the unfolding of the canon of the sages' Judaism, the documents before us contain the first explicit and emphatic statement of the age-old genealogy of God's people. So while the framers of Leviticus Rabbah may have stated in their own medium a familiar and routine message, still, the setting turns out to supply the catalyst of significance. Content, out of political context, is mere theology. But in political context, the theological issues, fully understood in all their awful urgency, focus on matters of social life or death. The doctrines of history and merit, of Israel's identity, selection and grace – these turn out to deal with the very life and identity of a people and its society.

BIBLIOGRAPHY

General:

N. H. Baynes, *Constantine the Great and the Christian Church* (New York, 1972: Oxford University Press). Second ed., preface by Henry Chadwick.

Erwin R. Goodenough, *The Church in the Roman Empire* (N.Y., 1931: Henry Holt. Repr, N.Y., 1970: Cooper Square Publishers, Inc.), pp. 41-61.

Adolf Harnack, *The Mission and Expansion of Christianity in the First Three Centuries*. Translated and edited by James Moffatt (London, 1908. Repr. Gloucester, 1972: Peter Smith).

J. R. Palanque, G. Bardy, P. de Labriolle, G. de Plinval, and Louis Brehier, *The Church in the Christian Roman Empire*. I. *The Church and the Arian Crisis* (N.Y., 1953: Macmillan). With special reference to Pierre de Labriolle, "Christianity and Paganism in the Middle of the Fourth Century," p. 220-257.

Rosemary Radford Ruether, *Faith and Fratricide. The Theological Roots of Anti-Semitism* (N.Y., 1979: Seabury Press).

Rosemary Radford Ruether, "Judaism and Christianity. Two Fourth-Century Religions," *Sciences Religieuses Studies in Religion* 1972, 2:1-10.

Marcel Simon, *Verus Israel. Etude sur les relations entre chrétiens et juifs dans l'empire romain* (135-425) (Paris, 1964: Editions E. de Boccard).

Judaism in the Land of Israel and in Babylonia

Jacob Neusner, *A History of the Jews in Babylonia* (Leiden, 1969) III. *The Age of Shapur II*.

Jacob Neusner, *Judaism in Society. The Evidence of the Yerushalmi. Toward the Natural History of a Religion* (Chicago, 1983: University of Chicago Press). I have made use of materials in that work for the description given in this section, cf. pp. 117-121, 196-197, 247-253.

Aphrahat and Judaism

John G. Gager, *The Origins of Anti-Semitism. Attitudes toward Judaism in Pagan and Christian Antiquity* (N.Y., 1983: Oxford University Press), pp. 247-264.

Adolf Harnack, *The Mission and Expansion of Christianity in the First Three Centuries*. Translated and edited by James Moffatt (London, 1908. Repr. Gloucester, 1972: Peter Smith), pp. 240-278.

Colm Luibheid, *The Essential Eusebius* (N.Y., 1966: Mentor Omega), p. 41.

Rosemary Radford Reuther, *Faith and Fratricide. The Theological Roots of Anti-Semitism* (N.Y., 1979: Seabury Press).

Marcel Simon, *Verus Israel. Etude sur les relations entre chrétiens et juifs dans l'empire romain* (135-425) (Paris, 1964: Editions E. de Boccard), on Christians as a third type of people, pp. 135-139; on the *Adversus Judaeos* literature in general, pp. 166-176.

Aphrahat and the People Which Is No People

Robert Murray, *Symbols of Church and Kingdom. A Study in Early Syriac Tradition* (Cambridge, 1975: Cambridge University Press).

Jacob Neusner, *Aphrahat and Judaism. The Christian-Jewish Argument in Fourth-Century Iran* (Leiden, 1971: E. J. Brill).

Chapter Six

The Sage and The Emperor

Yohanan ben Zakkai, Julian the Apostate and the Destruction of the Temple of Jerusalem

A Methodological Experiment

When the covenanted community of Qumran concluded that the Temple in Jerusalem did not conform to God's law, for that community the Temple was destroyed.[1] The problem at hand is this: when did the unfolding Judaic system of sages, fully documented in the canon of the dual Torah, from the Mishnah through the Bavli, recognize as finalities of history the destruction of the Temple and the cessation of the cult? What we want to know, therefore, is when, in the unfolding of the Judaism of the dual Torah, the Temple was destroyed. The framing of the question and method of answering it involves an unfamiliar approach to historical study of the rabbinic corpus of late antiquity, which the honoree and other readers may find of interest. Let me begin, therefore, with a statement of method.

I

The Documentary Approach

The sources of the Judaism of the dual Torah, oral and written, accurately and factually testify to particular moments in time. But how shall we identify the right time, the particular context to which the documents and their contents attest – and those to which they do not provide reliable testimony? Using the canonical sources of Judaism for historical purposes requires, first of all, a clear statement of why, in my view, these sources tell us about one period, rather than some other.

The problem, specifically, is that the documents preserved by Judaism refer to authorities who, we generally suppose, flourished in the early centuries of the Common Era. But at the same time, we also know, these documents were brought to closure in the later centuries of late antiquity. The Talmud of the

---

[1] I owe this formulation of matters to my sometime colleague, Yigael Yadin, who remarked to me that for the Essenes of Qumran, the Temple was destroyed before 70.

Land of Israel, ca. 400-450, Fathers According to Rabbi Nathan, ca. 400-500, the Talmud of Babylonia, ca. 600, all contain numerous sayings attributed to, and stories told about, first- and second-century figures. At the same time, we cannot show, and therefore do not know, that these sayings really were said by the sages to whom they are assigned, and we frequently can demonstrate that the sayings are attributed by diverse documents of the same canon to two or more figures. Along these same lines, stories that purport to tell us what really happened exhibit marks of stylization that show reworkings, and, more important, we rarely find independent evidence, e.g., corroboration by outside observers, of other views of what happened. Not only so, but where sages' stories about events can be compared to stories told by outside observers, we rarely can find any correlation at all, either as to causes, or as to circumstances, let alone as to actual events. Accordingly, we cannot show that attributions of sayings are valid and therefore do not know what what is assigned to a sage really was said by him.

We therefore turn for a picture of the circumstance and context of sayings and stories to the documents that preserve sayings and stories, therefore, and ask about the setting in which those documents' authorships have selected and organized the materials they have given us. We inquire into the role of redaction in the formulation of sayings and stories. We pursue that range of critical questions commonplace in biblical and historical studies since the Enlightenment. We take as our range of inquiry the relationship between the contents of the document, including the sayings and stories selected by its authorship, and the context in which the authorship of the document did its work. We ask whether we can find in context a mode of analyzing and interpreting contents, and, vice versa, whether the contents point to concerns contributed by the circumstance in which the authorship made its selections.

Let me review the order of the documents[2] as the consensus of scholarship presently sees it. The system of Judaism attested by the canon at hand reached its first literary expression in ca. 200 C.E. and its last in ca. 600 C.E. The first

---

[2]The contents of the documents varies according to the manuscript evidence. Therefore we cannot assume that everything now presented as a document was included in its first formulation. We know a number of different versions of what constituted, for instance, Genesis Rabbah or Leviticus Rabbah. In translating the received literature, I have always selected for translation the most widely available version of the Hebrew, e.g., Theodor-Albeck's Genesis Rabbah, Schechter's Fathers According to Rabbi Nathan, Albeck's Mishnah, and so forth. But in my studies of these documents, I have centered upon the document as a whole, its modes of discourse, its recurrent points of emphasis. I have never constructed an argument resting on the authenticity of one manuscript's version of a document as against another's, or based upon a single pericope and its message. To do so would be to commit the same error commonplace among those who take at face value everything attributed to or told about a given sage as evidence of things really said and done in the time in which that sage lived and by that sage. Working on documents requires us to work on whole documents, to characterize their plan and program not in detail but in the entirety, whole and complete, and, over all, to build hypotheses on the premise that the representation of the document as we now have it may well prove flawed and partial – or, more commonly, excessive.

document, the Mishnah, drew together teachings of authorities of the period beginning in the first century, before 70, when the Temple was destroyed and autonomous government ended, and ending with the publication of the code in ca. 200. The last, the Talmud of Babylonia (Bavli) provided the authoritative commentary on thirty-seven of the sixty-two tractates of the Mishnah as well as on substantial portions of the Hebrew Scriptures. In joining sustained discourse on the Scriptures, called, in the mythic of the present system, the Written Torah, as well as on the Mishnah, held to be the Oral, or memorized Torah, the Bavli's framers presented a summa, an encyclopaedia, of Judaism, to guide Israel, the Jewish people, for many centuries to come.

Between ca. 200, when autonomous government was well established again, and ca. 600 the continuous and ongoing movement of sages, holding positions of authority in the Jewish governments recognized by Rome and Iran, as political leaders of the Jewish communities of the Land of Israel (to just after 400 C.E.) and Babylonia (to about 500 C.E.), respectively, wrote two types of books. One sort extended, amplified, systematized, and harmonized components of the legal system laid forth in the Mishnah. The work of Mishnah-exegesis produced four principal documents as well as an apologia for the Mishnah.

This last – the rationale or apologia – came first in time, about a generation or so beyond the publication of the Mishnah itself. It was tractate Abot, ca. 250 C.E., a collection of sayings attributed both to authorities whose names occur, also, in the Mishnah, as well as to some sages who flourished after the conclusion of the Mishnah. These later figures, who make no appearance in that document, stand at the end of the compilation. The other three continuators of the Mishnah were the Tosefta, the Talmud of the Land of Israel (the Yerushalmi), and the Bavli. The Tosefta, containing a small proposition of materials contemporaneous with those presently in the Mishnah and a very sizable proportion secondary to, and dependent, even verbatim, on the Mishnah, reached conclusion some time after ca. 300 and before ca. 400. The Yerushalmi closed at ca. 400. The Bavli, as I said, was completed by ca. 600. All these dates, of course, are rough guesses, but *the sequence* in which the documents made their appearance is not. I know for example of no one who maintains that the Tosefta came to closure after the Bavli, or that Avot derives from an authorship prior to that of the Mishnah.

The Tosefta addresses the Mishnah; its name means "supplement," and its function was to supplement the rules of the original documents. The Yerushalmi mediates between the Tosefta and the Mishnah, commonly citing a paragraph of the Tosefta in juxtaposition with a paragraph of the Mishnah and commenting on both, or so arranging matters that the paragraph of the Tosefta serves, just as it should, to complement a paragraph of the Mishnah. The Bavli, following the Yerushalmi by about two centuries, pursues its own program, which, as I said, was to link the two Torahs and restate them as one.

The stream of exegesis of the Mishnah and exploration of its themes of law and philosophy flowed side by side with a second. This other river coursed up out of the deep wells of the written Scripture. But it surfaced only long after the work of Mishnah-exegesis was well underway and followed the course of that exegesis, now extended to Scripture. The exegesis of the Hebrew Scriptures, a convention of all systems of Judaism from before the conclusion of Scripture itself, obviously occupied sages from the very origins of their group. No one began anywhere but in the encounter with the Written Torah. But the writing down of exegeses of Scripture in a systematic way, signifying also the formulation of a program and a plan for the utilization of the Written Torah in the unfolding literature of the Judaism taking shape in the centuries at hand, developed in a quite distinct circumstance.

Another fruitful path also emerged from the labor of Mishnah-exegesis. As the work of Mishnah-exegesis got under way, in the third century, exegetes of the Mishnah and others alongside undertook a parallel labor. It was to work through verses of Scripture in exactly the same way – word for word, phrase for phrase, line for line – in which, to begin with, the exegetes of the Mishnah pursued the interpretation and explanation of the Mishnah. To state matters simply, precisely the types of exegesis that dictated the way in which sages read the Mishnah now guided their reading of Scripture as well. And, as people began to collect and organize comments in accord with the order of sentences and paragraphs of the Mishnah, they found the stimulation to collect and organize comments on clauses and verses of Scripture. As I said, this kind of work got under way in the Sifra and the two Sifrés. It reached massive and magnificent fulfillment in Genesis Rabbah, which, as its name tells us, presents a line-for-line reading of the book of Genesis.

Beyond these two modes of exegesis and the organization of exegesis in books, first on the Mishnah, then on Scripture, lies yet a third. To understand it, we once more turn back to the Mishnah's great exegetes, represented to begin with in the Yerushalmi. While the original exegesis of the Mishnah in the Tosefta addressed the document under study through a line by line commentary, responding only in discrete and self-contained units of discourse, authors of units of discourse gathered in the next, the Yerushalmi, developed yet another mode of discourse entirely. They treated not phrases or sentences but principles and large-scale conceptual problems. They dealt not alone with a given topic, a subject and its rule, but with an encompassing problem, a principle and its implications for a number of topics and rules. This far more discursive and philosophical mode of thought produced for Mishnah-exegesis, in somewhat smaller volume but in much richer contents, sustained essays on principles cutting across specific rules. And for Scripture the work of sustained and broad-ranging discourse resulted in a second type of exegetical work, beyond that focused on words, phrases, and sentences.

Discursive exegesis is represented, to begin with, in Leviticus Rabbah, a document that reached closure, people generally suppose, sometime after Genesis Rabbah, thus in ca. 400-500, one might guess. Leviticus Rabbah presents not phrase-by-phrase systematic exegeses of verses in the book of Leviticus, but a set of thirty-seven topical essays. These essays, syllogistic in purpose, take the form of citations and comments on verses of Scripture to be sure. But the compositions range widely over the far reaches of the Hebrew Scriptures while focusing narrowly upon a given theme. They moreover make quite distinctive points about that theme. Their essays constitute compositions, not merely composites. Whether devoted to God's favor to the poor and humble or to the dangers of drunkenness, the essays, exegetical in form, discursive in character, correspond to the equivalent, legal essays, amply represented in the Yerushalmi.

So in this other mode of Scripture interpretation, too, the framers of the exegeses of Scripture accomplished in connection with Scripture what the Yerushalmi's exegetes of the Mishnah were doing in the same way at the same time. We move rapidly past yet a third mode of Scriptural exegesis, one in which the order of Scripture's verses is left far behind, and in which topics, not passages of Scripture, take over as the mode of organizing thought. Represented by Pesiqta deR. Kahana, Lamentations Rabbati, and some other collections conventionally assigned to the sixth and seventh centuries, these entirely discursive compositions move out in their own direction, only marginally relating in mode of discourse to any counterpart types of composition in the Yerushalmi (or in the Bavli).

At the end of the extraordinary creative age of Judaism, the authors of units of discourse collected in the Bavli drew together the two, up-to-then distinct, modes of organizing thought, either around the Mishnah or around Scripture. They treated both Torahs, oral and written, as equally available in the work of organizing large-scale exercises of sustained inquiry. So we find in the Bavli a systematic treatment of some tractates of the Mishnah. And within the same aggregates of discourse, we also find (in somewhat smaller proportion to be sure, roughly 60% to roughly 40% in the sample I made of three tractates) a second principle of organizing and redaction. That principle dictates that ideas be laid out in line with verses of Scripture, themselves dealt with in cogent sequence, one by one, just as the Mishnah's sentences and paragraphs come under analysis, in cogent order and one by one.

The reason that the foregoing, somewhat protracted theory of the development and organization of the sources of formative Judaism requires attention is simple. If we are to trace the unfolding, in the sources of formative Judaism, of a given theme or of ideas on a given problem, the order in which we approach the several books, that is, components of the entire canon, gives us the sole guidance on sequence, order, and context, that we are apt to find. How so? We have no way of demonstrating that authorities to whom, in a given composition, ideas are attributed really said what is assigned to them. The sole fact in hand therefore is that the framers of a given document included in their book sayings imputed to named authorities. Are these dependable? Unlikely on the face of it. Why not? Since the same sayings will be imputed to diverse authorities by different groups of editors, of different books, we stand on shaky ground indeed if we rely for chronology upon the framers' claims of who said what. More important, attributions by themselves cannot be shown to be reliable. *What we cannot show we do not know.* Lacking firm evidence, for example, in a sage's own, clearly assigned writings, or even in writings redacted by a sage's own disciples and handed on among them in the discipline of their own community, we have for chronology only a single fact.

It is that a document, reaching closure at a given time, contains the allegation that Rabbi X said statement Y. So we know that people at the time of the document reached closure took the view that Rabbi X said statement Y. We may then assign to statement Y a position, in the order of the sequence of sayings, defined by the location of the document in the order of the sequence of documents. The several documents' dates, as is clear, all constitute guesses. But the sequence Mishnah, Tosefta, Yerushalmi, Bavli for the exegetical writings on the Mishnah is absolutely firm and beyond doubt. The sequence for the exegetical collections on Scripture Sifra, the Sifrés, Genesis Rabbah, Leviticus Rabbah, the Pesiqtas and beyond is not entirely sure. Still the position of the Sifra and the two Sifrés at the head, followed by Genesis Rabbah, then Leviticus Rabbah, then Pesiqta deR. Kahana and Lamentations Rabbati and some related collections, seems likely. What then constitutes the history of an idea in formative Judaism? We trace what references we find to a topic in accord with the order of documents just now spelled out. In such a study we learn the order in which ideas came to expression in the canon. We begin any survey with the Mishnah, the starting point of the canon. We proceed systematically to work our way through tractate Abot, the Mishnah's first apologetic, then the Tosefta, the Yerushalmi, and the Bavli at the end. In a single encompassing sweep, we finally deal with the entirety of the compilations of the exegeses of Scripture, arranged, to be sure, in that order that I have now explained.

Insisting on the "historicity" of attributions, which characterizes the bulk of work done these days as in times past, leads to asking the wrong questions, namely, questions of historical fact. More consequentially, that same attitude of mind obscures the right questions, specifically, questions of cultural order, social system and political structure, to which the texts respond explicitly and constantly. Confronting writings of a religious character, we err by asking questions of a narrowly historical character: what did X really say – or think! – on a particular occasion, and why. These questions not only are not answerable on the basis of the evidence in hand. They also are trivial, irrelevant to the character of the evidence. How little of real interest and worth we should know, even if we were to concede the historical accuracy and veracity of all the many allegations the canonical authorships! How little we should know – but how much we should have *missed* if that set of questions and answers were to encompass the whole of our inquiry. Since the honoree of this volume has read the religious writings of canonical Judaism as testimonies not to the mind of the authorship but to the views of those to whom sayings are attributed and about whom stories are told, this other approach may prove of interest to him in particular.

When studying topics in the Judaism of the sages of the rabbinic writings from the first through the seventh centuries, as we have seen, the scholarship represented by him among many others routinely cites sayings categorized by attribution rather than document. That is to say, they treat as one group of sayings whatever is assigned to Rabbi X. This is without regard to the documents in which those sayings occur, where or when those documents reached closure, and similar considerations of literary context and documentary circumstance. The category defined by attributions to a given authority rests on the premise that the things given in the name of Rabbi X really were said by him. No other premise would justify resort to the category deriving from use of a name, that alone. Commonly, the next step is to treat those sayings as evidence of ideas held, if not by that particular person, then by people in the age in which the cited authority lived. Once more the premise that the sayings go back to the age, if not the person, of the authority to whom they are attributed underpins further inquiry. Accordingly, scholars cite sayings in the name of given authorities and take for granted that those sayings were said by the authority to whom they were attributed and, of course, in the time in which that authority flourished. By contrast, as I said at the outset, I treat the historical sequence of sayings only in accord with the order of the documents in which they first occur.

Let me expand on why I have taken the approach that I have. Since many sayings are attributed to specific authorities, why not lay out the sayings in the order of the authorities to whom they are attributed, rather than in the order of the books in which these sayings occur? It is because the attributions cannot be validated, but the books can. In this study, I present a small component of such a systematic account of the response to the destruction of the Temple in the writings of the ancient sages, from the Mishnah through the Bavli. At issue is the treatment by the authorships of some of the fifth and sixth century documents, in particular the Talmud of the Land of Israel and Fathers According to Rabbi Nathan, and the Bavli, of the destruction of the Temple and Yohanan ben Zakkai's role in it.[3] We have, to begin with, to point to the single public event that, in my view, defined the public consciousness of Israel in the Land of Israel from the end of the fourth century and for a long time to come. It is the failure of Emperor Julian's plan to rebuild the Temple of Jerusalem. In my

---

[3]In this study I move beyond my *Development of a Legend. Studies on the Traditions Concerning Yohanan ben Zakkai* (Leiden, 1970: E. J. Brill) and *Messiah in Context. Israel's History and Destiny in Formative Judaism* (Philadelphia 1982: Fortress Press).

view, that event constituted a catastrophe for the morale and consciousness of
Israel in the Land of Israel.

II
Emperor Julian and the Rebuilding of the Temple

One noteworthy event took place in the public history of Judaism in the
fourth century.[4] That was the fiasco of Emperor Julian's plan of rebuilding the
Temple. To state what happened simply, the Emperor encouraged the Jews to
rebuild the Temple in Jerusalem and to restore the animal sacrifices there. After
a brief effort, the work collapsed, and nothing came of the plan. What was at
issue, and why did it matter to both Judaic sages and Christian theologians?
Christians had long cited the destruction of the Temple of Jerusalem as proof of
the prophetic powers of Jesus, who, in the Christian record, had predicted the
matter before it happened. The ruin of Jerusalem there had served for three
centuries to testify to the truth of Christianity. The emperor Julian, as part of
his policy of opposing Christianity, in 362-363 gave orders to permit the Jews
to rebuild their temple and resume animal sacrifices, just as the pagan temples
were to be restored and their animal sacrifices renewed. Julian in general favored
Jews, remitted taxes that had applied to them in particular, and as part of that
broader policy undertook to rebuild the Jews' temple. Unable to offer animal
sacrifices in the Jerusalem Temple for the preceding three hundred years, Jews
took the emperor's decree as a mark of friendship. Some may have assumed that
the emperor's action forecast the coming of the Messiah.

Julian had moreover issued edicts of toleration, but, singling out
Christianity, he pressured Christians to give up the faith and revert to paganism.
He further declared war on Christianity by forbidding Christians to teach in the
schools, since Christians could not teach the classical authors, for Christians
"despise the gods the [classics] honored." He took away the clergy's former legal
power, withdrew recognition of bishops as judges in civil matters, and subjected
the clergy to taxation. So, as Bowersock says, "Julian and the Jews had a
common enemy in the Christians; their allegiance could be valuable in the Near
East, particularly in Mesopotamia, where the emperor was going to conduct his
campaign against the Persians." Julian undertook a more general policy of
restoring temples Christians had closed, and for their part, the Christians had
turned Jerusalem into a Christian city. Constantine and his mother had built
churches and shrines there. Since, moreover, Julian had in mind to restore
sacrifices as part of normal prayer, Julian wanted the Jews to restore their cult as
well. By securing the restoration of the temple, he moreover would invalidate
the prophesy of Jesus that not one stone of the temple would be left upon

---

[4]What follows depends upon the bibliography found at the end of the chapter.

another (Bowersock, p. 89). But when Julian died in battle, in 363, nothing had been accomplished.[5] Frend explains the matter very simply:[6]

> His aim may have been...to strike at the heart of Constantinian Jerusalem, to upstage the Holy Places by a new, rebuilt "sacred city of Jerusalem." Unfortunately workers struck hidden gaseous deposits when they began to lay the new foundations. Explosions and fire greeted their efforts, and the attempt was abandoned in confusion.

So ended the last attempt to rebuilt the Temple of Jerusalem from then to now. Julian's successors dismantled all of his programs and restored the privileges the Church had lost.[7] We need hardly speculate on the profound disappointment that overtook the Jews of the Empire and beyond. The seemingly trivial incident – a failed project of restoring a building – proved profoundly consequential for Judaic and Christian thinkers. We know that a quarter of a century later, John Chrysostom dwelt on the matter of the destruction of the Temple – and the Jews' failure to rebuild it – as proof of the divinity of Jesus.

Whether some, or many, Jews reached the same conclusion in the aftermath of the fiasco we do not know. We have no reference in the sages' writings to the matter. But we can readily reconstruct an appropriate response, if not one particular to the event: the Temple will be rebuilt when the Messiah comes, not before; the Messiah will come when Israel attains that sanctification that the Torah requires, and the model of the sage provides the ideal for which Israel should strive. The attitude of mind required of Israel was humility and acceptance, humility before God and acceptance of sages' authority. These attitudes, joined with actions aimed at living the holy life, will in due course prove Israel worthy of receiving the Messiah. That message, written across the pages of the Talmud of the Land of Israel but so far as we know not in any prior document in the sages' movement, assuredly addressed the crisis of disappointment.[8]

The Christian restoration, after Julian, intensified over time the prior abridgement of the civil status of the Jews. That fact underlined the full meaning of the fiasco of 361-2. Referring to the view that the Jews should be kept in a condition of misery but should not be exterminated, Ruether says,[9] "Between 315 and 439 (from the reign of Constantine to the promulgation of the Theodosian Code), this view of the Jew was enforced through a steadily worsening legal status." Avi-Yonah divides the period after Julian into three

---

[5]Lietzmann, p. 282, Bowersock, pp. 87-90, Jones, p. 60, Frend, p. 606, Labriolle, pp. 232-236.

[6]P. 606.

[7]Goodenough, p. 61.

[8]See my *Messiah in Context. Israel's History and Destiny in Formative Judaism* (Philadelphia, 1984: Fortress Press).

[9]P. 186.

parts, the first, 363-383, until the accession of Theodosius, a period of "a truce between the hostile religions." The second, from the accession of Theodosius I to the death of his son, Arcadius, was marked by an

> ...energetic attack on Judaism by the leaders of the church, mainly through pressure on the imperial government. The government ceded here and there but did not cause serious injury to the Jewish community as a whole or to Jews as individuals. This campaign against Judaism was part of a larger program of physical attacks on paganism and pagans and their places of worship, which sharpened after 380.[10]

The third sub-period lasted from the accession of Theodosius II till the publication of his third Novella (408-438). During this time the power of the church overcame the scruples of the government and both turned against the Jews."[11] So through to the end of the period at hand, the judgment with which we began, that the problems were those of morale, not of politics and economics, remains valid.

III

The Christian Response to Julian's Fiasco

John "of the golden tongue" (Chrysostom), took as his principal point that Christians cannot believe in Christ and also worship in synagogues and observe Judaic rites. Judaism is over, offering no salvation, as the fiasco of the rebuilding of the Temple has proved just now. Preacher in Antioch, Chrysostom, who was born in 347 and died in 407, in a set of sermons preached in 386-7 addressed the issue of Judaism in a series of sermons accusing Christians of backsliding. Not concurring on the honorable title, "golden-mouthed," some, represented by Ruether, would call John foul-mouthed: "The sermons of John Chrysostom are easily the most violent and tasteless of the anti-Judaic literature of the period."[12] Christianity by the end of the century hardly enjoyed security as the religion of the empire. Julian had called into doubt the future of the Church in the state, and Judaism remained a vital faith and force. The issue, therefore, proved urgent for political reasons to both Christianity and Judaism. For the one, at stake was the future of a Church resting on the messiahship of Christ, for the other, the future of the holy people awaiting the Messiah in the future.

But the specific issue framed by Chryusostom was his own – and that of the Church. For while the messianic question confronted both sides, each framed the matter in terms of its own distinctive situation. Chrysostom's target was "Judaizing" Christians who attended synagogue worship and observed Judaic

---

[10]MacMullen, p. 119.

[11]Avi Yonah, p. 208.

[12]Reuther, p. 173.

rites. Judaism exercised great attraction to Christians, who had in mind to observe Jewish festivals. They attended synagogue worship, resorted to Jewish courts, listened to the reading of the Torah in the synagogue on the Sabbath and on the next day came to join in the Eucharist. At issue for John was not "anti-Semitism," a wholly anachronistic category. What troubled John was the state of Christian belief. Specifically, John regarded Christian participation in Jewish worship and customs as "Judaizing," so backsliding, that is, an act of disbelief. The backsliders not believe that Jesus is Christ, and that is why they kept the law, that is, the Torah. Clearly at the heart of the matter was the Messiahship of Jesus. All else depended on that question. There was a common and conventional program of rhetoric: the Jews are guilty of "apostasy, faithflessness, rejection of God, and hardheartedness." Wilken summarizes the theological matter:

> Embedded in these passages is to be found a theological argument about the status of the Jews after the death of Christ and the destruction of the temple at Jerusalem. Since Christians claimed to be the inheritors of the ancient Jewish tradition, the destruction of the temple was taken to be a sign that Jewish law had lost its legitimacy. Yet, three hundred years after the destruction of the temple and the loss of Jerusalem, the Jews were still observing the ancient laws.

Jesus had predicted the destruction of the Temple. Not a few years back, the apostate emperor and the Jews had tried to rebuild it. They did not succeed. That proves that the temple no longer serves to legimate Jewish religion. All of these commonplaces point to a single issue: was, and is, Jesus the Christ? That is why Chrysostom plays a part in our invention of a common program of thought for both Judaic and Christian writers in Constantine's age.[13]

Chrysostom's eight sermons, *Adversus Judaeos* , given in Antioch probably in 386 and 387, dealt with Christians soft on Judaism. As a set the sermons addressed Christians who observe and defend Jewish rites, keep the Passover, and, in general treat the law of Judaism as valid. The response to these views drew upon the exile of the Jews, the destruction of the Temple as Jesus had predicted, and, it must follow, the divinity of Jesus. Judaism as such was not the issue; the audience comprised backsliding Christians. The preacher referred to festivals of the autumn season, the New Year, Day of Atonement, and Tabernacles, and he evidently did not wish Christians to keep those festivals, or to observe Easter coincident with Passover. What concerned him transcended attendance on Judaic festivals and fasts. Christians were keeping the Sabbath, attending synagogue worship, and did not know the difference between Christian and Judaic worship. Chrysostom claimed that Jews' supposed magical power attracted Christians,

---

[13]Wilken: pp. 32-3, 66-7, 76, 132, xvi.   On "anti-Semitism," compare Gager, "The very violence of Chrysostom's language demonstrates the potential for a linkage between anti-Jewish beliefs and anti-Semitic feelings."

who went to synagogues for healing. So Chrysostom had to demonstrate that the Judaic rites were rejected by God and invalid.

In Chrysostom's case the relationship of the destruction of Jerusalem and the divinity of Jesus took pride of place. The longest homily and the most theological-historical, the fifth, is summarized by Wilken as follows:

> ...the chief topic of the sermon: The greatest proof that Christ is truly God is that he "predicted the temple would be destroyed, that Jerusalem would be captured, and that the city would no longer be the city of the Jews as it had been in the past." If only ten, twenty, or fifty years had passed since the destruction of the temple, one might understand doubts about Jesus" prophecy, but over three centuries have passed and there is not "a shadow of the change for which you are waiting." ...If the Jews had never attempted to rebuild the temple during this time, one might say that they could do so only if they made the effort. But the course of events shows the reverse, for the Jews have attempted to rebuild the temple, not once, but three times, and were unsuccessful in every effort....The failure of Julian's effort to rebuild the temple in Jerusalem, then, is proof that Christ was not an ordinary man among men, but the divine son of God. His word was more powerful than the feeble efforts of men, for by his word alone he defeated the emperor Julian and the "whole Jewish people" ...The prophecy of Christ is proven true by the historical "facts"...the fulfillment of the ancient prophecies and the continued existence of the Church is evidence of the power and divinity of Christ.[14]

And from this all the rest followed. So Wilken concludes,

> ...by keeping the Law, by celebrating Jewish festivals, by seeking out Jewish magicians, the Judaizers proclaimed that Judaism was spiritually more potent than Christianity. What greater proof of the truth of Judaism than for the followers of Christ to observe Jewish law?[15]

For Chrysostom at stake was not Judaism but Christianity:

> I ask you to rescue your brothers, to set them free from this error and to bring them back to the truth. There is no benefit in listening to me unless the example of your deeds match my words. What I said was not for your sakes but for the sake of those who are sick. I want them to learn these facts from you and to free themselves from their wicked association with the Jews.[16]

The upshot is that, as Chrysostom framed the issue, everything depended upon the Messiahship of Jesus, on the one side, and the confirmation of that Messiahship by the events of the age – the power of the Church, the humiliation of the Jerusalem temple, on the other. Everything depended on the Temple,

---

[14]P. 155-8.

[15]P. 160.

[16]Wilken, p. 158.

restored or in permanent ruin. Jesus had said no stone would rest on stone, and none did. Julian had tried to rebuild the Temple and had failed. Chrysostom therefore pointed to the Jews' exile as proof of their defeat: "It is illegitimate to keep their form way of life outside of Jerusalem...for the city of Jerusalem is the keystone that supports the Jewish rite."[17] The argument recurs throughout the homilies on the Judaizers and forms the centerpiece. No wonder then that sages would join the rebuilding of the Temple to the future coming of the Messiah.

IV

Judaic Sages and Julian's Fiasco:
The Fifth-Century Documents

Now that we have heard from the outsider on the centrality of the destruction of the Temple and the probative character of Julian's failure, we have every reason to expect to find, in the writings of sages that came to closure in the century after Julian, a contrasting and counterpart message. But sages' idiom taught them a more circumspect and subtle mode of discourse. They spoke not through proposition and explicit, philosophical syllogism. They framed their syllogisms in a more subtle way, proving their point by drawing upon facts of Scripture, on the one side, the Mishnah, on the second, and the lives and deeds of sages, on the third. Through their choice of topics and the points they made in telling stories about those topics, sages found it possible to deliver with great power and enormous effect the syllogistic message that others presented in a more abstract and general mode of discourse. In the present case, we find that the the Temple in which a sage, typically, Yohanan ben Zakkai, figures as a principal actor all occur in fifth-century documents. If we survey the stories about Yohanan ben Zakkai and the destruction of the Temple, we find that none of them occurs in the Mishnah, Tosefta, Avot, or the other documents that reached closure prior to 400. Among the eighty-eight distinct components of which the tradition and legend of Yohanan ben Zakkai is composed,[18] his role in the encounter with Vespasian figures in these: Zechariah 11:1 predicted the destruction, first in Bavli; Isaiah 14:14 and the destruction of the first Temple, first in Bavli; escape in a coffin, first in Fathers according to Rabbi Nathan; and the Temple rites are really hocus pocus, first in the Pesiqta deRab Kahana. In the fifth and sixth century documents therefore we first uncover the stories about Yohanan ben Zakkai as the critical figure in both predicting the destruction of the Temple and then forming the bridge between the destruction and the continuing life of Israel through the way of the Torah.

Stating matters more generally, we may say that the account of Israel's history as embodied in the figure of the sage, who balances and outweighs the

---

[17]Cited by Wilken, p. 149.

[18]See *Development*, pp. 267ff.

emperor, who embodies Rome's history, makes its original appearance in the documents of the fifth and sixth centuries. That is not to say that the destruction of the Temple does not figure in earlier writings. To the contrary, that event forms an astral presence in all rabbinic literature, from the Mishnah forward. But the particular role of the sage in opposition (as I shall now show) to the emperor awaits the authorships of the fifth and sixth century writings for full recognition. A simple contrast between the role of Yohanan ben Zakkai in the story in The Fathers According to Rabbi Nathan of the destruction of the Temple and the equivalent story in the Talmud of Babylonian (the one in the Yerushalmi omits all reference to him) shows how an authorship reworks the theme of the destruction to make its statement that the sage forms the counterpart to the emperor, just as does Israel to Rome, in the history of humanity and its salvation.

V

The Destruction of the Temple
With and Without Yohanan ben Zakkai

Let us now compare the account of the destruction of the Temple as it occurs in Babylonian Talmud with the counterpart as it is given in The Fathers According to Rabbi Nathan. On the escape from Jerusalem, we have a sizable story at b. Git. 56a. It comprises a pastiche of materials, only at a few points intersecting with The Fathers According to Rabbi Nathan's version. In this way we see how the sages of the Land of Israel chose to frame matters in The Fathers According to Rabbi Nathan, specifically by contrasting the way in which the same theme was worked out in the Talmud of Babylonia.

Where the text is cited, it is in the translation of M. Simon, *Gittin*, pp. 254-260. I insert the pertinent parallels of the story as it occurs in The Fathers According to Rabbi Nathan, in my own translation.[19]

1. Superscription: R. Yohanan said, "What is illustrative of the verse, *Happy is the man who fears always, but he who hardens his heart shall fall into mischief* (Prov, 28:14)? The destruction of Jerusalem came through Qamsa and Bar Qamsa; the destruction of Tur Malka through a cock and a hen; the destruction of Betar through the shaft of a leather."
2. Because of the contention between Qamsa and Bar Qamsa: the one gave a party and did not invite the other, who came anyhow and got thrown out. The sages present did not object. The injured party informed against them, saying, the Jews are rebelling against you. This led to the destruction of the Temple.
3. The emperor sent Nero, who produced an omen to indicate the city will fall. He had a boy repeat the verse of Scripture he had just learned,

---

[19]See my *Fathers According to Rabbi Nathan. An Analytical Translation* (Atlanta, 1986: Scholars Press for Brown Judaic Studies), and my *Judaism and Story: The Evidence of The Fathers According to Rabbi Nathan* (in press).

which was Ez. 25:14, predicting that Edom-Rome would destroy the
Temple. He became a proselyte, from whom Meir was descended.

4. He sent against them Vespasian. Three wealthy men in the city,
   Naqdimon, Ben Kalba Shabua, and Ben Sisis Hakkesset were there. Each
   had enough to keep the city in food, drink, and fuel. The sages in the
   city wanted to make peace with the Romans. The zealots would not
   agree, but burned the stories of wheat and barley, so producing a famine.

5. Martha daughter of Boethius, rich woman, could not get food. She
   ultimate went without her shoes to find food, some dung stuck to her
   foot, and Yohanan b. Zakkai invoked the verse, *The tender and delicate
   woman   which would not adventure to set the sole of her foot upon the
   ground* (Deut. 28:5).

6. Sadoq fasted for forty years so that Jerusalem would not be destroyed.

7. Abba Sikra, head of the zealots, was son of the sister of Yohanan b.
   Zakkai. Yohanan asked himn how long he was going to starve the
   people to death. The nephew said he could do nothing about it.
   Yohanan said, "Devise some plan for me to escape, perhaps I shall be
   able to save a little." Abba Sikra advised him to pretend to be sick, then
   to die, "Let then your disciples get under your bed but no others, so that
   they will not notice that you are still light, since they know that a
   living being is lighter than a corpse." He did so and R. Eliezer went
   under the bier from one side, Joshua from the other. When they reached
   the door, some men wanted to put a lance through the bier. He said to
   them, "Shall they say, 'They have pierced their master'?" They wanted to
   give it a push, etc. He got out.

The focus of this story is not on Yohanan b. Zakkai, who takes a subordinate
part. It provides a cause for the catastrophe, explaining who brought the
Romans down on the Jews. The Fathers According to Rabbi Nathan does not
answer that question. The story further stresses the zealots' destruction of the
stores of food and drink and fuel, then proceeds to the further story of Martha,
yielding the homily on Deut. 28:5; then turns to Sadoq. Yohanan is introduced
only by making him an uncle of the head of the zealots, who form the principal
actor in this version. The initiatives all belong to Abba Sikra, who tells
Yohanan what to do. The disciples or Abba Sikra ("he") have the wit to get
Yohanan out safely. As we shall see in a moment, Yohanan does nothing to
impress Vespasian, and gets little enough from him. In a word, the Bavli's
version of events does not accomplish what the story of the destruction of the
Temple does when it is told in the version of The Fathers According to Rabbi
Nathan, which is to place the sage into the balance as the opposite and equal of
the emperor and Israel's principal actor and active intellect. The contrast
between the one and the other comes out in a review, as follows:

The Fathers According to Rabbi Nathan IV:VI

1. A. Now when Vespasian came to destroy Jerusalem, he said to [the
      inhabitants of the city,] "Idiots! why do you want to destroy this city
      and burn the house of the sanctuary? For what do I want of you, except
      that you send me a bow or an arrow [as marks of submission to my rule],
      and I shall go on my way."

B. They said to him, "Just as we sallied out against the first two who came
    before you and killed them, so shall we sally out and kill you."

C. When Rabban Yohanan ben Zakkai heard, he proclaimed to the men of
    Jerusalem, saying to them, "My sons, why do you want to destroy this
    city and burn the house of the sanctuary? For what does he want of you,
    except that you send him a bow or an arrow, and he will go on his way."

D. They said to him, "Just as we sallied out against the first two who came
    before him and killed them, so shall we sally out and kill him."

E. Vespasian had stationed men near the walls of the city, and whatever
    they heard, they would write on an arrow and shoot out over the wall.
    [They reported] that Rabban Yohanan ben Zakkai was a loyalist of
    Caesar's.

F. After Rabban Yohanan ben Zakkai had spoken to them one day, a
    second, and a third, and the people did not accept his counsel, he sent
    and called his disciples, R. Eliezer and R. Joshua, saying to them, "My
    sons, go and get me out of here. Make me an ark and I shall go to sleep
    in it."

G. R. Eliezer took the head and R. Joshua the feet, and toward sunset they
    carried him until they came to the gates of Jerusalem.

H. The gate keepers said to them, "Who is this?"

I. They said to him, "It is a corpse. Do you not know that a corpse is not
    kept overnight in Jerusalem."

J. They said to them, "If it is a corpse, take him out," so they took him out
    and brought him out at sunset, until they came to Vespasian.

The critical element now follows: Yohanan and Vespasian. In the Bavli's
particular Yohanan's role is reduced, Vespasian taking the initiatve at each point:

8. When he reached the Romans, he said, "Peace to you O king..."
    Vespasian: Your life is forfeit on two counts, first, I am not a king, and
    you call me one, and, second, if I am a king, why did you not come until
    now?" Yohanan: You are a king + Is. 11:34. But Yohanan had no
    answer to the other question.

9. A messenger from Rome brought word that he had been made king.
    Vespasian could not put on his boot, or take off the one alreay on his
    foot, because his foot had swelled with pride. Yohanan explained wny
    and solved the problem.

10. "You can make a request of me." "Give me Yavneh and its sages, the
    chain of Gamaliel, and physicians to heal Sadoq."

The counterpart in The Fathers According to Rabbi Nathan is as follows:

K. They opened the ark and he stood before him.

L. He said to him, "Are you Rabban Yohanan ben Zakkai? Indicate what I
    should give you."

M. He said to him, "I ask from you only Yavneh, to which I shall go, and
    where I shall teach my disciples, establish prayer [Goldin: a prayer
    house], and carry out all of the religious duties."

N. He said to him, "Go and do whatever you want."

O. He said to him, "Would you mind if I said something to you."

P. He said to him, "Go ahead."]

Q. He said to him, "Lo, you are going to be made sovereign."

R. He said to him, "How do you know?

S. He said to him, "It is a tradition of ours that the house of the sanctuary will be given over not into the power of a commoner but of a king, for it is said, *And he shall cut down the thickets of the forest with iron, and Lebanon* [which refers to the Temple] *shall fall by a mighty one* (Is. 10:34)."

T. People say that not a day, two or three passed before a delegation came to him from his city indicating that the [former] Caesar had died and they had voted for him to ascend the throne.

It remains to note the two components of The Fathers According to Rabbi Nathan's story that make no appearance in the counterpart at b. Git. 56a-b:

IV:V.

1. A. ...**on deeds of lovingkindness:** how so?

    B. Lo, Scripture says, *For I desire mercy and not sacrifice, [and the knowledge of God rather than burnt offerings]* (Hos. 6:6).

2. A. One time [after the destruction of the Temple] Rabban Yohanan ben Zakkai was going forth from Jerusalem, with R. Joshua following after him. He saw the house of the sanctuary lying in ruins.

    B. R. Joshua said, "Woe is us for this place which lies in ruins, the place in which the sins of Israel used to come to atonement."

    C. He said to him, "My son, do not be distressed. We have another mode of atonement, which is like [atonement through sacrifice], and what is that? It is deeds of lovingkindness.

    D. For so it is said, *For I desire mercy and not sacrifice, [and the knowledge of God rather than burnt offerings]* (Hos. 6:6)."

The omission of the foregoing story seems to me a considerable matter. The following picture of the destruction of Jerusalem and Yohanan's reaction to it simply underlines the narrator's intent of placing Yohanan at the center of the entire story:

U. They brought him a [Goldin:] catapult and drew it up against the wall of Jerusalem.

V. They brought him cedar beams and put them into the catapult, and he struck them against the wall until a breach had been made in it. They brought the head of a pig and put it into the catapult and tossed it toward the limbs that were on the Temple altar.

W. At that moment Jerusalem was captured.

X. Rabban Yohanan ben Zakkai was in session and with trembling was looking outward, in the way that Eli had sat and waited: *Lo, Eli sat upon his seat by the wayside watching, for his heart trembled for the ark of God* (1 Sam. 4:13).

Y. When Rabban Yohanan ben Zakkai heard that Jerusalem had been destroyed and the house of the sanctuary burned in flames, he tore his garments, and his disciples tore their garments, and they wept and cried and mourned.

There is no counterpart in Bavli at all to Yohanan's colloquy with Joshua that deeds of lovingkindness constitute the counterpart to sacrifices of atonement. While the Bavli's version of the destruction of Jerusalem goes over a few of the same motifs as does the story in The Fathers According to Rabbi Nathan, nonetheless the two stories are essentially autonomous of one another. Let me state with emphasis what I believe we learn from this comparison and contrast:

What is fresh and indicative in The Fathers According to Rabbi Nathan is every major point of emphasis of the story of Yohanan's escape. The sage takes the central part; he undertakes all initiatives. He does more than merely react to the decisions and errors of others. He moreover forms the bridge from Temple to Torah, in that, rising from his bier, he points toward a center of Torah-study as the next step, out of Jerusalem. He further identifies a surrogate for the offerings, so long as the Temple lies in ruins, in acts of loving kindness, a doctrine that, in concrete deed, forms the counterpart to the sages' stress on the tamed emotions, conciliatory attitude, and ethic of self-abnegation, characteristic of both The Fathers and The Fathers According to Rabbi Nathan.

The upshot is that the sage now forms the model of Israel's salvation, and, therefore, by the way, also the definition of the Messiah as of other eschatological components of Judaism. This comparison of the two versions has carried us a long way from our original methodological statement. What we have seen indeed raises more questions than it settles. Once we view documents as the first issue of analysis, we compare two documents' picture of a single event.[20] These contrasting pictures require us to ask about the interests of the diverse authorships. They lead us in a direction scarcely imagined.

If I may say in conclusion what I think lies ahead, it is an issue of salvific theology. Who saves Israel? It is not the emperor but his counterpart, the sage. That conclusion (to us banal and commonlace) then points toward the further theological principle that the sage stands for Israel's salvation, with the consequence that the Messiah will be the quintessential sage, just as the later rabbinical compilations represent David as rabbi. The many stories about the sagacity of David, therefore of the Messiah, his mastery of the Torah, his formation in the model of the ideal sage, point toward profound reflection on Israel's true history and destiny. The Messiah will be not the charismatic wonder-worker portrayed by Vermes' *Jesus the Jew*, but the sage, master of the Torah *par excellence*. And yet, in honor of a scholar, I can think of no more fitting conclusion than to point to the power, imputed by the Judaism of the dual Torah, of learning to save humanity.

---

[20]G. Alon, *Mehqarim be toledot yisrael* (Tel Aviv, 1957), 1: 273ff., did the same, but he drew conclusions about what really happened in the first century, rather than about the interests of the story-tellers half a millenium later. Nonetheless, Alon must stand as the exception to the rule that all "Talmudic history" done in times past rested on a totally uncritical, indeed gullible and puerile, attitude of mind.

BIBLIOGRAPHY

Christianity and the Roman Empire in the Age of Constantine

Kurt Aland, *A History of Christianity. I. From the Beginnings to the Threshold of the Reformation*. Translated by James. L. Schaaf (Philadelphia, 1985: Fortress), pp. 171-204.

Roland Bainton, *The Penguin History of Christianity*. Volume 1. (Harmondsworth, 1964: Penguin Books).

N. H. Baynes, *Constantine the Great and the Christian Church* (New York, 1972: Oxford University Press). Second ed., preface by Henry Chadwick.

Peter Brown, *The Cult of the Saints. Its Rise and Function in Latin Christianity* (Chicago, 1981: University of Chicago Press).

Peter Brown, *Religion and Society in the Age of Saint Augustine* (N.Y., 1972: Harper & Row), pp. 46-73, 147-150.

Peter Brown, *The World of Late Antiquity. A.D. 150-750* (N.Y., 1971: Harcourt Brace Jovanovich, Inc.), pp. 7-95.

Jacob Burckhardt, *The Age of Constantine the Great* (N.Y., 1958: Doubleday Anchor Books). Translated by Moses Hadas.

F. L. Cross, *The Early Christian Fathers* (London, 1960: Gerald Duckworth & Co., Ltd.).

Louis Duchesne, *Early History of the Christian Church. From its Foundation to the End of the Fifth Century* (N.Y., 1922: Longmans Green & Co.).

W. H. C. Frend, *The Rise of Christianity* (Philadelphia, 1984: Fortress), pp. 473-650.

Erwin R. Goodenough, *The Church in the Roman Empire* (N.Y., 1931: Henry Holt. Repr., N.Y., 1970: Cooper Square Publishers, Inc.), pp. 41-61.

Adolf Harnack, *The Mission and Expansion of Christianity in the First Three Centuries*. Translated and edited by James Moffatt (London, 1908. Repr. Gloucester, 1972: Peter Smith).

J. M. Hussey, *The Byzantine World* (N.Y., 1961: Harper & Brothers).

A. H. M. Jones, *The Decline of the Ancient World* (London, 1966: Longmans) pp. 28-86.

J. N. D. Kelly, *Jerome. His Life, Writings, and Controversies* (New York, 1975: Harper & Row).

Samuel Laeuchli, *The Serpent and the Dove. Five Essays on Early Christianity* (Nashville, 1966: Abingdon), pp. 102-150.

Hans Lietzmann, *From Constantine to Julian. A History of the Early Church*, Volume III. Translated by Bertram Lee Woolf (N.Y., 1950: Charles Scribner's Sons).

Ramsey MacMullen, *Christianizing the Roman Empire (A.D. 100-400)* (New Haven, 1984: Yale University Press), pp. 43-51.

Ramsay MacMullen, *Constantine* (N.Y., 1969: Dial).

Arnaldo Momigliano, "Christianity and the Decline of the Roman Empire," in Arnaldo Momigliano, ed., *The Conflict between Paganism and Christianity in the Fourth Century* (Oxford, 191-16.63: Clarendon).

J. R. Palanque, G. Bardy, P. de Labriolle, G. de Plinval, and Louis Brehier, *The Church in the Christian Roman Empire. I. The Church and the Arian Crisis* (N.Y., 1953: Macmillan). With special reference to Pierre de Labriolle, "Christianity and Paganism in the Middle of the Fourth Century," pp. 220-257.

James Parkes, "Jews and Christians in the Constantinian Empire," *Studies in Church History* (Oxford, 1964: Basil Blackwell & Mott) 1:69-79.

Jaroslav Pelikan, *The Emergence of the Catholic Tradition (100-600). The Christian Tradition. A History of the Development of Doctrine.* Vol. 1. (Chicago, 1971: University of Chicago Press).

Rosemary Radford Ruether, *Faith and Fratricide. The Theological Roots of Anti-Semitism* (N.Y., 1979: Seabury Press).

Rosemary Radford Ruether, "Judaism and Christianity. Two Fourth-Century Religions," *Sciences Religieuses Studies in Religion* 1972, 2:1-10.

Marcel Simon, *Verus Israel. Etude sur les relations entre chrétiens et juifs dans l'empire romain* (135-425) (Paris, 1964: Editions E. de Boccard).

Robert L. Wilken, *The Christians as the Romans Saw Them* (New Haven, 1984: Yale University Press).

Robert L. Wilken, *John Chrysostom and the Jews. Rhetoric and Reality in the Late Fourth Century* (Berkeley, 1983: University of California Press. *The Transformation of the Classical Heritage*, ed. Peter Brown. Vol. VI).

The Jews in the Land of Israel in the Fourth Century

Michael Avi-Yonah, *The Jews under Roman and Byzantine Rule* (N.Y., 1976: Schocken, and Jerusalem, 1976: Magnes), pp. 158-231. On Julian, pp. 185-207.

Salo Wittmayer Baron, *A Social and Religious History of the Jews.* Second Edition, Revised and Enlarged. Volume II: *Ancient Times*, Part II (Philadelphia, 1952: Jewish Publication Society of America), pp. 172-214.

G. W. Bowersock, *Julian the Apostate* (Cambridge, 1978: Harvard University Press), pp. 120-122.

Peter Brown, *The World of Late Antiquity. A.D. 150-750* (N.Y., 1971: Harcourt Brace Jovanovich, Inc.), on Julian: pp. 92-93.

Louis Duchesne, *Early History of the Christian Church. From its Foundation to the End of the Fifth Century* (N.Y., 1922: Longmans Green & Co.). On Christianity in Palestine, pp. 486-491.

Frend, cited above, pp. 593-613.

John G. Gager, *The Origins of Anti-Semitism. Attitudes toward Judaism in Pagan and Christian Antiquity* (N.Y., 1983: Oxford University Press).

Johannes Geffcken, *The Last Days of Greco-Roman Paganism.* Translated by Sabine MacCormack (Amsterdam, N.Y., Oxford, 1978: North Holland Publishing Co.) Julian and paganism: pp. 136-159. I owe this reference to Robert Berchman.

Goodenough, cited above, pp. 58-61.

Kurt Hruby, *Juden und Judentum bei den Kirchenvaetern* (Zuerich, 1971: TheologischerVerlag).

A. H. M. Jones, *The Decline of the Ancient World* (London, 1966: Longmans) pp. 28-86.

A. H. M. Jones, *The Later Roman Empire, 284-602. A Social, Economic, and Administrative Survey* (Oxford, 1964: Basil Blackwell), pp. 944-950.

Hans Lietzmann, *From Constantine to Julian*, p. 281-283.

Ramsey MacMullen, *Christianizing the Roman Empire (A.D. 100-400)* (New Haven, 1984: Yale University Press), pp. 43-51.

Rosemary Radford Ruether, *Faith and Fratricide. The Theological Roots of Anti-Semitism* (N.Y., 1979: Seabury Press), pp. 183-195.

Marcel Simon, *Verus Israel. Etude sur les relations entre chrétiens et juifs dans l'empire romain* (135-425) (Paris, 19654: Editions E. de Boccard). On Julian: pp. 139-143.

Robert L. Wilken, *John Chrysostom and the Jews. Rhetoric and Reality in the Late Fourth Century* (Berkeley, 1983: University of California Press. *The Transformation of the Classical Heritage*, ed. Peter Brown. Vol. VI), on Julian, pp. 138-148.

Chrysostom and Judaism in the Land of Israel

Jacob Neusner, *Judaism in Society. The Evidence of the Yerushalmi. Toward the Natural History of a Religion* (Chicago, 1983: University of Chicago Press).

John G. Gager, *The Origins of Anti-Semitism. Attitudes toward Judaism in Pagan and Christian Antiquity* (N.Y., 1983: Oxford University Press), pp. 118-120.

Fred Allen Grissom, *Chrysostom and the Jews: Studies in Jewish-Christian Relations in Fourth-Century Antioch* (Ann Arbor, 1978: University Microfilms International).

C. Mervyn Maxwell, *Chrysostom's Homilies against the Jews. An English Translation.* Diss., University of Chicago, 1966. Unpublished. I did not see this item, which is listed in Grissom.

Rosemary Radford Ruether, *Faith and Fratricide. The Theological Roots of Anti-Semitism* (N.Y., 1979: Seabury Press), pp. 170-182.

Wayne A. Meeks and Robert L. Wilken, *Jews and Christians in Antioch* (Missoula, 1978: Scholars Press. Society of Biblical Literature Sources for Biblical Study Vol. 13).

Robert Payne, *The Holy Fire. The Story of the Fathers of the Eastern Church* (London, 1958). Chrysostom: pp. 222-262.

Marcel Simon, *Verus Israel. Etude sur les relations entre chrétiens et juifs dans l'empire romain* (135-425) (Paris, 1954: Editions E. de Boccard)., pp. 239-276.

Robert L. Wilken, *John Chrysostom and the Jews. Rhetoric and Reality in the Late Fourth Century* (Berkeley, 1983: University of California Press. *The Transformation of the Classical Heritage*, ed. Peter Brown. Vol. VI).

Part Three

ISSUES IN THE STUDY OF JUDAISM

Chapter Seven

Sociology and the Study of Judaism:
Nathan Glazer's *American Judaism*
after Thirty Years

When in 1954-1956 (the book came out in 1957) Nathan Glazer was writing his *American Judaism*, he was an editor of *Commentary*, and, scarcely 22 years old, I was a writer assigned to his editorship. So I knew him well and had the privilege of following the unfolding of his work on American Judaism. His act of generosity in thanking me in his preface attests to the character and conscience of a truly splendid person, all the more so since it was an act of grace, totally unearned by me. In many ways the book speaks for the man. It is graceful, lucid, encompassing, a wise and insightful work. No one has written a better book on the subject, and much recent work, e.g., Abraham Karp's, suffers by comparison. Karp's *Haven and Home, A History of the Jews in America*, is richer in narrative strength, telling story after story in an engaging way. But unlike Glazer, Karp asks no important questions, sustains no serious inquiry, and in the end tells the story for the story's sake, a kind of non-fiction fiction. The book makes a powerful case for the intellectual bankruptcy of the field of history. By contrast *American Judaism* places much into perspective, just as Glazer has in his important sociological writings placed into proper proportion long-term trends and developments of a variety of sorts.

Let us first appreciate the book's strengths. As history it is systematic and orderly. The periodization of American Judaism seems to me to have stood the test of time. No one has revised Glazer's picture of the important stages, the German immigration, 1825-1894, the relationship of Reform and Conservative Judaism, 1880-1900, the impact of the East European migration, 1880-1900, Judaism and Jewishness, 1920-1945 – all of these are classic and enduring contributions. It is difficult to find in later histories of Judaism in America any important innovations beyond the observations made by Glazer. His reflections on "the religion of American Jews" point toward the evolution, in America, of a Judaism different from all prior systems. The book moreover is literate, concise, engaging, readable, deserving of the vast audience it enjoyed. In outlining what went wrong, I pay Glazer the tribute of taking his work at utmost seriousness. More than that no one can ask. Glazer taught us to look at Judaism as a religion. I know of no prior work of its character and perspective. But Glazer himself did not grasp what religion is. And in that one judgment, I find the book's flaw.

I wonder whether one has to be religious to appreciate and understand religion. I hope not. But Glazer, rich in good will and understanding, amiable and brilliant, but secular to his bones, in the end could scarcely sort out what was really happening. He took so secular a perspective that, to him, religion found its testimonies in merely conventional data. So Glazer in no way understood what was happening even in his own time, and, fifteen years later, in the 1972 revision, he still did not grasp what was changing.

In *American Judaism* Glazer argues that religion in the crucible of modernity was in a process of disintegration, and we now know that that could not have been more wrong. Like the journalists who covered the Shah of Iran and missed the rebirth of Islam as a powerful force in the shaping of that nation, so Glazer saw nothing of what was about to change the face of American Judaism. The impact of the destruction of European Jewry and of the creation of the State of Israel upon the American Judaic imagination would write the next chapters in the history of American Judaism. Glazer in no way grasped that fact. He was right in understanding that American Jews would remain Jews. He missed the question that that fact was raising even then: what does it mean to be a Jew in America, a Jew of the third or fourth of fifth generation out of all contact with the emotional and psychological experiences of the inherited Judaism? As to American Judaism in its basic phenomenology, Glazer saw only that "the Jews have not stopped being Jews." "They still choose to be Jews." But they make little of that fact, so he thought. We now know that that fact would prove definitive, that a new Judaism was aborning. It would be a Judaism accessible to Jews without knowledge or experience of the received Judaism – and it would be powerful and dominant. The American Judaism of Holocaust and Redemption, gathering its earliest strength in the 1950s and fully in command of the American Jews' inner life by the 1970s, plays no role in Glazer's account of American Judaism. My guess is that his grasp of religion continued to limit itself to wholly conventional data. But today the Judaism of Holocaust and Redemption generates most of the (now-) conventional data.

Even the update of 1972 stresses essentially external facts, to the near-exclusion of what was happening in the inner life of the community. Radicalism now appears to have marked a passing phase, and the powerful reengagement of the American Jewish community with its own distinctive heritage and experience did not even then make an impression on Glazer. This is an essentially political reading of American Judaism. That is why it was, and remains, readily accessible. But it is also why Glazer provided guidance only about the politics of American Judaism, not about the religion of American Judaism. He faithfully replicated the inner strengths and weaknesses of the second generation Jewish scholar of good will and loyalty. He understood what he understood – that alone. And so do we all.

I
Two Problems of Method

1. From Impressionism to Analysis

Let us take up first of all the matter of method. Glazer's argument that religion and religious institutions and thought are not the same thing is both right and disastrous. No one can differ with his view that religion matters in "its place in the lives of ordinary people" (p. 129). But Glazer's explicit and powerful rejection of demographic evidence derived from sociological and social psychological studies, e.g., polling, would prove his undoing. In this book, as in nearly all of his other work, Glazer carries forward the humanistic tradition of sociology as a field defined by its topics. When a person writes about social questions, that person is a sociologist. Method then consists of making sound observations, developing worthwhile hypotheses, offering perceptive insights: high class free association. None would denigrate the power of that free association to produce insight received as self-evidently valid. But the possibility of testing that insight, building on it, producing further theses for future testing – that was closed off. Glazer's work, joined but another classic, Marshall Sklare's *Conservative Judaism*, as well as the numerous, equally impressionistic and journalistic – if equally insightful – writings, in the 1960s and 1970s, of Charles Liebman, relied on intuition, educated guess-work.

The approach of the now-obsolete school of sociology as a set of topics yielded slight opportunity for the falsification and verification of encompassing theses. But soon after the appearance of this version of American Judaism and how it was to be studied, a revolution was to take place which would render all former work obsolete, a mere curiosity. For impressionism would give way to the collection and analysis of facts through solid demographic method. Within a decade of the appearance of *American Judaism*, a totally fresh reading of American Judaism would draw upon different data to reach far more suggestive conclusions. The principal figure in the social scientific description of Judaism and the Jews, Calvin Goldscheider, completed his first book, *Jewish Americans: Three Generations in a Jewish Community*, not ten years after Glazer's book, yet in approach and conception, it might as well have been a century. His subsequent books, on the more encompassing methodological themes, e.g., *Population, Modernization, and Social Structure* (1971), *The Ethnic Factor in Family Structure and Mobility* (1978), and the newest and most important work, *Jewish Continuity and Change: Emerging Patterns in America* (1985) took the guess work out of the social study of American Judaism. Goldscheider and his co-workers transformed the field from one that relied on impressions to one that generated hypotheses for testing against solid facts.

2. From The Ethnic to the Academic, Comparative Perspective on the Jews

A second methodological flaw should not escape attention. The work reflects that ethnocentrism that from then to now commonly characterizes Judaic studies. *American Judaism* totally lacks a comparative dimension. Whatever was happening to the Jews affected them alone. Glazer failed to propose a broader context in which to interpret his observations. In this regard, Will Herberg's *Catholic Protestant Jew* was in method a far superior interpretation of the Judaism of that time. That context can have derived from a larger theory of what was happening in America, on the one side, or from a serious and sustained interest in the comparison of the Jews to other groups, on the other. Even before *American Judaism*, Oscar Handlin had presented his classic work, *The Uprooted*, to provide a theoretical framework within which to study diverse ethnic groups. But, while obviously literate in the comparative study of ethnic groups – in which, after all, Glazer was to make his principal contributions in the 1960s in his study, *Beyond the Melting Pot* – Glazer here made remarkably little use of Handlin's broader insights. The failure to compare and contrast American Judaism to its counterpart systems in American society, Protestant or Catholic for instance, or American Jews to their corresponding structures, Poles or Italians or Irish, for example, derives the work of the power to persuade. For its propositions prove episodic and not systematic. They do not relate the detail to a larger whole.

The failure to compare proves still more deleterious when we call to mind Glazer's exclusive attention to American Judaism, as though that Judaism in its day (and not solely in its past, to which he does attend) bore no points of comparison and contrast with the Judaisms of Jews elsewhere in the world. Accordingly, we look in vain for attention to what marked American Judaism as American, and to what joined American Judaism to other Judaisms of the same day and age. We do not therefore find the answers to the two questions that in my judgment must define the agenda of anyone claiming to describe, analyze, and interpret American Judaism: how is it American, and how is it Judaic, that is, how does it stand (in the present, not only in the past) in a linear and incremental relationship with Judaism under like conditions and unlike as well. These questions do not win a warm reception in the American Jewish Historical Society. When I raised them in my address to the Society, the Quarterly refused to print that address, though the invitation to give the paper included a pledge to print it. Its failure to review my books that have a bearing on American Jewish studies for twenty-five years is matched by the character of the reviewing that has taken place since the *Todschweigen* – murder by silence – came to an end. So Glazer's failure replicates the prevailing ethnocentrism joined to the American exceptionalism characteristic of the field as a whole.

In a word, the book is utterly descriptive, completely lacking a broader interpretive framework, an exercise in high class show and tell. Here too we may invoke for contrast the work of Calvin Goldscheider and Alan Zuckerman, *The Transformation of the Jews* (1984), a field theory for the comparative study of Jewish communities in modern times. Goldscheider and Zuckerman cover not a single community but all of them, all together, and show, once again on demographic and other solid factual bases, the possibilities for comparison and contrast, on the one side, and the essential unities of contemporary Judaic experience, on the other. In treating American Judaism out of phase with the rest of the Judaic world, Glazer repeated the error of American exceptionalism. In placing that Judaism into its broader international context, Goldscheider and Zuckerman provided that encompassing perspective that, at last, made sense of everything all together and all at once. Glazer here too marks the end of an age of history and sociology. Within a very short time, it would be clear, people would not carry forward the approach he took and the method he adopted.

II
Problems of Substance:
Glazer's Failure of Perception

This brings us to that other matter, the one of substance. Does the work stand the test of time in its description of American Judaism? The answer is an unqualified negative. In no way can we find in Glazer's picture the precursors of the principal developments of American Judaism in the 1960s and beyond. In fact, nothing we now know mattered in American Judaism beyond Glazer's book makes its appearance – even on the distant horizon – in that book. Glazer thought that American Judaism was disintegrating. But it was only changing. And the following decades showed that, in the aggregate, the changes would testify not to disintegration but to astounding energy and renewal. Let me point to four stunning omissions, all of which, we now realize, originated in the very age in which Glazer did his work.

1. The Renaissance of Orthodoxy and the Decline of the Judaism of "Jewish-But-Not-Too-Jewish"

The second and third generations in general sought a Judaism that would not separate Jews from other Americans. To state matters in a rough and ready way, they wanted to be Jewish, but not too Jewish – not so Jewish that they could not also find a place in that undifferentiated American society ("Americans all") which existed mostly in their minds. Integrationist Judaisms therefore flourished to the near demise of Orthodoxy as segregationist. Glazer accurately described that attitude, that Judaic system of Americanism. Glazer's perspective on integrationist-Orthodoxy clearly reflects the inexorable decline, from generation to generation, from the immigrant to the third generation. He however did not perceive that Orthodoxy in a renewed immigration, that of the period after World War II, was even then gathering strength. That Orthodoxy, shaped in the experience of Europe in World War II, would not only exhibit a resilience not shown by the earlier version, but it also would reshape Orthodox Judaism in America into a more militant, more aggressive, and less apologetic statement than anyone had ever known. The rebirth of violently segregationist Orthodoxy, both Hasidic and otherwise, plays slight role in Glazer's picture, even though Glazer did pay some attention to pockets of Hasidism. Glazer saw none of this, although it was even then taking root and gathering strength. He treated the renewal of Orthodoxy as part of the much more limited phenomenon of the growth of Hasidism. This was an error of judgment and perspective; he did not see what he did not expect to see.

2. The Demise of the Rabbinate and of Classroom Jewish Education

When Glazer wrote this book, the rabbinate was a powerful and effective force in American Judaism. Glazer in no way perceived the astonishing demise of the rabbinate as an effective and shaping element in American Judaism. True, he noted that the new ideas were coming from theologians and writers, outsiders to the rabbinate. But he did not realize that the conventional synagogue with its strong rabbinical voice was losing hold, and the rabbinate as the single most influential force in American Judaism was passing from the scene. This failure of perception forms part of his larger failure to assess the long-term decline of Jewish education in its formal expression. Yet even in the 1950s the standards of education were declining, and the informal educational system that was to develop outside of the synagogues or on their fringes, for instance in Community Centers and in summer camps and youth movements, was taking shape. Glazer missed the shift in the media of education as well as the remarkable failure of formal education to make an impact of a lasting sort on the values of the third generation of American Jews. Once more he looked backward. The second generation knew a powerful rabbinate, of articulate and politically consequential personalities. He did not grasp that, over the next twenty years, the rabbinate would turn into something far less important than it had been. The second generation took for granted that the afternoon Hebrew school would persist and that, in the main, Jewish education would take place in formal structures. But the day school for the most committed would dominate, and the afternoon school would gradually deteriorate.

Glazer took for granted that the synagogue of the third generation, in inheriting the educational system built by others altogether, would carry forward the system. The opposite happened. The synagogue's control of Jewish education weakened the educational system, just as the synagogue as the base for the rabbinate led to a diminished version of the rabbinate. In both cases the reason is clear, the growth of an assertive lay leadership, no longer subservient to the synagogue and its values, let alone to the rabbinate.

3. The Rise of the "Organized Jewish Community" and the Organizational Model for American Judaism

The third generation enjoyed a self-confidence lacking in the first and the second, because it was secure in its mastery of American life and values, and because it was, in the main, highly educated through the baccalaureate degree. Consequently lay leadership no longer deferred to the rabbinate, since the rabbi (like the lawyer or the doctor) was not the only college graduate in the community, and the values of the laity were set in judgment over the programs and activities of the synagogue as well. But this development of an assertive laity taking over Jewish community life, which Glazer missed completely, came about because of the events of the period in which Glazer himself reached maturity. Specifically, because of the crisis presented by the German nation's war against the Jews, the Jews had to do what they could to constitute themselves into a political entity, capable of mass action. So the leadership of the sort that came to the fore responded to the requirement of the times. What was what was needed was administrators, not intellectuals, bureaucrats, not charismatic thinkers formed the cadre of the hour. In an age in which, to survive at all, Jews had to address the issues of politics and economics, build a state (in the State of Israel) and a massive and effective set of organizations capable of collective political action (in the USA), not sages but *politicians* in the deepest sense of the word, namely, those able to do the work of the polity, alone could do what had to be done . And they did come forward and they did take over.

4. The Mythopoeic Dominance of "the Holocaust" within the Judaism of "Holocaust and Redemption"

The power of the State of Israel to shape the values of American Jewry in no way is recognized in this book. Yet by the mid-1950s it was clear that the State of Israel had made important changes in the mind and imagination of American Jewry. Glazer wrote before jet travel had made commonplace the pilgrimage to the Holy Land. He cannot have been expected to foresee the powerful impact of the events of 1967 on the messianic imagination of American Jewry. But he did not even raise for speculation the issues at hand. American Judaism works with the raw materials made available by contemporary experience – emotions on the one side, politics on the other. Jews in the American, European, African, and Australian worlds no longer regard "being Jewish" as a matter of intellect at all, and so far as they frame a worldview for themselves, it bears few points of intersection with the Judaic canon. The experiences that elicit immediate response in emotions, that dictate immediate and palpable action in political terms, relate to the destruction of European Jewry, "the Holocaust," and the maintenance of the State of Israel, "redemption." Together these two matters – "Holocaust and Redemption" – form the dominant and powerful theme of Judaism in America today. Glazer scarcely mentioned either one. Recognizing too late what had already happened, the deracinization of the Jews, the third generation then attempted to create a domestic Judaism resting on experiences no one had undergone or would want to.

But, as we have noted in treating the rabbinate and Jewish education, American Jewry form a community of Jews without books. They have focused such imaginative energies as they generated upon "the Holocaust," and they centered their eschatological fantasies on "the beginning of our redemption" in the State of Israel. But they had not gone through the one nor chosen to participate in the other. Not having lived through the mass murder of European Jewry, American Jews restated the problem of evil in unanswerable form and then transformed that problem into an obsession. Not choosing to settle in the State of Israel, moreover, American Jews further defined redemption, the resolution of the problem of evil, in terms remote from their world. Glazer – to his credit – could not imagine such a situation. His book on American Judaism took for granted that the Judaism of America would remain Judaism. He never foresaw that it would lose all touch with the inherited Judaism of the dual Torah, either in its classic form or in its modern continuations in Reform, Orthodoxy, Reconstructionism, and Conservative Judaism alike.

III

What Went Wrong with *American Judaism*

In fact the immediate and deserved success of the book masked its long-term failure. It gave no clue about what would happen. It offered no model on how to find out. In substance and in method the work in no way stood the test of time. The book exhibits limitations in both method and substance. *American Judaism* is episodic and unsystematic, impressionistic and lacking in rigorous testing of theses. Superficial and shallow like many other works, so common in American Jewish history and sociology, of mere collecting and arranging of facts, it emphasizes description to the exclusion of sustained analysis: the framing and testing of hypotheses of general intelligibility. In American Jewish history the model is the antiquarian, mindless gathering of information. In American Jewish sociology (then, not now, as I have explained), the hunters and gatherers treat the Jews in isolation from other groups in America as well as from other Jewish communities elsewhere.

Taken as a model of its genre, *American Judaism*'s strengths are those of a brilliant observer, that is, the essential journalist: what you see is what you get. Its weaknesses are those of the same sort of scholar. A work of guesswork, of show and tell, it led nowhere – though other books of the same age and the following decade would rehearse its strengths, to be sure. Not only so, but we now realize that its account of American Judaism would be rendered obsolete within a moment of its publication. It captured not what was happening but what had already run its course. In its acute description of how things were then, the work missed what was even at that moment starting to develop. That is what happens when show and tell takes the place of the asking of interesting questions, the positing of hypotheses worth testing, the framing of the issues such as *why? why not? what if?* and, above all, *why this, not that?*

In method therefore Glazer's *American Judaism* did not generate further work along the (essentially descriptive) lines it laid out. The book (and many like it) stands at the end of an era of sociology defined by the topics one studies. Glazer explicitly rejected the methods that would demonstrate their power in the years between the first and the second editions of his book. In substance *American Judaism* looks not to the future but to its even-then-dated present. In no way did the book point toward what, in fact, was to take place in the next phase of American Judaism. So the dying version of American Judaism, the one described by Glazer, scarcely outlived the age of the writing of the book that would form its epitaph. Glazer saw himself as the biographer, but turned out to write the obituary, of the Judaism he called American. But as an obituary the book will long serve as the definitive account of its subject: the brief moment of passing, the poised movement from the second generation to the third, the end of the old compromises, the beginning of the hard choices.

IV

What Changed in America:
The Next Thirty Years

In the past hundred years in American Judaism, Israel – being Jewish – has become only one of several things that Jews would be: we are also Americans, also workers, also Republicans or Democrats or many things, – but never only Israel, God's people. And that theory of Israel matches in social terms the conception of the individual person as well. For in the received Torah Israel, the Jew, lived out life in the rhythm of sanctification of the hear and now, realizing in concrete deeds the Torah's words, once more, not only always but also Israel. It was not a romance, it was a marriage: not a brief intense encounter in a motel room, but a long-term, if sometimes unexciting, meeting in bed every night.

A Jew in Eastern Europe, within the received system, wore Jewish clothes and talked a Jewish language and in it said thoughts he or she took for granted were uniquely Jewish. Jews in America do not – and do not want to. Nor are things different in the State of Israel. Zionism in its Israeli realization produced Jews whose commitment to profession – state-building, army-building, institution-building – in no way demanded particularly Judaic (in context: Zionist) action and activity. Now as the century draws to its close, the divisions within a human existence, setting apart the Jewish from the not-Jewish, have yielded two modes of Judaic existence. The large majority likes things as they are: we are many things, and an important one is being Jewish.

For a small minority, "being Jewish" in the partial definitions of available systems leaves dissatisfaction. This small minority now determines to find a mode of "being Jewish" – in our terms, a Judaic system – that would encompass not part but the whole of life. And it is the most interesting thing happening in American Judaism today. The evidences accumulate within Reform as much as Orthodoxy, with Reform day schools taking root, with a strong Reform movement growing in the State of Israel, and with a powerful Reform commitment to a rejudaiziation of the assimilated or non-Jewish Jew defining the policy of Reform Judaism in America. The Conservative movement's institutions are in disarray these days, but Conservative Judaism as the vital center remains positioned at the center of things, and its capacity to hold conflicting commitments in the balance appeals to the generation of return. The center, for example, of all egalitarian Judaism is in the Conservative movement, for the Orthodox cannot accommodate the cultic equality of women, and the Reform cannot meet the demands of the observant egalitarians. And that is only one example of the astonishing power of the vital center. Orthodoxy, for its part, has provided the road to Judaism for the bulk of the generation of return in its most serious components. American Orthodox, in particular, gets the credit. In the State of Israel, the yeshivot that welcome baalei teshuvah were founded by American Orthodox rabbis and are maintained by them. They had nthe imagination to understand what was happening, the wit to know what to do about it. Orthodoxy in this country enjoys a rebirth of popularity because of the movement of reversion and because people quite fairly identify with Orthodoxy when they look for the authentic and the true Judaism to which to return. True enough, Orthodoxy often has not known what to do with the reversioners. But, in the main, the record is clear.

The generation of return to Judaism, which marks today and points toward the future, is made up of Jews who wish not a protracted romance but a marriage: something permanent, whole, enduring, and complete. For larger numbers in American Judaism, "being Jewish" represents a kind of on-going romantic attachment: episodic but intense. American Judaism has left Jews free to be many things, some of them Jewish (or, in our terms, Judaic), others not. That represents its appeal. But that appeal now finds significant competition with a different ideal, and the result is only to the good.

No permanent and encompassing commitment requires American Jews to be only or mainly Jewish (that is, in our language, devotees of the American Judaic system). But the romantic attachment did mean that, when these Jewish Americans chose to "be Jewish," they entered into an intense and exhausting encounter. And, when not, not. The emotional appeal of Holocaust and Redemption should not be missed in any account of romantic or "motel" Judaism. "The Holocaust" in its rites and rituals allows ready access to deep feelings, direct encounter with transcendental experience. But it does not demand, or even make provision for, protracted feelings and lasting encounter with that transcendent moment of redemption. Israelism (not a disciplined Zionism but a generalized sentiment) presents us with another expression of "motel" Judaism. When carrying out the critical act within the American Judaic way of life of visiting the State of Israel, American Judaists end up not as pilgrims, come to celebrate and stay, but as tourists. They go home and re-enter those other dimensions of human experience that they share with others in the same time and place: undifferentiated Americans. While in the State of Israel they nod sagely when Israelis tell them to come on aliyah, and the young people come back from their high school or summer programs committed to make aliyah (just as long as they are committed to the boyfriend or girlfriend of the moment, that is, teen-age romance with its half-life of three weeks).

So it might be said that, as to the diverse Judaic systems of the modern age, what they had in common was a certain transient intensity: romance, not marriage. Deep, enduring commitment for about fifteen minutes is what people were prepared to give. By the end of the twentieth century, however, we see that some want in, and, so far as new and vigorous efforts as system-building take place, they find their power and vitality in the magnetism of the received Judaism, not in its Orthodox form as a well-explained and well-considered world, but in its version as a self-evidently valid statement of how things "really" are. But things are not all that simple. The road from outside to inside, of course, can never open again, for as Al Ghazali said, "There is no hope in returning to a traditional faith after it has once been abandoned, since the essential condition in the holder of a traditional faith is that he should not know he is a traditionalist."

On that account, the reversioners to the received Judaism of the dual Torah, paramount in the system-building of the Judaisms of the day, rightly point to themselves as the single important and influential Judaism of the day. Theirs is the energy, theirs is the power of renewal, and theirs is the Judaism that, at this moment, appears to enjoy the richest promise in the twenty-first century. Their numbers prove less then their influence. But their competition does not add up to much in either intellectual or social dimensions. What we shall make of all this only the next ten years will tell. For we shall soon complete a quarter-century since the 1967 war, which marks the beginning of the age of reversion and the generation of return. What is going to come of it all we may soon assess. Who can claim to see the next thirty years more or less perceptively than, between 1957 and 1987, Glazer perceived the future?

Chapter Eight

Art and the Study of Judaism

I

The Problem of Synagogue Art in the Study of Ancient Judaism

What we learn about Judaism from the art of the ancient synagogues has been debated for most of the twentieth century. When we follow those debates, we shall understand how the visual arts – with stress on the problem of interpreting the meaning of art and symbolism – affect our understanding of the religious life of people we know, otherwise, only from holy books. The particular case at hand brings us to the critical issue in the study of ancient Judaism, from the first to the seventh centuries. The literary evidence overall portrays that Judaism in one way, the artistic evidence, in a quite different way. That is why synagogue art presents a problem in the study of ancient Judaism.

The visual materials we shall now consider contribute in three ways to the study of Judaism as a religion. First, any introduction to Judaism, beginning to the present, will raise questions about modes and media of religious expression, and, among these, art in iconic and other graphic form will take pride of place. The intense interest in the art and architecture of synagogues, ancient, medieval, and modern, finds full justification. For these speak vividly and concretely about the world-view and way of life of the Judaism for which those synagogues have been constructed. Second, a study of ancient Judaism will require attention to the varieties of the Judaic systems of late antiquity. As I shall emphasize, critical to such a study – hence to all courses on ancient Judaism – will be the interpretation of synagogue art, with special attention to its symbolism. Finally, a course on art in religion will derive from Judaism a most interesting case study of a religious tradition that, at one and the same time, prohibits the representation of God and also makes ample use of representational art (not merely abstraction) for religious expression. These three types of courses only begin the list of the important ways in which we learn about religion from the study of the art of Judaism – not to mention of the complex relationships between Judaism and the arts.

Most ancient synagogues, both in the land of Israel and abroad, reveal important decorations on their walls. The decorations turn up fairly consistently. Some symbols recur nearly everywhere. Other symbols never make an appearance at all. A *shofar*, a *lulab* and *ethrog*, a *menorah*, all of them

Jewish in origin, but also such pagan symbols as a Zodiac, with symbols difficult to find in Judaic written sources – all of these form part of the absolutely fixed symbolic vocabulary of the synagogues of late antiquity. By contrast, symbols of other elements of the calendar year, at least as important as those that we do find, turn out never to make an appearance. And, obviously, a vast number of pagan symbols proved useless to Judaic synagogue artists. It follows that the artists of the synagogues spoke through a certain set of symbols and ignored other available ones. That simple fact makes it highly likely that the symbols they did use meant something to them, represented a set of choices, delivered a message important to the people who worshipped in those synagogues.

Because the second commandment forbids the making of graven images of God, however, people have long taken for granted that Judaism should not produce an artistic tradition. Or, if it does, it should be essentially abstract and non-representational, much like the rich decorative tradition of Islam. But from the beginning of the twentieth century, archaeologists began to uncover in the Middle East, North Africa, the Balkans, and the Italian peninsula, synagogues of late antiquity richly decorated in representational art. For a long time historians of Judaism did not find it possible to accommodate the newly discovered evidence of an on-going artistic tradition. They did not explain that art, they explained it away. One favorite explanation was that "the people" produced the art, but "the rabbis," that is, the religious authorities, did not approve it or at best merely tolerated it. That explanation rested on two premises. First, because talmudic literature – the writings of the ancient rabbis over the first seven centuries of the common era – made no provision for representational art, therefore representational art was subterranean and "unofficial." Second, rabbis are supposed to have ruled everywhere, so the presence of iconic art had to indicate the absence of rabbinic authority.

Aware of the existence of sources which did not quite fit into the picture that emerged from talmudic literature as it was understood in those years or which did not serve the partly apologetic purposes of their studies, scholars such as George Foot Moore in his *Judaism. The Age of the Tannaim* [1] posited the existence of "normative Judaism," which is to be described by reference to talmudic literature and distinguished from "heretical" or "sectarian" or simply "non-normative" Judaism of "fringe sects." Normative Judaism, exposited so systematically and with such certainty in Moore's *Judaism*, found no place in its structure for art, with its overtones of mysticism (except "normal mysticism"), let alone magic, salvific or eschatological themes except within a rigidly reasonable and mainly ethical framework; nor did Judaism as these scholars understood it make use of the religious symbolism or ideas of the Hellenistic world, in which it existed essentially apart and at variance.

---

[1] Cambridge, 1927: Harvard University Press.

Today no informed student of Judaism in late antiquity works within the framework of such a synthesis, for this old way is no longer open. The testimony of archaeology, especially of the art of the synagogues of antiquity, now finds a full and ample hearing. In understanding the way in which art contributes to the study of the history of a religion, we find in Judaism in late antiquity a fine example of the problems of interpretation and how they are accommodated and solved. Let us trace the steps by which people began to accept the importance of art – symbolic, representational, abstract, iconic – and survey the more important figures in the labor, now completed, of absorbing art as evidence of religious belief.

II
Erwin R. Goodenough and the Symbolism of Judaism

In teaching about ancient Judaism through reference to the art of the synagogue, we deal with one towering figure. Erwin Ramsdell Goodenough was the greatest historian of religion America ever produced, and his *Jewish Symbols in the Greco-Roman Period* is his major work.[2] Goodenough provided for the artistic remains of the synagogue a complete and encompassing interpretation, and, to the present time, his view remains the principal theory by which the art of the synogogue is approached.

Along with Moore's *Judaism* and Goodenough's *Jewish Symbols* no other single work has so decisively defined the problem of how to study religion in general, and, by way of example, Judaism in particular. Goodenough worked on archaeological and artistic evidence, so took as his task the description of Judaism out of its symbolic system and vocabulary. Moore worked on literary evidence, so determined to describe Judaism as a systematic theological structure. Between the two of them they placed the systematic study of Judaism in the forefront of the academic study of religion and dictated the future of the history of religion in the West. It would encompass not only the religions of non-literate and unfamiliar peoples, but also of literate and very familiar ones. In all, Moore and Goodenough have left a legacy of remarkable power and intellectual weight. Through the study of Judaism they showed how to describe, analyze, and interpret religious systems, contexts and contents alike.

The importance of reading Judaism's art with Goodenough cannot be overstated. Goodenough frames issues as they should be addressed in teaching religious studies. That is because he treats the study of religion as a generalizing

---

[2]The complete bibliography of his writings, by A. Thomas Kraabel, appears in J. Neusner, ed., *Religions in Antiquity. Essays in Memory of Erwin Ramsdell Goodenough* (Leiden, 1968: E. J. Brill), pp. 621-632. My abridged edition of his *Symbols* will be published shortly by Princeton University Press. In what follows I have drawn on parts of my introduction to that book, as well as on my introduction to the literature on Goodenough's work, printed in the appendix of the same book.

science, and he examines a particular case because it serves to exemplify matters of wider interest. Through the specific case of the symbolism of ancient Judaism and problems in its interpretation, Goodenough raises a pressing general question. It is how to make sense of the ways in which people use art to express their deepest yearnings. And how are we to make sense of that art in the study of the people who speak, without resort to words, through it. The importance of Goodenough's work lies in his power to make the particular into something exemplary and suggestive, to show that, in detail, we confront the whole of human experience in some critical aspect. Goodenough asks when a symbol is symbolic. He wants to know how visual symbols speak beyond words and despite words. Goodenough studied ancient Jewish symbols because he wanted to explain how that happens and what we learn about the human imagination from the power of symbols to express things words cannot or do not convey. It is difficult to point to a more engaging and critical problem in the study of humanity than the one Goodenough took for himself. That is why, twenty years after the conclusion of his research, a new generation will find fresh and important the research and reflection of this extraordinary man.

III

Goodenough's Review of the Archaeological Evidence for Jewish Art in the Synagogue

The first three volumes of Goodenough's *Jewish Symbols* collect the Jewish realia uncovered in the past by archaeologists working in various parts of the Mediterranean basin. Goodenough's interest in these artifacts began, he reports, with the question of how it was possible, within so brief a span as fifty years, that the teachings of Jesus could have been accommodated so completely to the Hellenistic world. Not only central ideas, but even widespread symbols of early Christianity appear in retrospect to have been appropriated from an environment alien to Jewish Palestine. "For Judaism and Christianity to keep their integrity, any appropriations from paganism had to be very gradual" (I, p. 4). Yet within half a century of Jesus' death, Christian churches were well established in Hellenistic cities, and Christian teachings were within the realm of discourse of their citizens. If the "fusion" with Hellenistic culture occurred as quickly as it did, then it seems best explained by reference to an antecedent and concurrent form of Hellenistic Judaism that had successfully and naturally achieved a comfortable accommodation with Hellenism. Why so? Goodenough maintains that the Judaism known from the writings of the ancient rabbis, hence, "rabbinical Judaism," could not accommodate itself to Hellenism. Goodenough's main point follows: "While rabbinical Judaism can adjust itself to mystic rites ... it would never have originated them."

That is to say, we should look vainly in the circles among whom Talmudic literature developed for the origins of the various symbols and ideas of

Hellenistic Judaism. It follows that evidences of the use of the pagan inheritance of ancient civilization for the specifically Jewish purposes derives from Jews whose legacy is not recorded in the pages of the Talmud. So Goodenough's first question is, if the rabbis whose writings we possess did not lead people to use the symbols at hand, then who did? If, as Goodenough contends, not all Jews (perhaps, not even many Jews) were under the hegemony of the rabbis of the Talmud, who did not lead the way in the utilization of pagan symbols in synagogue decoration, then what shall we think if we discover substantial, identifiably Jewish purposes of forms we should expect to uncover not in a Jewish but rather in a pagan setting?

One conclusion would render these finds insignificant. If illegal, symbolic representations of lions, eagles, masks, victory wreaths, not to mention the Zodiac and other astral symbols were made for merely ornamental purposes, "the rabbis" may not have approved of them, but had to "reckon with reality" and "accepted" them. That view was commonly expressed but never demonstrated. For his part Goodenough repeats litanously, symbol by symbol and volume by volume, (see I, p. 108) that it is difficult to agree that the handful of symbolic objects so carefully chosen from a great variety of available symbols, so frequently repeated at Dura, Randanini, Bet Alpha, Hammam Lif and elsewhere, used to the exclusion of many other symbols, and so sloppily drawn that no ornamental artist could have done them, constituted mere decoration. Furthermore, it begs the question to say that these symbols were "merely" ornamental: why specifically these symbols and *no others*? Why in these settings?

Goodenough attempts to uncover the meaning of various symbols discovered in substantial quantities throughout the Jewish world of antiquity. His procedure is, first, to present the finds *in situ*, second (and quite briefly), to expound a method capable of making sense out of them, and, third, to study each extant symbol with the guidance of this method. Goodenough presents a majestic array of photographs and discussion, for the first time presenting in one place a portrait of Jewish art in antiquity, one as magnificent as will ever appear. The Bollingen Foundation deserves credit for making possible Goodenough's remarkable edition of the art. Nothing like it has been done in the thirty years since the first three volumes made their appearance.

In his survey Goodenough begins with the art of the Jewish tombs in Palestine and of their contents, studying the remains by chronological periods, and thus indicating the great changes in funerary art that developed after 70 A.D. Goodenough proceeds (I, ch. 5) to the synagogues of Palestine, their inscriptions and contents, describing (sometimes briefly) more than four dozen sites. He concludes (I, p. 264):

> In these synagogues certainly was a type of ornament, using animals, human figures, and even pagan deities, in the round, in deep relief, or in mosaic, which was in sharp distinction to what was proper for Judaism

> ... The ornament we are studying is an interim ornament, used only after
> the fall of Jerusalem and before the completion or reception of the
> Talmud. The return to the old standards, apparently a return to the
> halakhic Judaism that the rabbis advocated, is dramatically attested by
> the destruction, obviously by Jews themselves, of the decorative
> abominations, and only for the abominations, in these synagogues.
> Only when a synagogue was abandoned as at Dura ... are the original
> effects preserved or the devastations indiscriminate.

The decoration in these synagogues must have seemed more than merely
decorative to those who destroyed them so discriminatingly.

Goodenough argues that distinction between fetishistic magic and religion is
generally subjective, and imposed from without by the embarrassed investigator.
He points out (II, p. 156) that magical characteristics, such as the effort to
achieve material benefits by fundamentally compulsive devices are common
(whether we recognize them as such or not) in the "higher" religions. It is
certainly difficult to point to any religious group before the present time that did
not quite openly expect religion to produce some beneficial consequence and if
that consequence was to take place after death, it was no less real. Hence
Goodenough concludes that "magic is a term of judgment," and thus the
relevance of charms and amulets is secured. Goodenough summarizes the
consequences of his evidence as follows (II, p. 295):

> The picture we have got of this Judaism is that of a group still intensely
> loyal to Yao Sabaoth, a group which buried its dead and built its
> synagogues with a marked sense that it was a peculiar people in the eyes
> of God, but which accepted the best of paganism (including its most
> potent charms) as focusing in, finding its meaning in, the supreme Yao
> Sabaoth. In contrast to this, the Judaism of the rabbis was a Judaism
> which rejected all of the pagan religious world (all that it could) ...
> Theirs was the method of exclusion, not inclusion.

The problem is then how to establish a methodology by which material amassed
in the first three volumes may be studied and interpreted.

IV

Goodenough's Interpretation of Symbols: The Method

Goodenough argues that the written documents, particularly the Talmudic
ones, do not suffice to interpret symbols so utterly alien to their spirit, and in
any case, so rarely discussed in them. Even where some of the same symbols
inscribed on graves or synagogues are mentioned in the Bible or Talmud, it is
not always obvious that those textual references engage the mind of the artist.
Why not? Because the artists follow the conventions of Hellenistic art, and not
only Hellenistic art, but the conventions of the artists who decorated cultic
objects and places in the same locale in which, in the Jewish settings, the

symbols have turned up.. Goodenough asks for a general theory to make sense of all the evidence, something no one else gives, and asks (IV, p. 10):

> Where are we to find the moving cause in the taking over of images, and with what objective were they taken over? It seems to me that the motive for borrowing pagan art and integrating it into Judaism throughout the Roman world can be discovered only by analyzing the art itself.

An interpretive method needs to be devised. Goodenough succinctly defines this method:

> The first step ... must be to assemble ... the great body of evidence available ... which, when viewed as a whole, demands interpretation as a whole since it is so amazingly homogeneous for all parts of the Empire. The second step is to recognize that we must first determine what this art means in itself, before we begin to apply to it as proof texts any possible unrelated statements of the Bible or the Talmud. That these artifacts are unrelated to proof texts is a statement which one can no more make at the outset than one can begin with the assumption of most of my predecessors, that if the symbols had meaning for Jews, that meaning must be found by correlating them with Talmudic and biblical phrases ... The art has rarely, and then only in details, been studied for its possible meaning in itself: this is the task of these volumes.

If the succeeding volumes exhibit a monotonous quality, as one symbol after another comes under discussion and produces an interpretation very close to the ones already given,it is because of his tenacious use of a method clearly thought through, clearly articulated and clearly appplied throughout. What is this method? The problem here is to explain how Goodenough determines what this art means in itself. Goodenough begins by asking (IV, p. 27):

> Admitting that the Jews would not have remained Jews if they had used these images in pagan ways and with pagan explanations, do the remains indicate a symbolic adaptation of pagan figures to Judaism or merely an urge to decoration?

Goodenough defines a symbol as "an image or design with a significance to one who uses it quite beyond its manifest content ... an object or a pattern which, whatever the reason may be, operates upon men and causes effect in the viewer beyond mere recognition of what is literally presented in the given form." Goodenough emphasizes that most important thought is in "this world of the suggestive connotative meaning of words, objects, sounds, and forms ..." He adds (IV, p. 33) that in religion, a symbol conveys not only meaning, but also "power or value." Further, some symbols move from religion to religion, preserving the same "value" while acquiring a new explanation. In the long history of Judaism religious "symbols" in the form of actions or prohibitions certainly endure through many, varied settings, all the while acquiring new explanations and discarding old ones, and perpetually retaining religious "force" or value or (in more modern terms) "meaning." Hence, Goodenough writes (IV, p. 36):

> Indeed when the religious symbols borrowed by Jews in those years are put together, it becomes clear that the ensemble is not merely a "picture book without text," but reflect a lingua franca that had been taken into most of the religions of the day, for the same symbols were used in association with Dionysius, Mithra, Osiris, the Etruscan gods, Sabazisus, Attis, and a host of others, as well as by Christianity later. It was a symbolic language, a direct language of values, however, not a language of denotation.

Goodenough is far from suggesting the presence of a pervasive syncretism. Rather, he points to what he regards as pervasive religious values applied quite parochially by various groups, including some Jews to the worship of their particular "Most High God." These values, while connotative and not denotative, may, nonetheless, be recovered and articulated in some measure by the historian who makes use of the insights of recent students of psychology and symbolism:

> The hypothesis on which I am working ... is that in taking over the symbols, while discarding the myths and explanations of the pagans, Jews and Christians admitted, indeed confirmed, a continuity of religious experience which it is most important to be able to identify ... for an understanding of man, the phenomenon of a continuity of religious experience or values would have much more significance than that of discontinuous explanations (IV, p. 42).

At this point Goodenough argues that the symbols under consideration were more than merely space-fillers. Since this matter is crucial to his argument, let me give his reasons with appropriate emphasis. These are:

first, they were all *living* symbols in surrounding culture;

second, the vocabulary of symbols is extremely limited, on all the artifacts not more than a score of designs appearing in sum, and thus highly selected;

third, the symbols were frequently not the work of an ornamental artist at all;

fourth, the Jewish and "pagan" symbols are mixed on the same graves, so that if the menorah is accepted as "having value" then the peacock or wreath of victory ought also to have "had value";

fifth, the symbols are found in highly public places, such as synagogues and cemeteries, and not merely on the private and personal possessions of individuals, such as amulets or charms.

Goodenough therefore must state carefully where and how each symbol occurs, thus establishing its commonplace quality; he must then show the meaning that the symbol may have had *universally*, indicating its specific denotative value in the respective cultures which used it. He considers its broader connotative value, as it recurs in each culture, because a symbol evokes in man, not only among specific groups of men, a broader, psychologically oriented meaning. Goodenough notes that the formal state religions of Athens, Rome, and Jerusalem, had a quite different basis, and had little (if any) use for the symbols at hand. These symbols, he holds, were of use "only in religions that engendered deep emotion, ecstasy, religions directly and consciously centered in the renewing of life and the granting of immortality, in the giving to the devotee of a portion of the divine spirit of life substance."

At the end these symbols appear to indicate a type of Judaism in which, as in Philonic Judaism, the basic elements of "mystery" were superimposed upon Jewish legalism. The Judaism of the rabbis has always offered essentially a path through this present life the father's code of instructions as to how we may please him while we are alive. To this, the symbols seem to say, was now added from the mystery religions, or from Gnosticism, the burning desire to leave this life altogether, to renounce the flesh and go into the richness of divine existence, to appropriate God's life to oneself.

These ideas have as little place in normative, rabbinic Judaism as do the pictures and symbols and gods that Jews borrowed to suggest them. That such ideas were borrowed by Jews was no surprise to me after years of studying Philo.

What is perplexing is the problem of how Jews fitted such conceptions into, or harmonized them with, the teachings of the Bible.

V

The Meaning of the Artistic Symbols

In volumes IV-VIII, Goodenough turns back to the symbols whose existence he traced in Volumes I-III. Now he attempts a systematic interpretation according to the method outlined in Volume IV, part I. In his discussion of symbols from the Jewish cult, Goodenough attempts to explain what these symbols may have meant when reproduced in the noncultic settings of synagogue and grave, specifically, the *Menorah*, the Torah shrine, *lulab* and *etrog, shofar*, and incense shovel. These symbols are, of course, definitely Jewish. But they seem to have been transformed into symbols (IV, p. 67), "used in devotion, to have taken on personal, direct value," to mean not simply that the deceased *was* a Jew but to express a "meaning in connection with the death and life of those buried behind them." It would be simple to assign the meaning of these symbols to their biblical or cultic origins, except for the fact that they are often represented with less obviously Jewish, or biblical symbols, such as birds eating grapes and the like.

Rather, Goodenough holds that these devices may be of some direct help in achieving immortality for the deceased, specifically

...the *menorah* seems to have become a symbol of God, of his streaming light and Law ... the astral path to God. The *lulab* and *ethrog* carried on the association of Tabernacles as a festival of rain and light, but took on mystical overtones, to become a eucharist to escape from evil and of the passing into justice as the immaterial Light comes to man....

He concludes:

They could take a host of pagan symbols which appeared to them to have in paganism the values they wanted from their Judaism and blend them with Jewish symbols as freely as Philo blended the language of Greek metaphysics with the language of the Bible.

In *Fish, Bread and Wine*, Goodenough begins by discussing the Jewish and pagan representations of creatures of the sea, in the latter section reviewing these usages in Egypt, Mesopotamia, Syria, Greece, and Rome (a recurrent inquiry), then turns to the symbolic value of the fish in Judaism, finally, to bread. The representations of "bread" often look merely like "round objects" however, and if it were not for the occasional representation of baskets of bread, one should be scarcely convinced that these "round objects" signify anything in particular. The section on wine is the high point of these volumes, both for its daring and for its comprehensive treatment of the "divine fluid" and all sorts of effulgences from the godhead, from Babylonia and Assyria, Egypt (in various periods), Greece, Dionysiac cults in Syria and Egypt, as well as in the late syncretistic religions. Goodenough finds considerable evidence in Jewish cult and observance, but insists that fish, bread and wine rites came into Jewish practice during and not before the Hellenistic period, and hence must be explained by contemporary ideas. Wine, in particular, was widely regarded as a source of fertility, but its mystic value was an expression of the "craving for sacramental access to Life."

Pagan symbols used in Jewish contexts include the bull, lion, tree, crown, various rosettes and other wheels (demonstrably not used in paganism for purely decorative purposes), masks, the gorgoneum, cupids, birds, sheep, hares, shells, cornucopias, centaurs, psychopomps, and astronomical symbols. Goodenough treats this body of symbols last because while some may have had biblical referents, the symbolic value of all these forms seems to him to be discovered in the later period. Of the collection, Goodenough writes (VIII, p. 220):

They have all turned into life symbols, and could have been, as I believe they were, interpreted in a great many ways. For those who believed in immortality they could point to immortality, give man specific hopes. To those who found the larger life in a mysticism that looked, through death, to a final dissolution of the individual into the All ... these symbols could have given great power and a vivid sense of appropriation ... The invasion of pagan symbols into either Judaism or Christianity ... involved a modification of the original faith but by no means its abandonment.

Symbolism is itself a language, and affected the original faith much as does adopting a new language in which to express its tenets. Both Christians and Jews in these years read their Scriptures, and prayed in words that had been consecrated to pagan deities. The very idea of a God, discussion of the values of the Christian or Jewish God, could be conveyed only by using the old pagan *theos;* salvation by the word *soteria;* immortality by *athanasia.* The eagle, the crown, the zodiac, and the like spoke just as direct, just as complicated a language. The Christian or Jew had by no means the same conception of heaven or immortality as the pagan, but all had enough in common to make the same symbols, as well as the same words, expressive and meaningful. Yet the words and the symbols borrowed did bring in something new ...

Goodenough continues (VIII, p. 224): "When Jews adopted the same lingua franca of symbols they must ... have taken over the constant values in the symbols."

Finally, Goodenough reviews the lessons of the evidence. From the cultic objects we learn that the Jews used images of their cultic objects in a new way, in the pagan manner, for just as the pagans were putting the mythological and cultic emblems of their religions on their tombs to show their hope in the world to come, so too did the Jews. From fish, bread and wine, we learn that the Jews were thus partaking of immortal nature. In reference to the symbols that had no cultic origins (VII and VIII) and, on the face of it, slight Jewish origins (apart from the bull, tree, lion, and possibly crown, which served in biblical times) Goodenough proposes that the value of these objects, though not their verbal explanations, were borrowed because some Jews found them "new depths for his ideas of ... his own Jewish deity, and his hope of salvation or immortality ..."

VI

The Debate on the Art of the Synagogue at Dura Europos:
Goodenough and Kraeling

When the painted walls of the synagogue at Dura-Europos emerged into the light of day in November 1932, the modern perspective on the character of Judaism in Greco-Roman times had to be radically refocused. Until that time, it was possible to ignore the growing evidence, turned up for decades by archaeologists, of a kind of Judaism substantially different from that described in Jewish literary remains of the period. It is true that archaeological discoveries had long before revealed in the synagogues and graves of Jews in the Hellenistic worlds substantial evidences of religious syncretism, and of the use of pagan symbols in identifiably Jewish settings. But before the Dura synagogue these evidences remained discrete and made slight impact. They were not explained; they were explained away.

After the preliminary report, the Dura synagogue was widely discussed, and a considerable literature, mostly on specific problems of art but partly on the interpretation of the art, developed; in the main, the Dura synagogue was studied by art historians, and not, with notable exceptions, by historians of religion or of Judaism. But, as I said, from 1932 to 1956 Goodenough was prevented by colleagues from discussing the finds at Dura since the final report on the excavation was still in preparation. In 1956, Carl H. Kraeling published *The Synagogue*.[3] Then the issue could be fairly joined. In no way can Goodenough's vols. IX-XI be considered in isolation from the other and quite opposite approach to the same problem. So as we take up Goodenough on the Dura synagogue, we deal with Goodenough only in the context of the debate with Kraeling.

Let me state the issue in a general way. Under debate is how we make use of literary evidence in interpreting the use of symbols, and, further, which evidence we consider. Goodenough looks at the symbols in their artistic context, hence in other settings besides the Jewish one, and he invokes literary evidence only as a second step in interpretation Kraeling starts with literary evidence and emphasizes the Jewish meanings imputed in literary sources to symbols found in Jewish settings. This he does to the near exclusion of the use and meaning of those same symbols in non-Jewish settings in the same town, indeed on the same street. Goodenough reads Hellenistic Jewish writings at his second stage, Kraeling reads rabbinic and related writings at his first stage. Now to make the matter concrete.

Kraeling opened the Talmud and Midrash and related writings and then looked at the walls of the synagogue. Kraeling argued that the paintings must be interpreted for the most part by reference to the so-called rabbinic literature of the period, and used the Talmudic, Midrashic, and Targumic writings for that purpose. He writes (pp. 353, 354):

> The Haggadic tradition embodied in the Dura synagogue paintings was, broadly speaking, distinct from the one that was normative for Philo and for that part of the ancient Jewish world that he presents. ... This particular cycle [of paintings] as it is known to us at Dura moves within a definable orbit of the Haggadic tradition, ... this orbit has Palestinian-Babylonian rather than Egyptian relations.

Goodenough took the opposite position. Characteristically, he starts with systematic statement of method, only then proceeding to the artifacts demanding interpretation.

Kraeling argues that the biblical references of the Dura paintings are so obvious that one may begin by reading the Bible, and proceed by reading the

---

[3]A. R. Bellinger, F. E. Brown, A. Perkins, and C. B. Welles, eds., *The Excavations at Dura Europos Conducted by Yale University and the French Academy of Inscriptions and Letters. Final Report*. VIII, 1. *The Synagogue*, by Carl H. Kraeling, with contributions by C. C. Torrey, C. B. Welles, and B. Geiger, Yale University Press.

paintings in the light of the Bible and its Midrashic interpretation in the Talmudic period. He says:

> Any community decorating its House of Assembly with material so chosen and so orientated cannot be said to have regarded itself remote from religious life and observance of the Judaism that we know from the Bible and the Mishnah .... It would appear [p. 352] that there is a considerable number of instances in which Targum and Midrash have influenced the pictures (p. 351).

Kraeling provides numerous examples of such influence. He qualifies his argument, however, by saying that the use of Midrashic and Targumic material is "illustrative rather than definitive." While he makes reference, from time to time, to comparative materials, Kraeling does not in the main feel it necessary to examine the broad iconographic traditions operating in Dura in general, and most manifestly in the synagogue art. Whatever conventions of pagan art may appear, the meaning of the synagogue art is wholly separated from such conventions and can best, probably only, be understood within the context of the Judaism known to us from literary sources.

Goodenough's argument, repeated in the later volumes from the earlier ones, is that literary traditions would not have led us to expect any such art as this. We may find statements in Talmudic literature which are relevant to the art, but we must in any case after assembling the material determine:

> what this art means in itself, before we begin to apply to it as proof texts any possible unrelated statements of the Bible or the Talmud. That these artifacts are unrelated to proof texts is a statement which one can no more make at the outset than one can begin with the assumption of most of my predecessors that if the symbols had meaning for Jews, that meaning must be found by correlating them with Talmudic and biblical phrases [IV, 10].

Even though the art of the Dura synagogue may at the first glance seem to be *related* to Midrashic ideas, even found in a few cases to reflect Midrashic accounts of biblical events, nonetheless one is still not freed from the obligation to consider what that art meant to a contemporary Jew, pagan, or Christian who was familiar with other art of the age. Since both the architectural and the artistic conventions of the Dura synagogue are demonstrably those of the place and age, and not in any way borrowed from pre-existent "rabbinic" artistic conventions – because there weren't any! – one must give serious thought to the meaning and value, or the content, of those conventions elsewhere and assess, so far as one can, how nearly that value and meaning were preserved in the Jewish setting.

Both Kraeling and Goodenough agree that there was a plan to the art of the synagogue. All concur that biblical scenes are portrayed not only as mere ornament or decoration but as a means of conveying important religious ideas, so that the walls of the sanctuary might, in truth, yield sermons. So we may now turn away from the argument that, anyhow, symbols are not always symbolic. *These* symbols were symbolic. One may continually say that the use of pagan art is wholly conventional, just as the critics of Goodenough's earlier interpretations repeat that the symbols from graves and synagogues were "mere ornament" and imply nothing more than a desire to decorate (none surely can say this of Dura, and no one has, for the meaningful character of Dura synagogue art is self-evident). But having asserted that pagan art has lost its value and become, in a Jewish setting, wholly conventional, we have hardly solved many problems. For by saying that the "art has lost its value," we hardly have explained *why* pagan conventions were useful for decoration.

Let us let the scholars speak for themselves, first, on the general meaning which emerges from the paintings as a whole and, second, on the nature of Judaism at Dura. While both scholars interpret the pictures in detail, each provides a summary of the meaning of the art as a whole. Kraeling's is as follows (pp. 350-51):

> A closer examination of the treatment of Israel's sacred history as presented in the Synagogue painting leads to a number of inferences that will help to appraise the community's religious outlook .... These include the following:
>
> a. There is a very real sense in which the paintings testify to an interest in the actual continuity of the historical process to which the sacred record testifies. This is evidenced by the fact that they do not illustrate interest in the Covenant relationship by a combination of scenes chosen from some one segment of sacred history, but provide instead a well-organized progression of scenes from the period of the Patriarchs and Moses and Aaron, from the early days of the monarchy, through the prophetic period, the exile, the post-exile period, to the expected Messianic age as visualized by prophecy ...
>
> b. There is a very real sense in which the history portrayed in the paintings involves not only certain individuals, but concretely the nation as a whole, and in which the course of events in time and space are for the individuals and the nation a full and completely satisfactory expression of their religious aspirations and ideals...
>
> c. There is a very real sense in which the piety exhibited in, and inculcated by, the paintings finds a full expression in the literal observance of the Law. This comes to light in the effort to provide the historical documentation for the origin of the religious festivals ... in the attention paid to the cult and its sacra, including the sacrifices: and in the opposition to idolatry.
>
> d. Because they have this interest in the historical process, in the people of Israel, and in the literal observance of the Law, the paintings can and do properly include scenes showing how those nations and individuals that oppose God's purposes and His people are set at naught or destroyed ...

In other words, the religious problem which the synagogue paintings reflect is not that of the individual's search for participation in true being by the escape of the rational soul from the irrational desires to a higher level of mystical experience, but rather that of faithful particpation in the nation's inherited Covenant responsibilities as a means of meriting the fulfillment of the divine promises and of making explicit in history its divinely determined purpose.

Since the West Wall contains the bulk of the surviving fresco, we turn to Goodenough's interpretation of that wall:

> The west wall of the synagogue as a whole is indeed coming to express a profoundly consistent Judaism. On the left side a miraculous baby is given by Elijah, but he ties in with the temporal hopes of Israel, exemplified when Persian rulership was humiliated by Esther and Mordecai. Divine intervention beings this about, but here brought only this. Above is the cosmic interpretation of the Temple sacrifice of Aaron, and Moses making the twelve tribes into the zodiac itself.

> On the right, just as consistently, the immaterial, metaphysical values of Judaism are presented. Moses is the divine baby here, with the three nyumphs and Anahita-Aphrodite. Kingship, as shown in the anointing of David by Samuel, is not temporal royalty, but initiation into the hieratic seven. Above these, the gods of local paganism collapse before the Ark of the Covenant, the symbol of metaphysical reality in Judaism, which the three men beside the ark also represented, while that reality is presented in a temple with seven walls and closed inner sanctuary, and with symbols from the Creation myth of Iran. At the top, Moses leads the people out to true spiritual victory.

> In the four portraits, an incident from the life of Moses is made the culmination of each of these progressions. He goes out as the cosmic leader to the heavenly bodies alongside the cosmic worship of Aaron, the menorah, and the zodiac. He reads the mystic law like the priest of Isis alongside the closed Temple and the all-conquering Ark. He receives the Law from God on Sinai beside a Solomon scene which we cannot reconstruct: but he stands at the Burning Bush, receiving the supreme revelation of God as Being, beside the migrating Israelites, who move ... to a comparable, if not the same, goal (X, 137-38).

The reader must be struck by the obvious fact that, in the main, both scholars agree on the substance of the paintings, but they disagree on both their interpretation and their implications for the kind of religion characteristic of this particular synagogue.

Concerning Dura Judaism, Kraeling argues that the Jews of Dura had fallen back "visibly" upon the biblical sources of religious life (p. 351). Kraeling says throughout that the Jews in Dura were, for the most part, good, "normative," rabbinic Jews:

> If our understanding of the pictures is correct, they reveal on the part of those who commissioned them an intense, well-informed devotion to the established traditions of Judaism, close contact with both the Palestinian

and the Babylonian centers of Jewish religious thought, and a very real understanding of the peculiar problems and needs of a community living in a strongly competitive religious environment, and in an exposed political position [p. 353].

Goodenough, in his description of Judaism at Dura (X, 196-209), holds that these were not participants in the "established traditions of Judaism," and that they did not have close contact with Babylonian or Palestinian Judaism. The walls of the synagogue are not, he argues, representations of biblical scenes, but *allegorizations* of them (as in the specific instances cited above). The biblical scenes show an acceptance of mystic ideas which the symbolic vocabulary of Jews elsewhere in the Groco-Roman world, studied in the first eight volumes, suggested. He says:

> While the theme of the synagogue as a whole might be called the celebration of the glory and power of Judaism and its God, and was conceived and planned by men intensely loyal to the Torah, those people who designed it did not understand the Torah as did the rabbis in general. Scraps stand here which also appear in rabbinic haggadah, to be sure ... But in general the artist seems to have chosen biblical scenes not to represent them but, by allegorizing them, to make them say much not remotely implicit in the texts ... On the other hand, the paintings can by no means be spelled out from the pages of Philo's allegories, for especially in glorifying temporal Israel they often depart from him altogether. Kraeling astutely indicated ... that we have no trace of the creation stories, or indeed of any biblical passages before the sacrifice of Isaac, sections of the Bible to which Philo paid almost major attention. This must not blind us, however, to the fact that the artist, like Philo, presumed that the Old Testament text is to be understood not only through its Greek translation, but through its re-evaluation in terms of Greek philosophy and religion. Again, unlike Philo in detail but like him in spirit, the artists have interpreted biblical tradition by using Iranian costumes and such scenes as the duel between the white and black horsemen ... The Jews here, while utterly devoted to their traditions and Torah, had to express what this meant to them in a bulding designed to copy the inner shrine of a pagan temple, filled with images of human beings and Greek and Iranian divinities, and carefully designed to interpret the Torah in a way profoundly mystical (X, p. 205).

Goodenough takes account of the high probability that, under such circumstances, Jews learned from their neighbors and commented, in a way they found appropriate, on their neighbors' religions. Kraeling's approach rests on the premise of a group of Jews quite separate from the diverse world around them. Yet so far as we know, there was no ghetto in Dura, and neither physical nor cultural isolation characterized the Jews' community there. They assuredly spoke the same language as others, and they knew what was going on.

The notion, moreover, of an "Orthodoxy," surely applies to the third century a conception invented in the nineteenth (a point students of religion will find particularly suggestive), and that anachronism has confused many, not only

Kraeling, in reading the artistic and literary sources at hand. There was no single Judaism, there was never an Orthodoxy, any more than today there is a single Judaism, Orthodox or otherwise. That conception is a conceit of Orthodoxy. Indeed, throughout Babylonia (present day Iraq) Jews lived in the same many-splendored world, in which diverse languages and groups worshipped different gods. And Jews themselves prove diverse: there were many Judaisms. And the art, properly interpreted, forms the principal testimony to the most widespread of the Judaisms of late antiquity. That is why the study of the art is essential for the study of ancient Judaism.

VII
The Debate on Goodenough's Interpretation:
Nock and Smith

Students will gain a clear picture of the difficulty of interpreting the religious life by reviewing the debate Goodenough precipitated. That will show them how to differentiate the main point from matters of detail. Anyone with an interest in symbolism will follow that debate with intense interest. A mark of the success of scholarship, particularly in a massive exercise of interpretation such as the one at hand, derives from how a scholar has defined issues. Did Goodenough succeed in framing the program of inquiry? Indeed he did. Nearly all critics concede the premise of his work, which, when he began, provoked intense controversy. Goodenough demanded that the Jewish symbols be taken seriously, not dismissed as mere decoration. That view formed the foundation of his work, and he completely succeeded in making that point stick. Few today propose to ignore what, when Goodenough began work, many preferred to explain away. So Goodenough's greatness begins in his power to reframe the issues of his chosen field. In his day in his area few scholars enjoyed equivalent influence, and, in ours, none in the field at hand.

But that fact should not obscure differences of opinion, both in detail and in general conclusions. Goodenough would not have wanted matters any other way. Teachers of ancient Judaism through art will find useful an account of two interesting approaches – those of Morton Smith and Arthur Darby Nock – to the criticism of Goodenough's *Jewish Symbols.*

ARTHUR DARBY NOCK (1902-1963): In *Gnomon* 27, 1955, 29, 1957, and 32, 1960, Nock presented a systematic critique of Vols 1-8, under the title, "Religious Symbols and Symbolism." Now reprinted in Zeph Stewart, ed., *Arthur Darby Nock. Essays on Religion and the Ancient World* (Oxford, 1972: Clarendon), II, pp. 877-918, Nock first summarizes the main lines of Goodenough's approach to the interpretation of symbols. He then expresses his agreement with what I regard as the principal result of Goodenough's work for the study of Judaism (pp. 880-882, *pass.*):

> G[oodenough] has made a good case against any strong central control of
> Judaism: it was a congregational religion and the local group or, in a
> large city such as Rome, any given local group seems to have been
> largely free to follow its own preferences. Again, in art as in other
> things, Judaism seems to have been now more and now less sensitive on
> questions of what was permissible. From time to time there was a
> stiffening and then a relaxing: down into modern times mysticism and
> enthusiasm have been recurrent phenomena; so has the "vertical path" as
> distinct from the "horizontal path." To speak even more generally, from
> the earliest times known to us there has been a persistent quality of
> religious lyricism breaking out now here, now there among the Jews....

The point conceded by Nock is central to Goodenough's thesis: that Judaism
yielded diversity and not uniformity. Again, since Goodenough repeatedly turns
to Philo for explanation of symbols, it is important to see that Nock concedes
how Philo may represent a world beyond himself:

> So again, in all probability, Philo's attitude was not unique and, deeply
> personal as was the warmth of his piety and his sense of religious
> experience, we need not credit him with much original thinking. The
> ideas which he used did not disappear from Judaism after 70 or even after
> 135. Typological and allegorical interpretation of the Old Testament
> continued to be common. G.'s discussion of the sacrifice of Isaac is
> particularly instructive; so are his remarks on the fixity and ubiquity of
> some of the Jewish symbols and (4.145 ff.) on lulab and ethrog in
> relation to the feast of Tabernacles, "the culminating festival of the year"
> with all that it suggested to religious imagination.

> Menorah, lulab, ethrog, Ark and incense-shovel were associated with the
> Temple and as such could remain emblems of religious and national
> devotion after its destruction; the details of the old observances were
> discussed with passionate zeal for centuries after their disuse. G. has
> indeed made a strong case for the view that, as presented in art, they refer
> to the contemporary worship of the synagogue (as he has produced
> serious arguments for some use of incense in this). It may well be that
> they suggested both Temple and synagogue.

But Nock provided extensive and important criticism, of Goodenough's ideas.
He expresses his reservations on detail (pp. 882-3):

> The improbability of many of G.'s suggestions on points of detail does
> not affect his main theses, but those theses do themselves call for very
> substantial reservations. Thus the analogy between Isis and Sophia is
> more superficial than real, and so is that between allegorical
> explanations of the two types of religious vestments used by Egyptians
> and the two used by the High Priest. No these are not minor matters; the
> first is one of the foundations of what is said about the "saving female
> principle" and the second is made to support the supposition of Lesser
> and Greater Mysteries of Judaism.

> The crucial question is: was there a widespread and long continuing
> Judaism such as G. infers, with something in the nature of a mystery
> worship? Before we attack this we may consider (a) certain iconographic

features regarded by G. as Hellenistic symbols – in particular Victories with crowns, Seasons, the Sun, and the zodiac; (b) the cup, the vine and other motifs which G. thinks Dionysiac; (c) the architectural features which he interprets as consecratory.

The important point to observe is how Nock calls into question not only detail but the general approach: the main results. That is how scholarly debate should go forward. But Nock concludes (p. 918):

> Once more such points do not destroy the essential value of the work. I have tried to indicate...what seem to be the major gains for knowledge which it brings and naturally there are also valuable details.

In the balance, Nock's systematic critique confirms Goodenough's standing as the scholar to insist that the symbols matter. More than that Goodenough could not have asked. More than that Nock did not concede.

MORTON SMITH (1915-   ): Smith's "Goodenough's Jewish Symbols in Retrospect" (*Journal of Biblical Literature* 1967, 86:53-68) provides a list of reviews of Goodenough's work,which he compiled from *L'Année philologique*, as well as a systematic reconsideration of the work as a whole. As a statement of an experienced of the history of Judaism and Christianity in the formative age, Smith's essay stands as the definitive account of his own   viewpoint on Goodenough's work.   Smith first calls attention to the insistence on distinguishing the value of a symbol from its verbal explanation (p. 55):

> The fundamental point in Goodenough's argument is his concept of the "value" of a symbol as distinct from the "interpretation." He defined the "value" as "simply emotional impact." But he also equated "value" with "meaning" and discovered as the "meaning" of his symbols a complex mystical theology. Now certain shapes may be subconsciously associated with certain objects or, like certain colors, may appeal particularly to persons of certain temperaments. This sort of symbolism may be rooted in human physiology and almost unchanging. But such "values" as these do not carry the theological implications Goodenough discovered.

The premise of a psychic unity of humanity, on which Goodenough's insistence on the distinction at hand must rest, certainly awaits more adequate demonstration. Smith proceeds (pp. 55-6):

> After this definition of "value," the next step in Goodenough's argument is the claim that each symbol always has one and the same "value."
>
> Goodenough's position can be defended only by making the one constant value something so deep in the subconscious and so ambivalent as to be compatible with contradictory "interpretations." In that event it will also be compatible with both mystical and legalistic religion. In that event the essential argument, that the use of these symbols necessarily indicates a mystical religion, is not valid.

So much for the basic theory of symbolism. Smith proceeds (p. 57) to the specific symbolism at hand:

> The lingua franca of Greco-Roman symbolism, predominantly Dionysiac, expressed hope for salvation by participation in the life of a deity which gave itself to be eaten in a sacramental meal. This oversimplifies Goodenough's interpretations of pagan symbolism; he recognized variety which cannot be discussed here for lack of space. But his thesis was his main concern, and drew objections from several reviewers, notably from Nock, who was the one most familiar with the classical material.

> It must be admitted that Goodenough's support of this contention was utterly inadequate. What had to be established was a probability that the symbols, as *commonly* used in the Roman empire, expressed this hope of salvation by communion. If they did not *commonly* do so *at this time*, then one cannot conclude that the Jews, who at this time took them over, had a similar hope. But Goodenough only picked out a scattering of examples in which the symbols could plausibly be given the significance his thesis required; he passed over the bulk of the Greco-Roman material and barely mentioned a few of the examples in which the same symbols were said, by those who used them, to have other significance. These latter examples, he declared, represented superficial "interpretations" of the symbols, while the uses which agreed with his theory expressed the symbols' permanent "values." The facts of the matter, however, were stated by Nock: "Sacramental sacrifice is attested only for Dionysus and even in his cult this hardly remained a living conception;" there is no substantial evidence that the worshipers of Dionysus commonly thought they received "his divine nature in the cup." So much for the significance of the "lingua Franca" of Greco-Roman Dionysiac symbolism.

Smith then points out that Goodenough "ruled out the inscriptional and literary evidence which did not agree with his theories." He maintains that Goodenough substituted his own intuition, quoting the following: "The study of these symbols has brought out their value for my own psyche...." By contrast, Smith concurs with Goodenough's insistence on the hope for the future life as a principal theme of the symbols. Still, Smith maintains that Goodenough failed "to demonstrate the prevalence of a belief in sacramental salvation" (p. 58). In Smith's view, therefore, "the main structure of his argument was ruined."

In reviewing the Goodenough debate, students will learn from examples of how not to pursue an argument. Smith provides a fine instance of a mode of discourse students will recognize as inappropriate. For, as is his way in general, Smith makes a long sequence of *ad hominem* points about Goodenough's background, upbringing, religious beliefs, and the like, e.g., "He is the rebellious son of G. F. Moore" (p. 65). In this way he personalizes and trivializes scholarship. He lays down such judgments as "enormous exaggerations," "his pandemic sacramental paganism was a fantasy," and on and on. Smith underscores his views with lavish use of italics., He declares a Goodenough's views nothing less than "incredible." He leaves in the form of questions a series of, to him "self-evident," claims against Goodenough's views. These claims in their form as rhetorical questions Smith regards as unanswerable and beyond all argument. For example: "But the difficulties in the supposition of a *widespread, uniform* mystical Judaism are formidable [italics his]. How did it happen that such a system and practice disappeared without leaving a trace in either Jewish or Christian polemics? We may therefore turn from the main argument to incidental questions" (p. 59). Those three sentences constitute Smith's stated reason for dismissing Goodenough's principal positions and turning to minor matters. Personalizing, then trivializing issues of scholarly interpretation forms a common mode of debate, and students will benefit from a direct encounter with this debate, since, after all, the evidence – the art itself – is there for them to interpret as well. Goodenough, for his part, had worked out answers to these questions, which he recognized on his own, and, had he lived, had every capacity of dealing with them to (at least) his own satisfaction.

Still Smith's criticism cannot be dismissed as that of a mere self-important crank. Nor should we wish to ignore his positive assessment (p. 61):

> Goodenough's supposition that the Jews gave their own interpretations to the symbols they borrowed is plausible and has been commonly accepted. His reconstructions of their interpretations, however, being based on Philo, drew objections that Philo was an upper-class intellectual whose interpretations were undreamt of by the average Jew. These, however, missed Goodenough's claim: Philo was merely one example of mystical Judaism, of which other examples, from other social and intellectual classes, were attested by the monuments. For this reason also, objections that Goodenough misinterpreted Philo on particular points did not seriously damage his argument; it was sufficient for him to show that Philo used expressions suggestive of a mystical and sacramental interpretation of Jewish stories and ceremonies. The monuments could then show analogous developments independent of Philo. Some did, but most did not.

The single most important comment of Smith is as follows (p. 65):

> Goodenough's theory falsifies the situation by substituting a single, anti-rabbinic, mystical Judaism for the enormous variety of personal, doctrinal, political, and cultural divergencies which the rabbinic and other evidence reveals, and by supposing a sharp division between rabbinic and anti-rabbinic Judaism, whereas actually there seems to have been a confused gradation.

Declaring Goodenough to have failed, Smith concludes (p. 66): "Columbus failed too. But his failure revealed a new world, and so did Goodenough's." For more than that no scholar can hope. For learning is a progressive, an on-going process, an active verb in the continuing, present tense. In teaching about ancient Judaism through the study of art, that is the principal lesson we impart – and the most important lesson of all education.

Chapter Nine

Literature and the Study of Judaism:
Intertextuality and the Text

I
The Issue of Intertextuality

The canon of Judaism as it took shape in late antiquity, comprises documents that relate both to a single common book, the Hebrew Scripture or Old Testament, and also to one another. Consequently the holy books of Judaism in its formative period provide an ideal example of the meanings and uses of the critical initiative represented by thought on intertextuality. But the urgency of the matter derives not from the traits of old writings, but from current interest in the use of those writings for consideration of today's issues. Specifically, the relevance of the category, intertextuality, derives from a broadly held and widely circulated characterization of the writings of the Judaic sages of late antiquity. Literary critics familiar with the writings of the ancient rabbis propose – as we see in the quotations above, reprsentative of widely held opinion – to treat the whole as harmonious, uniform, indivisible. That literary judgment further accords with theological convictions of faithful Jews, whether Orthodox or Reform, Conservative or Israeli or Reconstructionist. The received hermeneutic, long governing how the ancient texts are read, invokes all passages in the exposition of each, and each for all: intertextuality as the paramount hermeneutic, resting on theological principles. Contemporary expositions follow suit, so Handelman: "The rabbinic world is, to use a contemporary term, one of *intertextuality*. Texts echo, interact, and interpenetrate...."[1]

Proponents of the intertextualist approach to the canon of Judaism claim to discern deep connections between one document and the next, so that all documents impose meanings upon each, and each demands a reading solely in the setting of the whole literature. I propose to test that approach by asking what *intrinsic* traits of the entirety of the corpus of Judaism in late antiquity validate an intertextualist reading of that corpus. Of interest is not the well-known fact that one text relates to another. That truism will not have surprised anyone who has ever opened a single text, since all texts cite Scripture, or any passage of the

---

[1]*The Slayers of Moses* (Albany, 1982: State University of New York Press), p. 47.

Talmud, since the Talmud cites the Mishnah. The position at hand addresses the *entirety* of the writings of the ancient rabbis, all together, all at once, everywhere and all the time. Readers cannot imagine that I exaggerate the radical-intertextualist position on the Judaic canon: everything, everywhere, all at once. I do not impute to the proponents of the intertextualist theory of rabbinic writings positions they do not take: *"all units are so closely interwoven and simultaneously present that none can be considered in separation from any other at any given moment."*

We take up a genuinely orthodox hermeneutic, today advocated by nearly everyone. Now that hermeneutical claim is not only not true as a matter of literary fact (as distinct from theological conviction or social construction), it is in fact the exact opposite of the truth as a matter of literary fact. Viewed from the angle of their intrinsic traits, the documents scarcely connect at all. Intertextuality constitutes a social construction, a theological conviction, not a literary dimension of the canon at hand, not an operative category for hermeneutics. We can read these texts one by one, we do well to consult points of intersection with other texts of the same canon where relevant, but we have no reason as a matter of a literary interpretation to invoke that invitation to chaos represented by the counsel: read everything in light of everything, everywhere, all at once.

The writings of the sages of Judaism in late antiquity form a vast literature, each document exhibiting its own integrity, but in addition connected to others, and also continuous with the entire canon of which it forms a part. It follows that if you pick up any book written by ancient Judaic sages, you rightly expect to read what that book says on its own, beginning, middle, and end. You also will want to know how that book relates to others of its setting. That is because each book bears points in common with others. These include citing a common Scripture and addressing a shared program of interests. And, finally, one will wish to see a book in its broader role as part of the canon of Judaism, that is, of the Torah. For no document of the Judaism under discussion, that which came to its original expression in the Mishnah, ca. A.D. 200, and reached its full statement, in late antiquity, in the Talmud of Babylonia, stands on its own. All documents reach us through the medium of the Judaic community, and all of them join together because of their authority in that community, their standing as statements of the Torah. In all, therefore, we discern three dimensions by which any document of that Judaism may be measured: autonomy, connection, continuity. To review: a book in the canon at hand stands by itself, within its own covers; it also relates to other books of the same canon through specific connections, indicated by intrinsic traits of rhetoric, topic, and logic or by shared materials, common to a number of documents. And it also forms part of an undifferentiated canon, that is, the Torah, or Judaism, through the dimension of complete continuity. Hence among those three dimensions, autonomy, connection, continuity, we address the second.

To clarify this perspective, let me invoke the analogy of a library. Books brought together form a library. Each title addresses its own program and makes its own points. But books produced by a cogent community constitute not merely a library but a canon: a set of compositions each of which contributes to a statement that transcends its own pages. The books exhibit intrinsic traits that make of them all *a community of texts*. We should know on the basis of those characteristics that the texts form a community even if we knew nothing more than the texts themselves. In the Judaic system of the dual Torah, moreover, the documents at hand form a canon. All of them find a place in the Torah. But that is a fact we know only on the basis of information deriving from sources other than the texts at hand, which, on their own, do not link each to all and all to every line of each. Extrinsic traits, that is imputed ones, make of the discrete writings a single and continuous, uniform statement: one whole Torah in the mythic language of Judaism. The community of Judaism imputes those traits, sees commonalities, uniformities, deep harmonies: one Torah of one God. In secular language, that community expresses its system – its world view, its way of life, its sense of itself as a society – by these choices, and finds its definition in them. Hence, in the nature of things, the community of Judaism forms *a textual community*. That cogent community that forms a canon out of a selection of books therefore participates in the process of authorship, just as the books exist in at least two dimensions.

Let us turn to the problem of the community of texts. Since the present angle of vision may prove fresh, let me unpack its terms. I just now pointed to two dimensions, *autonomy*, on the one side, and *connection*, on the second. That is to say, a book enjoys its own autonomous standing, but it also situates itself in relationship to other books of the same classification. Each book bears its own statement and purpose, and each relates to others of the same classification. The community of texts therefore encompasses individuals who (singly or collectively) comprise (for the authorships: compose) books. But there is a set of facts that indicate how a book does not stand in isolation. These facts fall into several categories. Books may go over the same ground or make use in some measure of the same materials. The linkages between and among them therefore connect them. Traits of rhetoric, logic, and topic may place into a single classification a number of diverse writings. Then, as I said, there is the larger consensus of members who see relationships between one book and another and so join them together on a list of authoritative writings. So, as is clear, a book exists in the dimensions formed of its own contents and covers, but it also takes its place in the second and third dimensions of relationship to other books.

II

Intertextuality and Texts

If I now may invoke the suggestive word, intertextuality, we then treat the relationships in which a given document stands as one expressed in the prepositions *between* and *among*. That is to say, in its intellectual traits a document bears relationship, to begin with, to some other, hence we describe relationships between two documents. These constitute formal and intrinsic matters: traits of grammar, arrangements of words and resonances as to their local meaning, structures of syntax of expression and thought. But in its social setting a document finds bonds among three or more documents, with all of which it is joined in the imagination and mind of a community. These range widely and freely, bound by limits not of form and language, but of public policy in behavior and belief. Documents because of their traits of rhetoric, logic, and topic form a community of texts. Documents because of their audience and authority express the intellect of a textual community.

The principal issue worked out in establishing a community of texts is hermeneutical, the chief outcome of defining a textual community, social and cultural. The former teaches us how to read the texts on their own. The latter tells us how to interpret texts in context. When we define and classify the relationships between texts, we learn how to read the components – words, cogent thoughts formed of phrases, sentences, paragraphs – of those texts in the broader context defined by shared conventions of intellect: rhetoric, logic, topic. More concretely, hermeneutical principles tell me how, in light of like documents I have seen many times, to approach a document I have never before seenat all. Hermeneutics teaches me the grammar and syntax of thought. Let me give one example of the role of hermeneutics in an inductive inquiry into form. Memorizing a passage of a complex text will teach me the rhythms of expression and thought, for instance, that make of the sounds of some other document an intelligible music. Not only so, but documents joined into a common classification may share specific contents, not only definitive traits of expression – meaning and not solely method. So when I know how to assess the relationships between documents, I also come to a better way of sorting out the effects of those relationships: the intersections, the repetitions.

The upshot of defining a textual community, by contrast, is quite other. It is not hermeneutical, since at issue is not the reading and interpretation of texts but their social utility, their status as cultural indicators. When I know the choices a community has made for its canon, I find my way deep into the shared viewpoint of that community, moving from the contents of the texts to the contexts in which those texts bear meaning. And that brings us back to the basic matter: a text exists in diverse contexts, on its own, among other texts, and as part of a much larger social canon, e.g., a library or a court of appeal for authoritative judgments such as proof-texts supply.

The relationships among the documents produced by the sages of Judaism may take three forms: complete dependence, complete autonomy, intersection in diverse manner and measure. That second dimension provokes considerable debate and presents a remarkably unclear perspective. For while the dimensions of autonomy and continuity take the measure of acknowledged traits – books on their own, books standing in imputed, therefore socially verified, relationships – the matter of connection hardly enjoys the same clear definition. On the one side, intrinsic traits permit us to assess theories of connection. On the other, confusing theological and social judgments of continuities and literary and heuristic ones of connection, people present quite remarkable claims as to the relationships between and among documents, alleging, in fact, that the documents all have to be read as a single continuous document: the Torah. Some maintain that the connections between and among documents are such that each has to be read in the light of all others. So the documents assuredly do form a canon, and that is a position adopted not in some distant past or alien society but among contemporary participants to the cultural debate. While I take up a community of texts and explores those intrinsic traits that link book to book, my inquiry rests on the premise that the books at issue derive from a textual community, one which, without reference to the intrinsic traits of the writings, deems the set of books as a group to constitute a canon. My question is simple but critical:

If I in advance did not know that the community of Judaism treats the writings before us (among others) as a canon, would the traits of the documents have told me that the writings at hand are related?

I have in mind indications of a quite objective and material character, such as decisions of an authorship to refer to or not to refer to Scripture, to compose an intersecting set of agenda or to talk about essentially diverse things, to cite a prior text or not to cite one, to make ample use of materials common among a number of prior texts or to use only materials not earlier used, and on and on. These matters of fact tell us whether, and how, autonomous documents connect with one another and so form a communion of authorships and give expression in textual form to a community. The connections include materials used in common, formal preferences dominant in two or more documents, substantive inquiries into topics interesting to two or more authorships, modes of intelligibility that characterize two or more sets of writers. In a word, we deal with rhetoric, topic, and logic. We take up such considerations as symmetrical or asymmetrical plans of logic and rhetoric, programs of topic and proposition about a given topic, sharing materials, not sharing materials, and other perfectly objective and factual criteria.

III

Three Theories of Intertextuality in the Judaic Canon

Let me now give a representative specimen of the prevailing hermeneutic, so that readers will not conclude I argue against a moribund position. Only then will the persistence, even today, of a wrong approach to these writings prove an urgent problem. For the argument addresses not the faithful, who cannot – by definition – care about what comes first and what happened then, and for whom anachronism nourishes of true belief. It concerns those who here and now, in the world of the academy, claim to tell us how to read these texts and what they mean for the academy. When we give them their hearing, we listen to what is, in fact, the message of the Torah, speaking in its own categories: the hand is the hand of the academy, but the voice is the voice of Sinai: two media of a single Torah, timeless and eternal, everywhere harmonious and always cogent. Glorious faith, but dreadful history, the position at hand translates beliefs into facts. It moreover ignores the requirement to adduce in evidence traits of the documents themselves. Here is a single representative example of the position, as to hermeneutics and history, of both the received tradition of Judaism and also the contemporary intellectual avatars of that tradition in the academy (where they do not belong).

> Synoptic texts must always be studied synoptically, even if one text is "later" than another.
>
> Shaye J. D. Cohen

The second position introduces a somewhat different metaphor from the synoptic one.

> This system, composed of interlocking and re-interlocking parts possessed of an organic connection one to another, is never really divisible.
>
> Lawrence H. Schiffman[2]

This metaphor claims much more than the first. Now we are told that everything "interlocks" with everything else, and, in a hashing of the metaphor, we learn further that there is an "organic" connection, so that nothing is ever "really divisible" from anything else. Quite what that means in practice emerges from the third of the three spokesmen at hand.

---

[2]In his *Sectarian Law in the Dead Sea Scrolls* (Chico, 1983), p. 3.

It is Susan Handelman, who has provided the most ambitious theory of how rabbinic writings relate – and the least informed.[3] Her principal position, so far as the matter of connection and continuity is concerned (there is no room in her reading of the literature for the autonomy of documents), is stated as follows:

> ...all units are so closely interwoven and simultaneously present that none can be considered in separation from any other at any given moment; it is a world of "intertextuality"...[4]

> ....interpretation is not essentially separate from the text itself–an external act intruded upon it–but rather the extension of the text, the uncovering of the connective network of relations, a part of the continuous revelation of the text itself, at bottom, another aspect of the text.[5]

This represents a far more extreme position than that of Cohen, who refers only to synoptic texts, and an even more radical statement of matters than that of Schiffman.

Handelman makes a variety of generalizations about the character of the rabbinic writings, e.g., "In Rabbinic thought...it is often the obverse–the particular and concrete take precedence over the general and abstract." Her larger theory of hermeneutics is not at issue just now, only her characterization of the relationships among documents and her reading of intertextualityn as that interesting conception applies to those documents. These characterizations of the rabbinic canon express broadly-held opinion. In the closing unit of ,this essay we revert to these theories of intertextuality of Handelman's.

---

[3]Her discussion of "the development of the oral law," pp. 42-50, is breathtakingly uninformed. She grasps nothing of the scholarly issues and imperfectly understands the issues. What she does is merely recite in full guillibility the "Orthodox" doctrine, which itself has nothing to do with the diverse and interesting classical positions on the matter. She does not seem to realize, for example, that the heirs of the Mishnah took two conficting positions on the relationship of the laws of the Mishnah to Sinai. She reads the issue as a historical one, in terms of the origin of the law. But it was a question of *authority*, not origin – a matter critical to the work of mine that she cites. Evidence of her imperfect grasp of issues is easy to adduce from her botched report of my work. I am given the opinion "that the oral law is not a product of organic historical development from the written text but an entirely autonomous coexistent body of thought correlative to but independent of the written scriptures...." *I have no position*, what I am doing is outlining positions I claim to discover in a variety of continuator-documents of the Mishnah, e.g., Avot as against Sifra and Sifré to Numbers. Handelman's larger theory of the literature in fact rests on unsound historical premises, and these historical premises are critical to her literary theory. But I choose here to ignore that fact and discuss the theory of the literature solely in relationship to the traits and characteristics of the literature, as exemplified in the sizable sample in the reader's hands. Then people can decide on the basis of the literature Handelman claims to discuss whether or not her description and consequent theory are right. But her amateur status, as contrasted to Cohen's and Schiffman's, should not be missed. They know the sources they discuss and she scarcely compares in knowledge to them.

[4]Susan A. Handelman, *The Slayers of Moses. The Emergence of Rabbinic Interpretation in Modern Literary Theory* (Albany, 1982: State Universty of New York Press), p.78.

[5]Ibid., p. 39.

My purpose is to test that opinion, exemplified by Cohen, Schiffman, and Handelman, against the facts presented by the components of the canon. Specifically, how do documents of Judaism relate to one another? And, as to relationship, the specific issue here concerns connection of one document to the next and of all the documents together. We wonder whether, in Handelman's formulation, none can ever be considered in separation from any other, whether, in Schiffman's formulation, the documents cannot be read one by one because they are never really divisible, or, in Cohen's, whether (some of) the documents before us really do relate in a synoptic manner, a term to which we shall return so that when the documents interrelate, each must be read in light of the other. Cohen and Schiffman raise the issue of texts that clearly interrelate, Cohen invoking the analogy of the synoptic relationships among Matthew, Mark, and Q in Gospels' research, Schiffman phraising matters still more broadly.

I marvel at the certainty of Handelman, Schiffman, and Cohen, and of the broadly-held consensus that they represent. Let me spell out what I find puzzling. It is, specifically, why in the world we should ever have wondered how – on the basis of *intrinsic* and not imputed traits – one document connects to others. Seeing each document on its own or viewing all documents all together by reason of a social consensus pose no special problems of logic or interpretation. The one perspective derives from the very definitive trait of a book or a document: its uniqueness. The other constitutes a social, not a textual issue: why do people see as one what in fact are several? The answer derives not from documents and their traits but from communities and their choices. Common sense tells us that a given document should undergo examination within its own framework, and it is equally reasonable to ask how a number of discrete documents preserved by a single community related to the interests expressed by that community.

IV

Metaphors of Connection:
Genealogy through Dialectic vs. Structural Taxonomy

This brings us, at long last, to the matter at hand, connection. By connection I mean sharing like traits, including materials, and by the absence of connection I mean not sharing traits of plan and program. What is at issue is defining what we know as fact and avoiding what can come to us as mere impression. There are two appropriate metaphors, and we explore them both, genealogical and taxonomical. Genealogy serves for the relationships among texts some call synoptic in relationship, and I regard as dialectical in relationship. Taxonomy serves for all of the writings all together. The connections between the Mishnah, Tosefta, Yerushalmi, and Bavli are dialectical, in that each succeeding document takes up and responds to the problems and program of its predecessor, hence a moving, or dialectical, relationship and connection characterizes the whole.

The taxonomic metaphor derives from natural history, and it sees things as connected when they fall into a single category, and as not connected when they do not. The notion of connection as an essentially taxonomic issue requires some explanation, since it is not the more familiar of the two connections. First to define the matter: the diverse species of a genus are connected by reason of their taxonomic traits, and two or more genera are not connected when they lack in common any taxonomic points. The metaphor that derives the sense of connection from taxonomy, that is, relationship of like and unlike traits, established through systematic classification, directs us to data that we can readily find for ourselves. Since the data prove congruent to the work, we invoke as our sole useful metaphor the taxonomic one: things are connected when they fall into a common classification, and taxonomic relationship – like, unlike – serves as the criterion for connection. The analysis of the relationships., hence of the connections, between and among the principal documents of the Judaism of the dual Torah therefore pursues a program of comparison and contrast among those documents. The results of comparing and contrasting documents tell us how documents are or are not connected with one another.

Documents that fall into a single genus therefore may exhibit relationships, for instance points of rhetoric, logic, or topic, in common, and the speciation of those documents then tells us aspects in which they do not relate, that is, points not in common. Accordingly, by "community of texts" – within the metaphor deriving from taxonomy – I mean texts that coalesce, form a community and in that way establish connections with one another, thus texts that are connected are writings that fall within a single classification. The same traits exhibited by two or more texts will then indicate that the two texts form a single genus, falling into a shared category or classification – one defined by the traits they have in common. The connection, then, between one text and the next is established by shared traits of form or program or fixed relationship to a single document to which, in common, the texts relate. Such common characteristics therefore indicate that two or more texts connect with one another in a taxonomic framework, which seems to me the sole genuinely objective basis for establishing connection at all.

We may now turn to the more obvious metaphor, genealogical connection. The genealogical connection maintains the view that one thing is connected to some other because the one begat the other, a connection based on origin. One thing is not connected to another if there is no affinity based on genealogy. At issue, then, is how we may establish genealogy. It may derive from direct relationship or from indirect. A direct relationship requires that document B not only draw upon document A but also take shape in response to the contents of document A. An indirect relationship involves document A as proximate ancestor for document B, C, and D, in that(necessarily) later writings draw upon an earlier source in common. An example of a direct relationship between documents comes from Kings and Chronicles, with the later drawing upon, and reworking, the former. An example of an indirect relationship, also of a genealogical character, would point to Genesis and Exodus, both of which draw heavily upon common materials, e.g., J, E, JE, and P, but neither of which draws upon the other. In either sort of relationship, we may establish a genealogical connection between two documents, direct or through a third document, as well as the same sort of connection among three or more documents, upon the same basis. The genealogical metaphor for connection invokes not taxonomic but human relationships, e.g., family, filiation, affinity, cousin, uncle, mother-in-law, and the like. In the anthropomorphic setting in which our thought goes forward, the conception of relationship invariably evokes the metaphor of family, surely a more "self-evidently" accessible category than mere classification.

The choice between the two metaphors for connections of the canon as a whole is governed by the character of our data, and our knowledge of the traits and history of the data. So we turn from the definition of the metaphors of connection to the data before us. When we sift the meanings of connection, sorting out the metaphors we may invoke for our study, we see that one available metaphor proves congruent to all of the data at our disposal, and the other does not in its simple form fit any of it. Specifically, taxonomy – by definition – serves all data. Genealogy fits the part of the data to which the synoptic issue is relevant – Mishnah, Tosefta, Yerushalmi, Bavli – but does not fit those data very well.

In order to utilize the metaphor of genealogy, we should have to know that document A has generated document B. While more commonsensical and therefore attractive, the metaphor for connection provided by family invokes considerations of history and precedence, generations and offspring, that, at this stage in our knowledge, we cannot take up. For how shall I determine affinities, filiations, and the like? What objective and factual data can I adduce in evidence of the claim that two or more texts form a family, hence stand in relationship as mother and daughter, or that one text stands in a filial relationship to some other? The metaphor, filiation, draws in its wake the issues of history in the sense of temporal sequence, the conception, for example, that A begat B, so B represents a generation of A. That represents a quite different statement of what we mean by relationship from the one I have offered. But, except for the Mishnah, we do not know that document A's framers came prior to document B's, and our dates for the documents and the order we assign to them, if not wholly arbitrary, do not rest upon firm foundations. Everything is at best approximate and derives from impressions and guesses.

More weighty still, except for the Mishnah, Tosefta, Yerushalmi, and Bavli, we do not know that the authorship of B had access to the work of A and as a matter of decision adopted the model of A. Evidence to prove filiation must encompass demonstrations of points of contact and intersection. That is to say, connection as a direct and concrete category requires that we make judgments of a historical order: this first, then that. But I cannot demonstrate such connection as would have one set of authors meet with and make use of the work of another's writings. So that kind of connection lies beyond demonstration, and a different metaphor of connection will prove more useful.

True, we can show that some small portion of the materials of document A occur also in document B. That fact provides some variant readings of modest interest. But what fact flows from the sharing of a unit of discourse in common? The shared use of some materials in common, and proves that two sets of authorships drew upon a common corpus of materials. The connection then is common access to a third authorship – that alone. We cannot then posit direct relationship between group A and group B, but only indirect and adventitious relationship. And that sort of relationship hardly tells us the two groups, that is, the two documents, stand in a relationship of connection that we can exploit, e.g., for hermeneutical or historical purposes. It tells us the opposite. These and similar problems of demonstrating the presence of relationships comparable to families, filiations, and the like require us to look elsewhere for our notion of relationship. In place of connection, I posit a metaphor that rests on no more than demonstrated points of similarity and difference. Now that the metaphor and its rejected alternative have been fully exposed, let us turn to a clearer statement of connections between and among documents as I propose to investigate them.

The genealogical metaphor, which compares connection, a rather abstract category, to genealogical affinity therefore rests on an essentially historical premise. One thing is connected to some other because the one begat the other, a connection based on origin. One thing is not connected to another if there is no affinity based on genealogy. But that metaphor, while self-evidently illuminating, cannot serve most of our documents here. The reason is that the premise of the metaphor of connection as genealogy within families demands data we do not have. We do not know that the Mishnah begat Leviticus Rabbah, or that the Sifra begat Genesis Rabbah, so if materials occur in both documents, we cannot claim that the one document is connected in a relationship of filiation to its predecessor. I have already explained why we do not know the relationships, as to history, of documents, though we can classify documents in relationship to common points of origin and focus, Mishnah and Scripture, respectively. On the other hand, as I have suggested, there are clear relationships among documents that stand in a straight line, the later ones commenting on the earlier ones. Those relationships demand analysis, and they are the ones characteristic of the Mishnah, Tosefta, and two Talmuds. But for the literature as a whole we cannot show continuous unfolding out of a single, linear connection. The opposite is the case. Many of the documents stand quite independent of the generality of writings and intersect with the rest only casually and episodically.

V

A Community of Texts?
Cohen, Schiffman, and Handelman Revisited

Viewing the documents from the angle of their intrinsic traits, we find no single community of texts.[6] That position claims too much and finds no substantiation in the data. I see not only an absence of a collectivity, but a failure even of sustained imitation of later texts by earlier ones. Indeed I am struck by the independence of mind and the originality of authorships that pretend to receive and transmit, but in fact imagine and invent. True, individual texts do relate to other individual texts, either in a sustained dialectical relationship, as in the case of Mishnah and its continuator-exegeses, or in a taxonomic relationship of connection, as in the case of Sifra and Sifré to Numbers and of Genesis Rabbah and Leviticus Rabbah, or in an episodic and anecdotal relationship, as in the case of documents that make use of sayings or stories in common. (The connection between these sayings or stories that occur in two or more documents scarcely requires analysis in the present context; what we have is simply diverse versions of given units of discourse.) But the received position, outlined today by Cohen, Schiffman, and Handelman, maintains far more twill not find satisfaction in the modest points of intersection and overlap that we have noted. In fact, overall, there is no community of texts existence of which is proven by intrinsic traits. We conclude at the point at which we began, with three theories of how the documents and their units of discourse relate.

Cohen states, "Synoptic texts must always be studied synoptically, even if one text is 'later' than another." Schiffman says, "This system, composed of interlocking and re-interlocking parts possessed of an organic connection one to another, is never really divisible." Cohen is certainly right that we must take account of diverse versions of a given saying or story as these may occur in two or more documents in sequence. But if that is all he means, then he has not told us something anyone doubted. Since he borrows language from Gospels' research, he clearly intends something more than the admonition that we not ignore parallel versions of a single story or saying. But claiming to say more, he produces less than meets the eye. He errs, specifically, in invoking the metaphor of the Synoptic Gospels, or of synoptic relationships among some of the Gospels and Q. The metaphor does not pertain.

---

[6]In my *Canon and Connection: Intertextuality in Judaism* (Lanham, 1987: University Press of America) I have conducted extensive and detailed studies, which validate the statements made here.

Schiffman is right that sayings and stories do recur in two or more documents. He is wrong to maintain that, on that account, documents are not divisible (as he says), and what he further may mean by "possessed of an organic connection to one another" I cannot say. The formulation, so far as it pertains to literary and redactional traits, is murky, the sense unclear. My best guess is that Schiffman, like Cohen, refers to the mere fact that we have some sayings and stories occur in more than a single document. Cohen's and Schiffman's formulation of the issue of connection leads no where. My sense is that, despite Cohen's and Schiffman's rather portentous framing of matters, there is less than meets the eye.

Handelman presents a weightier claim, but her mastery of the texts, conspicuously less than that of Cohen and Schiffman, leads to some infelicities of thought and argument. By Handelman, we are told, "...all units are so closely interwoven and simultaneously present that none can be considered in separation from any other at any given moment; it is a world of 'intertextuality'...." And, she further states, "...interpretation is not essentially separate from the text itself–an external act intruded upon it–but rather the extension of the text, the uncovering of the connective network of relations, a part of the continuous revelation of the text itself, at bottom, another aspect of the text." The "connective network of relations," in Handelman's formulation, would correspond to that dimension of "continuity" in mine. For it is an extrinsic, not an intrinsic aspect of the document to which, in the nature of things, we speak when we ask about relations. People impute meanings to texts, and that too forms a dimension of interpretation. But we commit anachronism and so misinterpret a text if we find in a text of the second century issues otherwise first attested in the seventh. When we treat as indivisible the text and its later interpretation, what we describe is not the text and its author's meaning, but the community and its enduring values. These relate, but they are not one and the same thing.

The importance of Handelman's formulation of matters lies in her explicit invocation of the matter of interpretation. When, however, she says that no document or unit of discourse can be considered on its own, she lays down a claim that she does not – and cannot – make stick. Once more, if all she means is that when a unit of discourse occurs in more than a single document, we cannot consider one version in isolation from another, then she has found a remarkably extreme way in which to express a perfectly routine fact of everyday observation. If she means more than that, I cannot say what she wishes to propose. My guess is that she wants to say we have to read everything in light of everything else. Indeed we do, when we propose to describe, analyze, and interpret a system whole and complete, in light of all its literature. But if we ignore the lines of structure and order that separate one text from another and that account for the sequence in which the textual canon unfolds, we invite chaos. Then how to sort things out and find the rules of order? – That is the challenge to learning, which in time to come all parties to the debate will have to undertake. But Handelman's contribution is not only to set the terms for debate. She introduces the issue of intertextuality. That many-splendored jewel seems to refract whatever light people cast on it. Let me state the literary facts in their secular setting:

> *The texts recapitulate the system. The system does not recapitulate the texts. The system comes before the texts and defines the canon. No universally shared traits or characteristics, topical, logical, rhetorical, within the diverse texts can account by themselves for the selection of those texts for places in the canon.*

Cohen, Schiffman, and Handelman correctly express the consequences of theology – that is, of canon – in their incorrect literary judgments. This they do when they confuse theology with literary criticism, finding traits dictated by theological conviction in documents that, as a matter of fact, only occasionally exhibit the allegedly paramount traits. They therefore commit equivalent of creationism, confusing propositions of the faith with properties of the world out there. Creationism maintains that, since Scripture says God created the world this way, not that, therefore geology must be rejected. For hermeneutics the equivalent error is to maintain that, since the system joins the texts, therefore the texts are indivisible and have to be read each in the light of all, always all together and all at once.

But the correct theological conviction has misled the faithful into insisting that, because everything is Torah, and Torah is everywhere, therefore, in hermeneutical terms, nothing may be read in its own setting. We could not demonstrate the presence of those connections that would as a matter of fact validate theological convictions. So, as hermeneutic, they do not apply. But when Handelman, speaking for ages of faithful Judaists, says, "...interpretation is not essentially separate from the text itself–an external act intruded upon it–but rather the extension of the text, the uncovering of the connective network of relations, a part of the continuous revelation of the text itself, at bottom, another aspect of the text," as a matter of theology she speaks with accuracy. But it is solely from the aspect of theology, that is, of the canon. It is therefore a social judgment, extrinsic to the traits of the texts and intruded upon them. Once canonical texts then do participate in that common discourse, each contributing its component of the single, continuous discussion.

Let me account for the enormous error of imputing the traits of intertextuality to the canonical texts of Judaism: *We err when we seek to demonstrate that a system recapitulates its texts.* That is what leads us to impute to texts intrinsic traits of order, cogency, and unity. It is, further, what provokes us to postulate connection, rather than demonstrating it. The source of error flows from treating as literary facts what are, in fact, judgments of theology, that is, the reification of faith, the transformation of convictions of culture into facts of literature and – it must follow – a theory of hermeneutics. The fact is that the system not only does not recapitulate its texts, it selects and orders them, imputes to them as a whole cogency that their original authorships have not expressed in and through the parts, expresses through them its deepest logic, and – quite by the way – also dictates for them the appropriate and operative hermeneutics. The canon (so to speak) does not just happen after the fact, in the aftermath of the texts that make it up. The canon is the event that creates of documents holy texts before the fact: the canon is the fact. Since we cannot demonstrate connection, we must draw conclusions of a heuristic and hermeneutical character. These are readily stated. The simple rule may be laid down both negatively and positively. The documents do not (naturally, as a matter of fact) *coalesce* into a canon. They (supernaturally, as a gesture of faith) are *constructed* into a canon. Let me state my conclusion with appropriate emphasis:

> *The canon emerges not through recognition of mere facts, pre-existing unities, but of made up and imputed ones. The canon comes into being through a process not of post facto aggregation of like documents or connected ones drawn by a kind of unnatural magnetism to others of their kind, but of selection, choice, deliberation. The system does not recapitulate the canon. The canon recapitulates the system. In the beginning are not words of inner and intrinsic affinity, but the word: the system, all together, all at once, complete, whole, finished – the word awaiting only that labor of exposition and articulation that the faithful, for centuries to come, will lavish at the altar of the faith.*

Chapter Ten

Were the Rabbis Joking?
And Other Serious Issues

The basic unit of the Bible, for the midrashist, is the verse: this is what he seeks to expound, and it might be said that there simply is no boundary encountered beyond that of the verse until one comes to the borders of the canon itself.

James Kugel

At issue is whether, and to what extent, we are to read and interpret a work of literature initially within a particular social and historical context. In our reading of the received writings of former times may we ignore questions of circumstance and context, setting and society? In my view, in introducing Midrash, Kugel commits an act of gross ahistoricism. That is, he purports to read Scripture-exegesis out of the determinate past. He instead treats Midrash as a statement both deriving from, and directed toward, an indeterminate and eternal present: nothing in particular to whom it may concern. Indeed, his proposed introduction to, and therefore definition of, midrash is so encompassing as to include pretty much everything about anything to do with Scripture and much else. The definition signals confusion generated by an ahistorical and anti-contextual approach to interpretation of midrash, in which documents make no difference, and knowledge of the particular time and place and condition of a given authorship contributes in no way to our understanding of the genre in all its specificity.

Let me specify the statements of Kugel subject to discussion here, so that an accurate representation of his views, in his own words, may define the issues for debate. As I see it, in his "Two Introductions to Midrash," he makes these five important points:[1]

1. *Midrash stands for Judaic biblical interpretation in general:*

---

[1] I shall stipulate that minor errors of the representation of the Hebrew texts, translation, major errors of interpretation and even description, will not impede discourse. It is not about details or misunderstandings or misinterpretations that I conceive a book-length debate to be appropriate, but about a position fundamental to his entire position and, as I shall show, utterly in contradiction to the character of the literature Kugel claims to describe, analyze, and interpret.

At bottom midrash is not a genre of interpretation but an interpretative stance, a way of reading the sacred text...The genres in which this way of reading has found expression include...translations of the Bible such as the early Aramaic targumim; retellings of biblical passages and books such as the 'Genesis Apocryphon'...; sermons, homilies, exegetical prayers and poems, and other synagogue pieces; and of course the great standard corpora of Jewish exegesis..., in short, almost all of what constitutes classical and much of medieval Jewish writing....for at heart midrash is nothing less than the foundation stone of rabbinic Judaism and it is as diverse as Jewish creativity itself.[2]

2.   *Midrash is precipitated by the character of the verse subject to exegesis:*

...midrash's precise focus is most often what one might call surface irregularities in the text: a good deal of the time, it is concerned with...*problems.*[3]

3.   *Midrash is an exegesis of biblical verses, not of books:*

...midrash is an exegesis of biblical verses, not of books. The basic unit of the Bible for the midrashist is the verse: this is what he seeks to expound, and it might be said that there simply is no boundary encountered beyond that of the verse until one comes to the borders of the canon itself.[4]

4.   *The components of midrash-compositions are interchangeable:*

Our midrashic compilations are in this sense potentially deceiving, since they seem to treat the whole text bit by bit; but with the exception of certain patterns, these "bits" are rather atomistic, and, as any student or rabbinic literature knows, interchangeable, modifiable, combinable – in short, not part of an overall exegesis at all.[5]

5.   *Midrash is the way every Jew reads Scripture:*

Forever after, one cannot think of the verse or hear it recited without also recalling the solution to its problematic irritant–indeed, remembering it in the study-house or synagogue, one would certainly pass it along to others present, and together appreciate its cleverness and erudition.   And so midrashic explications of individual verses no doubt circulated on their own, independent of any larger exegetical context. Perhaps in this sense it would not be inappropriate to compare their manner of circulating to that of jokes in modern society; indeed, they were a kind of joking, a learned and sophisticated play about the biblical text, and like jokes they were passed on, modified, and improved as they went, until a great many of them eventually entered into the common

---

[2]Op. cit., pp. 91-2.

[3]P. 92.

[4]P. 93.

[5]P. 95.

inheritance of every Jew, passed on in learning with the text of the Bible itself.[6]

We shall pass by in silence the sleight of hand that transforms the *no doubt* of the middle of the paragraph into the factual historical statement at the end, that "a great many of them *eventually entered....*" These minor slips need not detain us; we may stipulate up front that Kugel is an honest scholar.

Before we enter the debate, however, I have to specify what is at stake. Why should anyone not in a rabbinical school or a synagogue pulpit care about introducing midrash, on the one side, and assessing the literary traits of the documents subject to description, on the other?[7] The stakes in fact are high. They concern whether and how we see literature in context, and what we may mean by the appropriate arena for discourse. Kugel is a Jewish species of the genus, literary critic, and he stands for a whole school of contemporary literary criticism, one which treats the critic as creator, not merely interpreter, of literature.

Let me spell out the issue, first in its particularity, then in more general terms. I maintain that midrash-exegesis of Scripture reaches us in distinctive documents, and the first (though not the last) point of entry into the reading and interpretation of midrash-exegesis finds location in the document: hence, documentary discourse. As he says explicitly and repeatedly in his "Two Definitions," Kugel treats documentary lines as null, just as he treats all data, deriving from all times and all places, as equally valid and wholly undifferentiated evidence for the genre he claims to define. That is how and why the very broad issue comes to concrete debate. If Kugel is right about the Midrash-documents, then, I am inclined to think, we may generalize as follows.

First, we may reasonably ignore the documentary limits pertaining to the very particular literature at hand. Second, even though the midrash-exegeses were formed into compilations of exegesis in circumstances we may identify, for a social group we may describe in detail, in response to issues we may define and describe, we may – so the argument runs – turn directly to the contents of all the books of midrash-exegesis, without paying any attention to the context of any one of them.

And, second, it must follow, then we surely may do so when we read literature not so definitively circumscribed by time, circumstance, and social setting. That conclusion will then permit us to maintain as a general principle of hermeneutics an essentially ahistorical, anti-contextual, and formal reading.

---

[6]P. 95.

[7]Felicities of style do not comprise one of the reasons to read the literary critical essays at hand. The papers assembled in the volume edited by Hartman and Budick seem to me remarkably prolix and verbose, using a great many fancy words to say a few simple things, most of them wrong. But we shall not dwell on trivialities, though, admittedly, it is no joy to read the circle represented by Kugel. Still, his paper is by no means the worst of the lot.

In interpreting all literature we may treat as null those considerations of society and history, particular sensibility and distinctive circumstance, to which documents in all their particularity and specificity point.

But it is the documentary definition of discourse – *this* particular compilation or book and its traits, *that* book and its aesthetic, its plan and its program – that to the present have guided us in our reading of the received classics of our culture in the West. It will not longer matter, in our understanding of the heritage of the West, that an author lived in one time, rather than some other, and addressed one situation, rather than a different one. Everything is the same as everything else, and no work of writing speaks to anyone in particular. The stakes therefore are high. It is probably unfair to Kugel to impute to him the confusion between mishmash and midrash, but in the approach to midrash exemplified in his circle, there does surface a tendency to put in one's thumb and pull out a plum, with slight regard to the ingredients or even the flavor of the pudding at hand.

Let me now broaden discourse and introduce the still larger issue, one of general intelligibility signaled by the contrast between mishmash and midrash. It concerns the textuality of a text: whether or not a document has integrity. Kugel's position rests on the prevailing, and theologically-correct but descriptively-wrong, notion that all the canonical writings of Judaism are to be read as a single document: "the one whole Torah of Moses, our rabbi." That hermeneutic derives from the theological conviction that at Sinai God gave the Torah, in two media, oral and written, to Our Rabbi, Moses, and, furthermore, everything that a great prophet or sage later on would say forms part of that one and seamless Torah. As believing Jews, Kugel and his Orthodox-religious colleagues (most of his circle, in *Prooftexts*, are Orthodox or Reversioners to "Tradition") maintain these convictions, and, as a believing and practicing but not Orthodox Jew, so do I. But for the inductive construction of intrinsic evidence, such a theological premise makes no contribution to hermeneutics.

When I systematically tested the claims framed within the literary-critical category known as that of "intertextuality," as these theological-literary claims are advanced by Shaye J. D. Cohen, Lawrence Schiffman, and Susan Handelman, I found no sustaining evidence in the canonical literature of Judaism in its formative age, down through the seventh century. Each test that I devised in support of each claim and definition of intertextuality produced negative results.[8] Kugel's treatment of midrash in particular rests upon the same deeply flawed construction of the Judaic canon in general and measured against the limns of actual documents, is equally groundless. It derives as much as do the misconstructions of Schiffman, Cohen, and others, from the received, Orthodox-Judaic reading of the holy books of Judaism. I state the Orthodox-Judaic position, represented in both the State of Israel and in Jewish seminaries in this country, as well as in the few universities possessed or controlled by the Orthodox, e.g., Yeshiva University and Harvard University. *That reading is ahistorical, ignoring all issues of specific time, place, and context; unitary, homogenizing all documents into a single Torah (as Kugel says, reaching out to the limits of the canon); linear and incremental, seeing a single Judaism, in a straight line from Sinai, and, therefore, triumphalist.* It also is – as a matter of fact – wrong. A debate such as this one, with its large and abstract issues, therefore involves real people, exchanging views (where they choose to address one another and not to debate – as they persist in doing – through *Todschweigen*[9]) on deeply held convictions. So we must ask, *cui bono?* Why is the issue raised as it is? Profound theological convictions intervene, and as I said, the issues are not literary nor even religious but narrowly theological. That explains why evidence and rigorous argument play so slight a role in the debate; it explains why episodic citation of self-evidently probative proof-texts takes the place of rigorous reasoning; and and it accounts for the deporable fact that books

---

[8]*Canon and Connection: Intertextuality in Judaism* (Lanham, 1987: University Press of America). That book forms the third in the sequence from *The Integrity of Leviticus Rabbah. The Problem of the Autonomy of a Rabbinic Document* (Chico, 1985: Scholars Press for Brown Judaic Studies), then *Comparative Midrash: The Plan and Program of Genesis Rabbah and Leviticus Rabbah* (Atlanta, 1986: Scholars Press for Brown Judaic Studies). But these two books just applied to the documents at hand the findings of my *History of the Mishnaic Law of Purities. VII. Negaim. Sifra* (Leiden, 1976: E. J. Brill), which demonstrated the documentary definition of Sifra. Kugel simply declines to consider the facts and arguments of those books. When in autumn, 1984, I asked him why he passed in utter silence by my work on many of the problems and texts he deals with in the section on the rabbinic literature of his work in his book on the parallelism of biblical poetry, he stated, "Your name is not on the canon of scholarship, and I do not have to pay attention to your work." Geoffrey Hartman just now, in a personal letter, took the same position. I cannot take it personally.

[9]I look in vain in an article purportedly defining midrash for debate with Gary G. Porton, "Defining Midrash," or to Porton's *Understanding Rabbinic Midrash. Text and Commentary* (N.Y., 1985: Ktav Publishing House) as noted elsewhere in this book. In Kugel's defense I note that his essay originally appeared in 1983, so was completed in 1982. But in presenting his published paper at the conference of which the Hartman volume is the report, he does not appear to have updating his original paper, nor has he tried to come abreast with current literature. Still, even as of 1983, Kugel appears to have learned very little from a very long list of scholars, whose books he does not cite or dismisses casually and routinely. The same traits of sectarianism characterize other writers in the book edited by Hartman and Budick, and call into question the effectiveness of the referee-system of Yale University Press. Scholarly responsibility requires all of us to debate with those with whom we disagree, not to pretend the other side does not exist and to assassinate through silence entire viewpoints and positions. That is not scholarship, except among orthodoxies, and, in the Judaic setting, within Orthodox Judaism.

and articles of the other side are not answered but ostentatiously ignored as though they did not exist. The viewpoint represented by Kugel proves particularly attractive to Orthodox Jews and formerly-non-Jewish Jews who have become reversioners to Judaism in what they imagine to be its "traditional" form. A sound theological reason yields that preference.

From the classical perspective of the theology of Judaism the entire canon of Judaism ("the one whole Torah of Moses, our rabbi") equally and at every point testifies to the entirety of Judaism. All documents in the end form components of a single system. Each makes its contribution to the whole. If, therefore, we wish to know what "Judaism" or, more accurately, "the Torah," teaches on any subject, we are able to draw freely on sayings relevant to that subject wherever they occur in the entire canon of Judaism. Guided only by the taste and judgment of the great sages of the Torah, as they have addressed the question at hand, we thereby describe "Judaism." And that same theological conviction explains why we may rip a passage out of its redactional context and compare it with another passage, also seized from its redactional setting. In the same way Kugel and his friends wish to move freely across the boundaries of documents alike, that is to say, ignoring all questions of time and condition in pursuit of the episodes of Torah, one by one, all alike, all equal on a single plane of circumstance and context: the one whole Torah of Moses, our rabbi, timeless and ubiquitous. But the theological *apologia* for doing so has yet to reach expression; and there can be no other than a theological *apologia*. In logic I see none; epistemologically there never was one.

Let me lay out the alternative to the theological reading of the canon. These are three dimensions to a document within the canon of the Judaism of the dual Torah. Documents stand in three relationships to one another and to the system of which they form canonical parts, that is, to Judaism, as a whole. The specification of these relationships constitutes the principal premise of my position and validates the approach to *the* primacy of documentary discourse in the study of midrash that I offer here.

1.   Each document is to be seen all by itself, that is, as autonomous of all others.

2.   Each document is to be examined for its relationships with other documents universally regarded as falling into the same classification, as Torah.

3.   And, finally, in the theology of Judaism (or, in another context, of Christianity) each document is to be allowed to take its place as part of the undifferentiated aggregation of documents that, all together, constitute the canon of, in the case of Judaism, the "one whole Torah revealed by God to Moses at Mount Sinai."

Simple logic makes self-evident the proposition that, if a document comes down to us within its own framework, as a complete book with a beginning, middle, and end, in preserving that book, the canon presents us with a document on its own and not solely as part of a larger composition or construct. So we too see the document as it reaches us, that is, as autonomous.

If, second, a document contains materials shared verbatim or in substantial content with other documents of its classification, or if one document refers to the contents of other documents, then the several documents that clearly wish to engage in conversation with one another have to address one another. That is to say, we have to seek for the marks of connectedness, asking for the meaning of those connections. For the purpose of definition, as much as of comparison, is to tell us what is like something else, what is unlike something else. We know what something is only when we also know what it is not, hence comparison and definition form twin-procedures. To begin with, we can declare something unlike something else only if we know that it is like that other thing. Otherwise the original judgment bears no sense whatsoever. So, once more, canon defines context, or, in descriptive language, the first classification for the labor of definition as well as for comparative study is the document, brought into juxtaposition with, and contrast to, another document.

Finally, – and this is the correct entry for theological discourse, whether in the philosophical or historical or literary idiom – we take the measure of the dimension of continuity, in which we see all documents together in a single statement. The community of the faithful of Judaism, in all of the contemporary expressions of Judaism, concur that documents held to be authoritative constitute one whole, seamless "Torah," that is, a complete and exhaustive statement of God's will for Israel and humanity, we take as a further appropriate task, if one not to be done here, the description of the whole out of the undifferentiated testimony of all of its parts. These components in the theological context are viewed, as is clear, as equally authoritative for the composition of the whole: one, continuous system. In taking up such a question, we address a problem not of theology alone, though it is a correct theological conviction, but one of description, analysis, and interpretation of an entirely historical order. It is at this third point of entry that Kugel and his associates join discourse.

Were they theologians, they would have chosen the right door. But if they propose to interpret the literature as literary scholars, they should have come in through the first entry. For, in my view the various documents of the canon of Judaism produced in late antiquity demand a hermeneutic altogether different from the one of homogenization and harmonization, the ahistorical and anti-contextual one represented by Kugel. It is one that does not harmonize but that differentiates. It is a hermeneutic shaped to teach us how to read the compilations of exegeses first of all one by one and in a particular context, and second, in comparison with one another.

Now back to Kugel's propositions. Is it the fact that, as he maintains, *Midrash is precipitated by the character of the verse subject to exegesis:*

> ...midrash's precise focus is most often what one might call surface
> irregularities in the text: a good deal of the time, it is concerned
> with...*problems.*[10]

In detail, Kugel may well be right. That is to say, once an exegete has chosen
the verse and knows what he wishes, in general, to prove, then a set of the
properties of a given verse may attract attention. Why one type of property,
rather than some other, why one issue, not another — these are questions to
which the discrete exegesis of a verse on its own does not respond. In the
comparison of such midrash-compilations as the two families we have examined,
Sifra and Sifré to Numbers, on the one side, Genesis Rabbah, Leviticus Rabbah,
and Pesiqta deRab Kahana, on the other, we can propose theses in response to
those questions — the ones of *why this, not that?* — and we can test those theses
against the traits of rhetoric, logic, and even topic. Accordingly, I do not
register a one-sided disagreement with the position represented by Kugel that the
traits of a given verse register in the formation of an exegesis of that verse. I am
certain that the received exegetical literature, the thousand-year tradition of
reading the midrash-exegeses precisely the way Kugel and others wish to read
them, enjoys ample proof in result in detail. But it begs the question to
conclude *post hoc, ergo propter hoc*, as Kugel and his friends do. So his
position is not necessarily wrong, merely lacking in rigorous logic.

Next case: *Midrash is an exegesis of biblical verses, not of books:*

> ...midrash is an exegesis of biblical verses, not of books. The basic
> unit of the Bible for the midrashist is the verse: this is what he seeks to
> expound, and it might be said that there simply is no boundary
> encountered beyond that of the verse until one comes to the borders of
> the canon itself.[11]

It is simply false to claim that there is no boundary between midrash-exegesis of
a single verse and the entirety of the canon of Judaism. The opposite is the fact.
Most documents exhibit a well-conceived program and plan, with clearly-defined
principles of rhetoric, logic, and topic, guiding compositors in shaping and
framing the document as a whole. Thee principles may be uncovered through
inductive inquiry into the forms and logic of cogent discourse exhibited in a
given document, then through the analytical comparison of the plan and program
of one document with those of another. I have done so for Genesis Rabbah and
Leviticus Rabbah, for Pesiqta deRab Kahana and Pesiqta Rabbati, and many
other rabbinic compilations and compositions. Kugel has yet to publish a line
in support of his position.

And yet here too, Kugel is not completely wrong. Some materials do travel
freely from document to document, though apart from verses of Scripture,

---

[10]P. 92.

[11]P. 93.

nothing known to me appears in every document of the dual Torah in its repertoire of late antiquity, through the Talmud of Babylonia. Hyman's *Torah hekketubah vehammesurah*, which lists pretty much all places in the corpus in which a given verse comes under discussion, sustains that judgment, as a rapid survey will show. Nonetheless, the peripatetic sayings and stories do journey hither and yon. So Kugel is talking about facts, if not (in proportion to the whole) a great many, and if not (in weight of evidence) probative ones.

But why they are accepted here and not there (where – to argue imaginatively, as Kugel and his friends do so elegantly – they *might have* appeared), what a given authorship has chosen to accomplish through citing a passage they have found in an earlier document, we cannot explain for the documents of late antiquity merely by saying things move from here to there. If a document's authorship exhibits a cogent program, then we should be able to explain why they have used a peripatetic saying or story or exegesis of a verse of Scripture in the way they have. Or, we should be able to state, we do not know what, if anything, they proposed to accomplish in resorting to the passage at hand. Or we should ask about the history of a composite unit of materials prior to the authorship's selecting it, for at least some travelling materials were composed into a larger conglomerate prior to their insertion in some of the several documents in which they occur. So the reason a given midrash-exegesis recurs may well be found in the history of the larger composite of which it forms a part. That proposition is fairly easy to demonstrate, as a matter of fact. And it calls into question the notion that authorships compose their documents essentially through free association.[12]

On to the critical issue: *The components of midrash-compositions are interchangeable:*

> Our midrashic compilations are in this sense potentially deceiving, since they seem to treat the whole text bit by bit; but with the exception of certain patterns, these "bits" are rather atomistic, and, as any student or rabbinic literature knows, interchangeable, modifiable, combinable – in short, not part of an overall exegesis at all.[13]

Kugel is stupefyingly wrong – totally, completely, utterly uninformed. He does not demonstrate that the components of midrash-exegesis are mere atoms, readily

---

[12]The concept that authorships play an active role in the formation of what they include in their documents is not new to me or particular to my school. It is in fact a routine inquiry, one that has produced interesting results for diverse scholars. I call attention, for example, to Steven Fraade, "Sifré Deuteronomy 26 (ad Deut. 3:23): How Conscious the Composition," *Hebrew Union College Annual* 1983, 54:245-302. Despite his certainty on these matters, I can find in Kugel's notes no reference to, or argument with, Fraade and his important work. My own debate with Fraade is in my *Religious Studies of Judaism. Description, Analysis, and Interpretation* (Lanham, 1986: University Press of America *Studies in Judaism* series) I:93-128, in particular, pp. 104-108, "Fraade vs. Fraade." But Fraade in his HUCA paper is certainly on the right track.

[13]P. 95.

interchanged, modified, combined in diverse ways. In his defense, I point to what I said at the third proposition. Some (few) midrash-exegeses do occur in a number of passages. Characterizing all of them as Kugel does, however, simply violates the facts of something on the order of 80-90% of the midrash-exegeses in the documents that in fact have been examined. Perhaps Kugel has facts in hand to prove his allegation correct, but he does not present them, and my suspicion is that he is talking off the top of his head or just making things up on the basis of impressions.

But there is another line of argument in support of Kugel's contention. The midrash-documents of medieval times are highly imitative, borrowing and arranging and rearranging whole tracts of received materials. The authorships intervene in various ways, in some cases making up exegeses and assigning them to named authorities of a thousand years earlier. They succeed because of their power of imitation. Now if Kugel wishes to propose that the pseudepigraphic character of the midrash-compilations of medieval and early modern times – the making of collections/*yalquts* continued into the nineteenth century! – demonstrates the interchangeable character of the received materials, I believe he can make a solid case. But that case testifies to the taste of the imitators and pseudepigraphs, rather than to the historical setting and point of origin of the earlier documents. Usefulness to later authorships tells us about the enduring appeal of the creations of earlier ones. It does not tell us that everything is everywhere interchangeable – unless as our premise we take the facticity of attributions, on the one side,[14] and the fundamental irrelevance of context and circumstance of the original formation of the document, on the other. But, as a matter of fact, Kugel and his friends build on both of these premises.

We come now to a triviality: *Midrash is the way every Jew reads Scripture:*

> Forever after, one cannot think of the verse or hear it recited without also recalling the solution to its problematic irritant—indeed, remembering it in the study-house or synagogue, one would certainly pass it along to others present, and together appreciate its cleverness and erudition. And so midrashic explications of individual verses no doubt circulated on their own, independent of any larger exegetical context. Perhaps in this sense it would not be inappropriate to compare their manner of circulating to that of jokes in modern society; indeed, they were a kind of joking, a learned and sophisticated play about the biblical text, and like jokes they were passed on, modified, and improved as they went, until a great many of them eventually entered into the common inheritance of every Jew, passed on in learning with the text of the Bible itself.[15]

---

[14]I shall refer to Kugel's history of midrash in a moment.

[15]P. 95.

Kugel does not prove that "every Jew" has received this "common inheritance," though as a matter of religious faith he may hold that every Jew should accept it. He does not demonstrate that we deal with "a kind of joking," and nothing in the propositions and syllogisms I have laid out in my research justifies his rather jejune characterization of this literature. How this literary judgment, which I regard as unproved and probably groundless, accords with the theological position at hand I cannot say. What I find stunning in the midrash-compilations as well as in their contents, the midrash-exegeses is the urgency and immediacy of matters, not the cleverness and erudition demonstrated therein. Israel, the people of God, turned to with deep anxieties about salvation to Genesis, Leviticus, and the sacred calendar. I find nothing amusing, merely clever, or particularly erudite in what the sages found there. In my description, analysis, and interpretation of the midrash-compilations, I find messages of self-evident truth in response to questions of life and death.

As a believing and practicing Jew, I too have a position to express. In this judgment of Kugel's I find no merit, since it treats as trivial and merely personal what is in fact a monumental theological statement of the founders of Judaism. Our sages were not scholars, mere clever erudites. They were holy men and they gave God's judgment, through the Torah, oral and written, to suffering Israel – then and now. As a religious Jew, that is my deepest conviction, on account of which I cannot find redeeming arguments in behalf of Kugel's amazing judgment.

Taking *midrash-meaning-exegesis* out of the documentary context, that is, *midrash-meaning-a-document* that organizes and presents midrash turns *midrash* into *mishmash*. That is not because of errors of judgment about trivialities, let alone because he does not know what he is talking about, but because of a fundamental error in the reading of the literature. Since, as I said, Kugel has evidently read the documents atomistically, he claims that they are made up only of atoms. When he works his way through complete compilations of midrash-exegeses and gives us his judgment on whether or not they form mere scrapbooks or purposely statements, documents of integrity, as I have done, we shall see whether or not he maintains the view he announces in the statement under discussion here.

Still, before concluding, I hasten to say a word in Kugel's defense. It would be an altogether too harsh judgment to conclude that Kugel is merely making things up as he goes along, though a certain distance does appear to have opened up between Kugel's allegations about the literature he purports to interpret and the actual character of documents of that same literature. I believe he has conscientiously done his best to represent things he has studied as well as he can. But it would be a bit generous to concede that he has done his homework awfully well. Since my description of the documents is accurate and available for all to study if they wish, and since that literary judgment on matters of rhetoric, logic, and topic stands at complete variance with Kugel's premises, I think we shall have to conclude that he has some considerable gaps in his mastery of the sources. And yet, by stating in a forthright and unabashed way the convictions of Orthodox Judaism as well as a fair part of ethnic Judaic scholarship concerning midrash, Kugel deserves our thanks for precipitating a fruitful debate. We in the academic sector of Judaic studies welcome that debate and intend to pursue it most vigorously.

In conclusion let us turn to the upshot of the matter, Kugel's claim to give us "two introductions to midrash." Kugel's two introductions yield not even one definition. Midrash in his definition is pretty much the same thing as "Jewish creativity itself." Let us return to Kugel's most general statement of the matter:

> At bottom midrash is not a genre of interpretation but an interpretative stance, a way of reading the sacred text...The genres in which this way of reading has found expression include...translations of the Bible such as the early Aramaic targumim; retellings of biblical passages and books such as the "Genesis Apocryphon"...; sermons, homilies, exegetical prayers and poems, and other synagogue pieces; and of course the great standard corpora of Jewish exegesis..., in short, almost all of what constitutes classical and much of medieval Jewish writing....for at heart midrash is nothing less than the foundation stone of rabbinic Judaism and it is as diverse as Jewish creativity itself.[16]

Kugel does not tell us what midrash is, when he says it is "a way of reading the sacred text." For until he explains precisely what *way* it is – *and what way it is not* – he has clarified nothing. And definition requires comparison, for when we define we exclude just as we include. But in this statement, Kugel encompasses everything Jews wrote as midrash. To me in this definition, Midrash is pretty much a mishmash.

And it is a mishmash of Judaisms, in the sense that "Jewish creativity" encompasses everything any Jew wrote anywhere (at least, within the canon of contemporary Orthodox Jewish scholarship). In making this bizarre judgment, Kugel not only declines to define midrash. He also fails to differentiate among the different groups behind the writings to which he makes reference. The Genesis Apocryphon is not a document produced and preserved by the same people who wrote and handed on Genesis Rabbah ("rabbinic Judaism" indeed!), for example, and no one has demonstrated the rabbinic provenience of the Targumim (except for Onqelos). Many have shown the opposite. So I do not exaggerate in concluding that Kugel homogenizes everything every Jew every wrote, so to speak, into one Judaism.

A further aspect of his "Two Definitions of Midrash" requires passing attention at this point, his history of midrash.[17] In that history, Kugel takes at

---

[16]Op. cit., pp. 91-2.

[17]See pp. 80-90, which I have neglected, and, especially, the repertoire of scholarly authorities cited in those pages. This is the connection to my *Reading and Believing: Ancient Judaism and Contemporary Gullibility*.

face value all attributions of sayings and most of books, so that if a given figure, rabbinical or otherwise, is assigned a statement, Kugel takes as fact that the man made that statement at the time at which he is supposed to have lived. Kugel furthermore invokes for his history of interpretation of Scripture works that rest upon the same gullible position, e.g., p. 100, n. 6: "For the historical setting of this transition and parallels to the inspired interpreter outside the rabbinic tradition see D. Patte, *Early Jewish Hermeneutic in Palestine*." Patte at that stage in his work took for granted and at face value pretty much everything he read in the rabbinic literature, so presenting a picture of the fourth century B.C. out of writings of the fifth century A.D., a mere nine hundred years later. On that basis Kugel presents us with his linear, incremental, and unitary picture of the history of midrash within Judaism: everything everybody ever wrote, more or less. That introduces nothing.

Accordingly, I believe that the authorships of the actual Midrash-documents will have found puzzling many aspects of Kugel's introduction and description of their work. The source of his misrepresentation of the literature is not trivial, and he has not made minor mistakes to be blown up out of all proportion into an indictment of the integrity of the man and his scholarship. On the contrary, no one doubts his scholarly ethics, his learning, his character, commitment, and conscience – only his critical judgment *on the issue at hand*. And the issue is not one of orthodoxy or heresy, but merely one of introduction: the accurate description, analysis, and interpretation of some old books. I think he has not accomplished an accurate description, because he read the parts but not the whole. I think he has not accomplished a rigorous analysis because he has read acutely but has not undertaken a program of comparison and contrast. I think he has not given us a plausible interpretation – that is, an introduction, a definition – because he has thought deeply but not worked inductively on the basis of intrinsic evidence and, alas, also has brought a set of convictions, I have shown of a theological character, that are inappropriate to the secular work of literary analysis.

Since Kugel clearly has worked hard on the study of Midrash-exegeses, readily invoking what everybody knows as proof for his premises or positions ("as any student or rabbinic literature knows"), we must conclude that – as in the case of all mortals – his strength is his weakness. What he knows he knows in one way, rather than in some other. Having spent a great deal of effort to explain how a given verse has precipitated a received exegesis, he quite reasonably concluded that exegeses begin with the problems of verses. Having reached that position, furthermore, he appears not to have spent a great deal of time in the analysis of rhetoric, on the one side, or in the inquiry into the principles of logical cogency and intelligible discourse, on the other. This has further discouraged him from asking whether a document as a whole proposes to make a point or to register a syllogism or a set of syllogisms. I suppose that, if you work in a pickle factory all day long, everything you eat for supper will taste like pickles.

And yet, I think there is a deeper premise than the one defined by scholarly habits, both bad and good. The clue lies in Kugel's explicit recognition of the category of canon: "there simply is no boundary encountered beyond that of the verse until one comes to the borders of the canon itself." That is another way of saying that the Torah is one and seamless, or that Judaism is Judaism. And so it is – at the end. But the problem of how diverse documents, with their premises and their distinct syllogisms, fit together is not solved merely by saying it is solved. Precisely how the diverse documents constitute a canon, where, when, and why a given document and its message made its way into the canon – these are questions Kugel and those he represents do not address. They treat as the premise of their literary critical reading of midrash-exegeses what in fact defines the most profound and difficult problem in the reading of all of the documents that, today, after the fact, constitute the canon, or the Torah.

In the academy we do not frame our hypotheses out of the detritus of theological conviction. In the sectarian world of seminary and yeshiva (and Harvard and Yale), people do just that. Kugel stands for a position – not limited to Orthodox Judaism by any means – that everything is one thing and bounded only at the outer limits. That is correct theology. But it is bad scholarship. The reason is not merely that, as a matter of fact, it is wrong. Bad scholarship treats as a premise what is in fact the issue; it begs the question. Kugel is a man of intelligence, sensibility, learning and industry. I am confident that, as he reflects on the case made here, he will learn to construct his argument and introduce midrash by framing hypotheses and testing them, crafting well-composed questions and exploring them, rather than, as he does here, by defining axioms and repeatedly *illustrating* them in the medieval-Yeshiva manner. Then, I am certain, he will find greater motivation than he has exhibited to date to study the work of others who have pursued the same inquiries – and to study the texts not bit by bit but as a whole. When he does, I do not think he will maintain that our sages of blessed memory were joking.

Index

BROWN JUDAIC STUDIES SERIES

140001	*Approaches to Ancient Judaism I*	William S. Green
140002	*The Traditions of Eleazar Ben Azariah*	Tzvee Zahavy
140003	*Persons and Institutions in Early Rabbinic Judaism*	William S. Green
140004	*Claude Goldsmid Montefiore on the Ancient Rabbis*	Joshua B. Stein
140005	*The Ecumenical Perspective and the Modernization of Jewish Religion*	S. Daniel Breslauer
140006	*The Sabbath-Law of Rabbi Meir*	Robert Goldenberg
140007	*Rabbi Tarfon*	Joel Gereboff
140008	*Rabban Gamaliel II*	Shamai Kanter
140009	*Approaches to Ancient Judaism II*	William S. Green
140010	*Method and Meaning in Ancient Judaism*	Jacob Neusner
140011	*Approaches to Ancient Judaism III*	William S. Green
140012	*Turning Point: Zionism and Reform Judaism*	Howard R. Greenstein
140013	*Buber on God and the Perfect Man*	Pamela Vermes
140014	*Scholastic Rabbinism*	Anthony J. Saldarini
140015	*Method and Meaning in Ancient Judaism II*	Jacob Neusner
140016	*Method and Meaning in Ancient Judaism III*	Jacob Neusner
140017	*Post Mishnaic Judaism in Transition*	Baruch M. Bokser
140018	*A History of the Mishnaic Law of Agriculture: Tractate Maaser Sheni*	Peter J. Haas
140019	*Mishnah's Theology of Tithing*	Martin S. Jaffee
140020	*The Priestly Gift in Mishnah: A Study of Tractate Terumot*	Alan J. Peck
140021	*History of Judaism: The Next Ten Years*	Baruch M. Bokser
140022	*Ancient Synagogues*	Joseph Gutmann
140023	*Warrant for Genocide*	Norman Cohn
140024	*The Creation of the World According to Gersonides*	Jacob J. Staub
140025	*Two Treatises of Philo of Alexandria: A Commentary on De Gigantibus and Quod Deus Sit Immutabilis*	David Winston/John Dillon
140026	*A History of the Mishnaic Law of Agriculture: Kilayim*	Irving Mandelbaum
140027	*Approaches to Ancient Judaism IV*	William S. Green
140028	*Judaism in the American Humanities*	Jacob Neusner
140029	*Handbook of Synagogue Architecture*	Marilyn Chiat
140030	*The Book of Mirrors*	Daniel C. Matt
140031	*Ideas in Fiction: The Works of Hayim Hazaz*	Warren Bargad
140032	*Approaches to Ancient Judaism V*	William S. Green
140033	*Sectarian Law in the Dead Sea Scrolls: Courts, Testimony and the Penal Code*	Lawrence H. Schiffman
140034	*A History of the United Jewish Appeal: 1939-1982*	Marc L. Raphael
140035	*The Academic Study of Judaism*	Jacob Neusner
140036	*Women Leaders in the Ancient Synagogue*	Bernadette Brooten
140037	*Formative Judaism: Religious, Historical, and Literary Studies*	Jacob Neusner
140038	*Ben Sira's View of Women: A Literary Analysis*	Warren C. Trenchard
140039	*Barukh Kurzweil and Modern Hebrew Literature*	James S. Diamond
140040	*Israeli Childhood Stories of the Sixties: Yizhar, Aloni, Shahar, Kahana-Carmon*	Gideon Telpaz
140041	*Formative Judaism II: Religious, Historical, and Literary Studies*	Jacob Neusner

BROWN JUDAIC STUDIES SERIES

BROWN JUDAIC STUDIES SERIES